H95/7. £11.99

Beyond the New Right

Beyond the New Right presents a critique of the political thought of the New Right from within, as developed by one of its principal theorists. John Gray criticises the New Right as a form of Enlightenment rationalism, alien to true conservative philosophy, whose essential insight is the imperfectibility of all human institutions, including the market.

All the major thinkers and themes of the New Right are examined, together with many major issues of current public policy such as the growth of the underclass and the future of the role of government in education and culture. In the final essay the author argues that there are deep affinities between conservative philosophy and Green thought. He advances radical proposals for the preservation and renewal of common life for an age in which the ideals of modernism, including continuous economic growth, are decreasingly viable. The last essay expresses the author's conviction that conservative philosophy will find its future in dissociating itself from the neo-liberalism that has lately dominated policy, and returning to the task of redefining traditional values in an historical context in which the tenets of modernism are no longer credible.

Beyond the New Right

Markets, government and the common environment

John Gray

London and New York

First published 1993
by Routledge
11 New Fetter Lane, London EC4P 4EE

Simultaneously published in the USA and Canada
by Routledge
29 West 35th Street, New York, NY 10001

New in paperback 1994

© 1993 John Gray

Typeset in Times by Michael Mepham, Frome, Somerset
Printed and bound in Great Britain by
Mackays of Chatham PLC, Chatham, Kent

British Library Cataloguing in Publication Data
A catalogue record for this book is available from the British Library.

Library of Congress Cataloging-in-Publication Data
Gray, John, 1948–
  Beyond the new right: markets, government, and the
  common environment / John Gray.
  p. cm.
  Includes bibliographical references and index.
  1. Conservatism. 2. Liberalism. 3. Libertarianism.
  4. Free enterprise. 5. Green Movement. I. Title.
  JC571.G73   1993
  322.4′4—dc20   92–40306
                                                              CIP

  ISBN 0–415–09297–3 (hbk)
  ISBN 0–415–10706–7 (pbk)

Contents

Acknowledgements

Limited Government: a Positive Agenda was published by the Institute of Economic Affairs; *A Conservative Disposition: Individualism, the Free Market and the Common Life* by the Centre for Policy Studies; *The Moral Foundations of Market Institutions* by the Institute for Economic Affairs. *An Agenda for Green Conservatism* is published here for the first time.

I am grateful to the Principal and Fellows of Jesus College, Oxford, for granting me periods of sabbatical leave without which the papers collected in this volume could not have been written. I am grateful to the Directors and staff of the Social Philosophy and Policy Center, Bowling Green, Ohio, for periods of residence there during which much of the thought and research that bore fruit in these papers was done. I thank Mary Dilsaver and Tammi Sharp for their labours in turning my handwritten manuscript pages into a bona fide typescript.

John Gray

Introduction

The papers collected in this volume reflect over a decade's involvement in the intellectual currents and political movements that came together to make up the New Right in Britain. In retrospect, it is now obvious – what some people suspected during its heyday – that the New Right was not a single, coherent system of ideas but rather an eclectic mixture of themes and policies brought together, in Britain and elsewhere, more by the contingencies of circumstance than by logic or sustained reasoning. During the period of its political hegemony, the miscellaneous intellectual ancestries of the New Right hardly mattered, even if they sometimes confused policy-makers. Developments such as the political victories of conservative parties throughout most of the English-speaking world and in much of continental Europe; the capture of the conservative parties, and in New Zealand of the Labour Party, by New Right ideologies; the spectacular collapse of the Soviet system, followed shortly by that of Swedish Social Democracy, when taken in the context of a global movement toward privatisation and marketisation of economic life and the political impotence of all of the traditional parties of the Left, encouraged among supporters and members of the New Right the triumphalist belief that their political hegemony was irreversible, and that it expressed an intellectual triumph that was no less decisive. If the ideas and policies of the New Right were sometimes inconsistent; if they rested on philosophical foundations that were precarious; if the coalition of political forces that supported them was to prove ephemeral and conflict-ridden; if the policies animated by the thought of the New Right were to have effects that were costly, in human and political terms, and sometimes self-defeating – these were shadows cast by the New Right, discerned by the seasoned eyes of conservatives of an older and wiser school, but unseen by the enthusiasts of the New Right itself. For them, the political victory of the New Right – transitory as it predictably was – embodied the triumph of an ideology as comprehensive, and as hubristic in its claims, as Marxism had been. For the libertarian and classical liberal ideologues of the New Right, their ideas were truly what Marxism had falsely promised to be: the riddle of history solved. And for a few years their confidence seemed, at least to them, well founded.

It was never altogether baseless. In its several varieties – Chicagoan, Virginian, Austrian, and so forth – New Right thought contained insights, long neglected or denied in the stagnant mainstream of academic life, that explained many of the failures of government in our time. The poverty, waste, malinvestment and industrial archaism disclosed by the Soviet *glasnost*, and confirmed in the best-case example of Eastern Germany, which confounded the witless prognostications of generations of Western experts, merely provided, belatedly, irrefutable evidence in support of what Austrian theorists such as Hayek and Mises had long claimed: that comprehensive economic planning was an epistemological impossibility, demanding of the socialist planning institutions knowledge – of relative resource scarcities and consumer preferences – that they could not possess; and that the attempt to institute comprehensive planning and to suppress market pricing could only issue in a calculational chaos whose practical upshot was impoverishment. Far from 'catching up with and overtaking' the West, Soviet-style economies remained always parasitic on the Western economies, for credit, technology and price information. Without the support provided for them by Western market institutions, Soviet institutions would have collapsed long before they did. Austrian theory, whatever its weaknesses in other areas, provided a deep theoretical explanation for the systematic failures everywhere of socialist planning. Its exponents, who had been marginalised in academic life throughout most of the post-war period, can be forgiven for concluding that their analyses, rejected by their peers, had been decisively vindicated on the terrain of history.

The political thought of the New Right also contained a powerful analysis of government failure in the Western democracies. The Virginia School of Public Choice gave intellectual rigour to arguments about governmental overload and over-extension by applying to the behaviour of democratic politicians and governmental bureaucracies the same economic models applied to behaviour in markets. It illuminated the absurdity of the conventional view of economics as being governed by an inexorable, impersonal logic of profit and loss, while political life was seen as a realm of voluntaristic choice-making, and it revealed how far modern democratic states have been transformed into agencies for rent-seeking by (often collusive) special interests. If the Virginia analysis was sound, we could expect government activity always to be fraught with the risks of government failure, of capture by collusive interest groups and of bureaucratic expansionism. The economics of political life, as theorised by the Virginia School, suggested that for every instance of market failure there might be a corresponding instance of government failure. Skewed as public choice theory undoubtedly was by the corrupt and elephantine bureaucracies of the US government, which are nowhere else precisely replicated, it nevertheless gave a theoretical statement of the limits of the efficacy of government which accounted for much in the post-war experience of the Western democracies.

Part of that experience had to do with inflation – with the adoption by governments of currency debasement as an instrument of policy. Here the analysis of the Chicago School was relevant and incisive. Insisting that inflation was, in the end, always a monetary phenomenon, it pointed out that the stimulant effect of inflationary monetary policy on economic activity depended upon its being unforeseen. In so far as inflation was anticipated by economic actors, who indexed their expectations accordingly, inflationary monetary policy ceased to be effective. Hence the rational expectations strand in monetarist theory, which affirmed that the behaviour of actors in the market was governed by the expectations they might reasonably form as to future rates of inflation. For monetarists, the policy implication of their analysis was obvious: what was required of government in respect of its control of the money supply was that its discretionary authority be severely restricted by a regime of rules or clear monetary targets. These would provide the stable framework within which actors in the market could make and implement their plans. The role of government, in this and other respects, was in the provision of a framework, not in intervention aiming at the production of specific outcomes. In so far as economic growth had faltered in the Western economies in the seventies, and the Keynesian policies that had sustained it before then seemed to be self-limiting or misconceived, the monetarist analysis and prescription was a system of ideas whose time had come.

The diverse strands of thought that came together in the New Right had elements in common, family resemblances among their central conceptions, which gave it a recognisable political identity. All strands of the New Right recognised that too much had been expected from government in the post-war period, indeed, since the New Deal, or even earlier. Government had been conceived as the positive guarantor of general welfare, rather than as an institution for alleviating the worst evils of the human lot and an agency which provided a framework within which persons and communities could pursue their various goals and goods. As a result of aspiring to an impossible omnicompetence, governments had failed in discharging their most essential tasks of keeping the peace, maintaining a sound currency, tending and sustaining the institutions of civil society, and assuring a decent provision for the poor. Such humble but vital tasks were neglected as governments embarked on grandiose schemes for world peace and for egalitarian redistribution and on myriad projects in social engineering. The common strand in the political thought of the New Right which had the deepest resonance, and which retains an enduring value, is that all of these projects of government ascribed to it an immunity from the imperfections that we know to be characteristic of every other human institution. This is the one lesson of permanent significance that the political thought of the New Right contains.

Unfortunately, the lesson of imperfectibility was, from the first, combined inconsistently in New Right thought with a rationalist attachment, inherited from the Enlightenment classical liberals in France and America, to system and to projects of world improvement. The mark of imperfectibility, rightly discerned in the institutions of government, was not also recognised in the institutions of the market, which were understood as a sort of perpetual motion machine for economic growth, which only the ill-advised interventions of governments could disturb or dislocate. Once the simple truths of Adam Smith and the Manchester School were grasped again, and so long as they prevailed in government, the turmoils and terrors of history were bound to be exorcised, and humankind would emerge on to a sunlit plateau of permanent betterment. It was this Whiggish fantasy that animated the enthusiasts of the New Right; the failure of its political projects, or the unanticipated consequences of their success, has rudely dispelled it. Among some of the enthusi-asts, indeed, as among some Marxists, failure has taught no lessons, and the illusions of Enlightenment remain intact: in both cases, it is argued that the system of ideas, Marxian or classical liberal, was incorrectly applied, or wilfully distorted; that its failures are due not to any lacunae in its foundations, nor to the intractability of the political condition, but to treachery or bad luck. In either case, it is the deeper conservative truth of the imperfectibility of all human things, and the ultimate vanity of all political projects, that is denied.

It was as a response to the hubris of the New Right, to its deficiencies in self-criticism, its unhistorical dogmatism and its ignorant neglect of the verities of an older conservative philosophy, that the four papers collected in this book were written. The first three were published originally by think-tanks of the New Right itself and were intended as exercises in immanent criticism, in which the presup-positions of New Right thought were explored and questioned, and its limits investigated. Three themes run through all four of the papers. The first is that the New Right brought into conservative discourse a sectarian spirit that belongs properly not with conservatism, which is sceptical of all ideology, but with the rationalist doctrines of the Enlightenment. This species of political rationalism, which entirely dominates public discourse in the United States, represents political reasoning as an application of first principles of justice or rights, rather than as circumstantial reasoning aiming at the achievement of a *modus vivendi*. It supposes that the functions and limits of state activity can be specified, once and for all, by a theory, instead of varying with the history, traditions, and circumstances that peoples and their governments inherit. It demands of political discourse a deter-minacy in its outcomes and a certainty in its foundations that it does not and never can possess. It denies the character of political life as a practical art of mutual accommodation, and represents it instead as the application of universal principles. It thereby contributes to the corruption of political practice by ideological hubris, which is one of the most distinctive vices of an age wedded to political religions.

Second, the New Right has also neglected, or actively denied, the dependency of civil society and its institutions on the resources of a common culture. Imbued as it was by economism, which understands all human conduct in terms of a calculus of exchange, New Right thought conceived market institutions as free-standing entities, outgrowths of natural human propensities or products of a spontaneous order, rather than as legal artefacts, sustained by cultural traditions and sheltered by governments. It did not grasp that market institutions fail insofar as they are not underpinned by trust, integrity and the other virtues of fair dealing. More seriously, the rationalist orientation of the New Right encouraged it to suppose that the political order which sustained a civil society, including the institutions of the market, could or should be one defined, primarily or solely, by abstract principles of rights or justice. The political thinkers of the New Right thereby neglected the historical basis of political allegiance in a shared history and a common culture. They did so because they had imbibed from liberal individualism the denatured fiction of the person, the Kantian subject that lacks any particular identity and has a history only by accident. This, in turn, led them to evade the issue of the legitimacy that market institutions must possess in the shared moral and political culture, if they are to survive periods of hardship and difficulty. If the cultural preconditions of stable and legitimate market institutions were considered at all, as they were on occasion by American neo-conservatives, it was by reference to American circumstances, values and beliefs that had little, if any, relevance elsewhere. In general, the cultural matrix of the market was altogether ignored, with the tacit assumption of neo-liberals being that their legitimacy could be secured soley by subscription to common rules in a context of ever-growing prosperity.

It was not recognised that a free society, if it was to endure, could not be an open society; rather, as Michael Polanyi observed in criticism of Popper, it must be closed – closed by the norms of a common culture, however liberal. Nor was it acknowledged that it is not a plan to end all planning that will protect us from collectivism; as Oakeshott says pointedly of Hayek, such a plan is of the same style of politics as that which it seeks to resist. It is only by strengthening the resources of a common culture – a culture of liberty and responsibility rather than of servility and dependency – that we can hope to renew the institutions of civil society across the generations. To assume that we can rely on a regime of abstract rules is the merest folly. The absurdity of this assumption, always evident to conservatives in the older, Tory tradition for whom allegiance is ever a precarious achievement, became evident to neo-liberals themselves, only as the collapse of the Soviet system released repressed ethnicities into new forms of ancient enmity, as the logic of world markets was thwarted by political forces propelling the formation of regional trade blocs, and as the decline of the United States into a sort of chronic, low-intensity ethnic civil war, a proto-Lebanon held together only by a dwindling capital of legalism, called into question the Enlightenment project of citizenship grounded in universal principles and excluding the contingencies of historical identity.

The rationalist tradition that was exemplified in New Right thought in its neglect of common culture and particular allegiances made it as vulnerable as the Left to most decisive developments of the late twentieth century – the shattering of transnational political institutions in the Soviet Union and in Eastern and Western Europe, the re-emergence of ethnicity and the rise of fundamentalism. This same rationalist tradition also infected the political prescriptions of the New Right, which all have the character of technical, or constitutional, fixes: if poverty is to be eliminated by a negative income tax, governmental profligacy is to be prevented by a balanced budget rule; fluctuations in the value of the currency are to be abolished by the establishment of an independent central bank governed by a regime of rules; and so on. What all of these projects of rationalism deny are the human imperfections, intellectual as well as moral, which prevent the solution of perennial problems by any single institutional device or rule. The proposal for a negative income tax, among its many other failings, disregards the fact that modern poverty – at least the poverty of the underclass, rather than of those whom illness or disability has struck – is not a monetary but a cultural phenomenon, caused by a breakdown in moral and familial traditions. It cannot be cured, and may be aggravated, by mechanical transfers of income of the sort envisaged in negative income tax schemes. Equally, monetarist prescriptions for the control of inflation disregard the systematic elusiveness of money in a modern credit economy, the consequent difficulties inherent in measuring it, and the historical fact that the comparative performance of central banks in controlling inflation has little to do with their constitutional positions but rather arises from the levels of tolerance of the broader political cultures with respect to inflation. (The Japanese central bank, which is not independent, has a far better record on inflation than the American Federal Reserve, which is independent, for precisely this reason.) The monetarist idea of a wholly independent central bank, guided in its policy by a regime of strict rules, exaggerates the independence that a central bank can have of governmental authority, and the importance such independence has in controlling its policy; and underestimates the difficulty of applying fixed rules of monetary policy, when the definition of money itself is always partly arbitrary and discretion in policy accordingly inevitable. (How, in any case, is the central bank to know what the right quantity of money is to be, always supposing that it can measure it and can control its supply?) For these reasons, the monetarist project – considered as a panacea for currency fluctuations – is merely another illusion of the New Right. It has in common with other utopian schemes of the New Right a neglect of the evidences of history, which teach us that it is the soundness and vitality of cultural traditions, not constitutional devices or rules, that constrain governments and renew civil societies.

This is the third theme of my argument: that the New Right, because of its neglect of history, reposes its trust in legalist and constitutionalist devices, when our only support is in the vitality of our cultural traditions. It is, indeed, this fundamental conservative insight that the political thought of the New Right systematically evades or suppresses.

The papers collected in this volume, which were conceived as exercises in immanent criticism of the New Right, trace a development of thought which issues in a radical criticism of neo-liberalism from a standpoint which I believe to be that of traditional conservatism. The central conception of traditional conservatism, as we find it expressed in Pascal, in Montaigne and in Hume, is the idea of human imperfectibility and even of the elusiveness (for merely human understanding) of the idea of perfection itself. We cannot know what is the best human society, if only because the goods that make up good human societies are not always combinable or commensurable, and the idea that there is a definite ranking among them is dubiously coherent. For a traditional conservative, human imperfection and its consequences are intractable and permanent, not to be conjured away by the petty and shallow half-truths of any ideology. This was an understanding of the human condition, and of the practice of politics, which was shared, in the British political tradition, as much by Disraeli as by Salisbury.

It was the error of twentieth century collectivism, in all its varieties, to ascribe to governments a wisdom and an efficacy denied to any human institutions. It was the error of the New Right to suppose that market institutions, if only they are left alone, will achieve a sort of natural coordination among human activities, which only the exogenous forces of government intervention disrupt. Such fideism about the market represses, or else interprets away with spurious a priori theorisings, the cycles of growth and decline in economic life, captured by Joseph Schumpeter in his writings on business cycles and on the waves of creative destruction released by entrepreneurship and by technological innovation. And it suppresses the insights into markets as kaleidic, sometimes chaotic processes, susceptible to massive endogenous discoordination through speculative panics and the subjectivity of expectations, that are theorised in the great work of G.L.S. Shackle. The political thought of the New Right, in short, suppresses recognition of the institutions of the market as being as fallible, as frail and as obdurately imperfectible as any other human institution. It is for this reason that the political thought of the New Right, in all of its Austrian, Chicagoan and Virginian varieties, runs aground on the frailties of market institutions. In seeking deliverance from the vicissitudes of history and the intractabilities of political life in the illusions of economism, legalism and constitutionalism, the political thought of the New Right reveals itself as yet another species of the ideology of Enlightenment that has presided over so many of the disasters of our age, and which now finds its nemesis in the return of repressed enmities and religious passions.

It is by returning to the homely truths of traditional conservatism that we are best protected from the illusions of ideology, which in the political thought of the New Right found a new lease on life. As the last chapter of this book aims to show, genuinely conservative thought will remain alive only insofar as it is ready to look afresh at received ideas and established practices, including the belief – held in common by all conventional political philosophies of our times – that incessant growth in goods and services is a feasible, and desirable, object of policy. As I conceive of it, it is a part of conservative philosophy to question such dogmas of modernism. In pursuing such questioning, the conservative thinker will find most sustenance in the thought not of Hayek or Popper but of Oakeshott and Polanyi. And, insofar as he or she seeks insight from the liberal intellectual tradition, it will be found in the stoical and agonistic liberalism of thinkers such as Keynes and Berlin rather than in the paleo-liberalism of the New Right. The lesson of the bankruptcy of the New Right, intellectual as well as political, that is exhibited in this book is that political life is not a project of world improvement in which are invested the transcendental hopes of an age without faith. It is instead an almost desperately humble task of endless improvisation, in which one good is compromised for the sake of others, a balance is sought among the necessary evils of human life, and the ever-present prospect of disaster is staved off for another day.

1 Limited government
A positive agenda

ECONOMIC POLICY FOR A FREE SOCIETY

> none of the precious 'freedoms' which our generation has inherited can be extended, or even maintained, apart from an essential freedom of enterprise – apart from a genuine 'division of labour' between competitive and political controls.
>
> (Henry Simon)[1]

The proper extent of the activity and authority of government is the chief question in political philosophy. The object of these reflections, nevertheless, is not to try to specify, once and for all, the appropriate functions of government and the limits of its authority. There are good sceptical reasons – which I shall invoke when I consider recent attempts to fix the frontiers of the state by reference to a set of abstract principles – for supposing that that object cannot be achieved. My purpose here is the humbler one of addressing the role of government in Britain today and in other, similar countries. Since I deploy arguments and considerations which ought to be accepted by anyone who cares for individual liberty, my reflections are intended to have application well beyond the present circumstances in Britain, but I harbour no aspiration of universality for them. This is intended to be a study in theory and policy, not primarily in political philosophy.

I shall not rehearse my arguments here, but instead simply summarise my conclusions. The scope of government activity in Britain remains vastly over-extended. The autonomous institutions of civil society are today threatened by an invasive state whose size and arbitrary power have not substantially diminished, and in important respects have indeed been enhanced, after over a decade of rule by a Conservative administration avowedly dedicated to whittling down government to its most indispensable functions. In recent years, the project of confining government to the task of assuring for individuals and enterprises a stable legal and monetary framework within which they may plan their own activities has been abandoned, and there has been a return to 'stop–go' policies of macro-economic management, with government conceiving itself as the sponsor or author of enterprise. According to most measures, the overall burden of taxation has not diminished but rather increased, and public expenditure as a fraction of national income has fallen, if at all, only slightly. It is, again, a depressing fact that, despite efforts to diminish the culture of dependency in Britain, the poorer half of the population still receives nearly half of its income from government. Most ominously, a tendency to increasing centralisation has become evident in many aspects of policy, most particularly in those concerning education, with substantial discretionary powers being appropriated by Ministers. As the *Economist* noted recently: 'Far from reducing the role of the central state, Mrs Margaret Thatcher's government has extended it.... Mr Kenneth Baker acquired 415 new powers when the Education Reform Act became law in July.... Mrs Thatcher's government has also broken all records in the quantity of legislation.'[2] There has also been an explosion of secondary legislation, with the first half of 1987 seeing as many pages of statutory instruments (allowing for subsequent ministerial orders) as the whole of 1959. Further, as the *Economist* went on to observe: 'Over the past two years the civil service has started to grow again. Its numbers are still higher than they were under Mr Edward Heath's Tory government of the early 1970s.... The numbers working for quangos have also started to rise. Recent and prospective legislation could make things worse. The new education bill has created four big new quangos, covering the national curriculum, school examinations and the financing of universities and polytechnics. The water-privatisation bill will set up an even bigger one, a national rivers authority employing up to 10,000 staff.'[3] The danger now is that in the ruins of a project of limited government a corporatist monolith is being built up, which in the inevitable effluxion of time will be inherited by an administration (of any party) that, by conviction or by force of circumstance, will regard the claims of individual liberty with indifference or hostility.

One of my two main claims in this chapter is that the project of limiting government in Britain stands in urgent need of reassertion. Measures must be conceived and implemented which halt and reverse the trend to centralisation, and which return power and initiative to civil society. Reviving the project of limited government involves adopting policies which effect a massive withdrawal of the state from many areas of social life and which subject its remaining interventions to radical amendment. It means reaffirming the conception of government, most profoundly theorised by Thomas Hobbes and eloquently defended in our own time by Michael Oakeshott, as first and foremost protector of the peace and guardian of civil society. This is the first of my claims: that government in Britain must to a very considerable extent relinquish a paternal role in the economy and society, substantially withdraw from the sphere of civil life and assume again its true office, which 'is not to impose other beliefs and activities upon its subjects, not to tutor or to educate them, not to make them better or happier in another way, not to direct them, to galvanize them into action, to lead them or to coordinate their activities so that no occasion for conflict shall occur'; the office of government is that of 'the umpire whose business is to administer the rules of the game, or the chairman who governs the debate according to known rules but does not himself participate in it'.[4] This is an understanding of government conspicuous by its absence in recent years from political discourse in Britain.

My second and perhaps more contestable claim is that a government which is limited has nevertheless an important positive agenda to fulfil. This is to say that, whereas government is presently vastly inflated in its activities, what is needed is certainly not a minimum state but instead a limited or framework government, with significant positive responsibilities. Let me mention the most weighty of these positive tasks, which are very inadequately discharged by current over-extended governments. Government has a duty to liberate the poor and the underclass from the culture of dependency and thereby empower them as full participants in civil society. It has an obligation to protect and promote independence and freedom of choice, by assisting all who wish to acquire a decent modicum of wealth and to exercise responsibility in the control of their health, education and provision for old age. It is a vital responsibility of government to facilitate the transmission of valuable cultural traditions across the generations. Accordingly it is a responsibility of government to acknowledge the diversity of cultural traditions among people in Britain by providing each with the opportunities and, where necessary, the resources whereby it can express and reproduce itself in peaceful coexistence with its neighbours, while at the same time seeking to nurture and enrich the undergirding common culture.

These three tasks are not intended to be exhaustive of the positive functions of government in Britain today, but they seem to me to mark the chief areas where a limited government may and indeed must go beyond its most essential role as umpire and peace-keeper. Discharging these tasks will require the abandonment by government of pernicious policies which have imposed on civil society the heavy burdens of chronic inflation and excessive taxation. Government can best discharge its positive duties, not by adding further to the ramshackle apparatus of the so-called welfare state, but rather by dismantling it progressively and returning its resources substantially to the domain of private provision. Nevertheless, a limited government will always have positive duties in respect of encouraging the relief of poverty and the diffusion of wealth, the support of education and health services and the protection of valued cultural traditions. Moreover, a limited government has good reason to concern itself with the distributive implications of its systems of taxation and welfare. In general, I will contend that, even though many of the central policies and institutions of the interventionist state need abolition rather than the sort of replacement for them that is envisaged in schemes for universal vouchers or negative income taxes, for example, there remains a range of positive services which government is entitled and in truth obliged to provide as means to the ends of greater independence, freedom of choice and diversity and harmony in communal life. A limited government does most to achieve these ends, however, when it acts to repair and renew the fabric of civil society – the institutions of private property and contractual exchange on which a market economy, and thereby all of the autonomous institutions of a free people, ultimately depend.

THE ARGUMENT FOR LIBERTY AND THE LIMITS OF PHILOSOPHY

Many who have sought to defend individual liberty in our times have supposed that its survival depends upon our having at our disposal the resources of a com-

prehensive doctrine, a systematic philosophy, on which our commitment to freedom is to be founded, and from which the principles specifying the limits of state
intervention may be deduced. Bentham and J.S. Mill, each of them classical liberals
by the standards of the revisionist liberalism of later times, thought that the
importance of individual liberty in both its personal and its economic aspects could
be demonstrated as a derivation of the Principle of Utility. Locke, Kant and, in
recent years, thinkers such as John Rawls and James Buchanan have developed a
more persuasive argument that the essential institutions of a liberal society can be
given a rational reconstruction as the outcome of a hypothetical choice under
conditions of uncertainty. Each of these perspectives contains something to enrich
the argument for liberty. Utilitarianism – at least in some of J.S. Mill's writings,
and in later writers such as Henry Sidgwick, before it was appropriated by the
theorists of welfare economics – comprehends the insight that voluntary exchange
in a market economy is the best guarantor of general welfare. Contractarian theory,
especially in the form in which it has been developed by James Buchanan, shows
why and how it is that a reconstitution of limited government may be in the interests
of each, and thereby of all. A third strand of argument, that which invokes
fundamental rights as the foundation of limited government, has less to offer the
argument for liberty, but serves as a useful reminder that the principal defence of
liberty is not in its promotion of efficiency or productivity but in its contribution
to the autonomy of the individual.

Each of these schools of liberal philosophy has something to offer the argument
for liberty, even though none succeeds in giving individual liberty a demonstrative
foundation in unshakeable first principles,[5] or is capable of serving as any very
definite guide to practice. As I see it, the value of political philosophy is prophylactic, in that it discourages us from expecting too much of general principles, and
teaches us that policy and practice are always underdetermined by them. The liberal
perspectives I have mentioned – utilitarian, contractarian and rights-based – are
illuminating and helpful principally as a compound of theory and rhetoric, rather
than as exercises in philosophical inquiry. My approach will not be that of the
liberal ideologue who seeks to give liberal values an unquestionable claim on
reason, but instead that of a theorist of the political experience and tradition of
Britain and similar countries. (The countries to which my reflections have most
relevance may seem to be restricted to the English-speaking democracies but I
hope that, in dissipating the hubristic claims of doctrinaire liberal ideology, they
have relevance to the post-communist lands also.) I will hold that its most essential
elements, as well as its current vicissitudes and disorders, are best expressed in the
thought of Thomas Hobbes, which (shorn of its contractarian metaphor and of its
over-simple psychology) best conceives of government as the guardian of the peace
that is attained in civil association. My approach will venture the paradox – a
genuine paradox, in that it expresses a truth in the form of an apparent contradiction
– that it is in such a Hobbesian conception, in which the state is unconstrained by
abstract rights in its pursuit of civil peace, that the best guide to an understanding
of the character of limited government today is to be had.

On the theoretical side, accordingly, my task will be to elicit from political experience a range of considerations which assist us in grasping the character of a civil society and defining the role of government in sustaining and reproducing civil society. Among such considerations are a concern for the autonomy and independence of the individual, the protection of these values by a rule of law, and the contribution made to individual liberty by freedom of enterprise in a market economy. These considerations, in turn, suggest on the policy side a series of maxims, intended to guide reform of the currently massively over-extended activity of governments such as that in Britain today, which in turn indicate a variety of broad policies to these ends. These maxims are not the 'unshakeable first principles' of liberal doctrine, since they are not intended to be universal in application, they are not derivable from any general theory of human nature or of historical development, and it is not supposed that they necessarily cohere into a system which obviates the need for trade-offs among conflicting values and interests. Such maxims are altogether humbler devices, aiming only to illuminate political experience in British tradition, and to suggest profitable directions in the reform of the inheritance of civil society. The defence of these maxims is ultimately in terms of their contribution to human well-being, that is, the well-being of concrete, historically specific human beings who inherit the liberal tradition of individuality.

THE FALLACY OF THE MINIMUM STATE AND THE VACUITY OF *LAISSEZ-FAIRE*

Freedom, like a recipe for game pie, is not a bright idea; it is not a 'human right' to be deduced from some speculative concept of human nature. The freedom which we enjoy is nothing more than arrangements, procedures of a certain kind.... And the freedom which we wish to enjoy is not an 'ideal' which we premeditate independently of our political experience, it is what is already intimated in that experience.

(Michael Oakeshott)[6]

The scope and limits of government are not able to be decided a priori. Time, place and historical circumstance are of crucial importance in determining the range and character of intervention by the state in civil society. To assert this necessary indeterminacy in the functions of government is to go against a powerful tradition in classical liberal thought, which has sought to specify the proper activities of government by a universal doctrine. The simplest (and by far the least compelling) of these is the doctrine of the minimum state, which asserts that the sphere of government action is exhausted by the protection of negative rights. This is the doctrine espoused by von Humboldt, by Herbert Spencer and, in our own day, by Robert Nozick. It has many difficulties, some of them fatal to it.

First, and perhaps most fundamental, there is the difficulty generated by the vagueness of those negative rights which it is claimed the state has the duty to protect. Is there only one such right – to liberty, say – and, if so, how is it to be defined? (How are conflicts between one person's liberty and another's – between a liberty of privacy and a liberty of expression or information, for example – to be adjudicated?) If there are many such rights, how is practical competition among them to be resolved? The history of judicial review in the United States, which is founded on the supposition that such rights exist, that they have a definite and ascertainable content, and that their content cannot generate conflicts among them, is a history of endemic and intractable conflict about them. In truth, because their content is open-ended and their very definition uncertain, the negative rights in terms of which the minimum state is theorised confer upon it all of the indeterminacy which characterises my own account of the proper functions of government. That this is indeed so is only confirmed by the many contemporary theories of government which restrict its duties to rights protection but affirm that there are positive as well as negative rights, such as rights to well-being or the satisfaction of basic needs.[7] Such theories are not (as contemporary classical liberals insist) distortions or perversions of an earlier and legitimate theory of negative rights, but rather inevitable developments of a discourse of rights whose contents are incorrigibly indeterminate.

Classical liberal conceptions of the role of the state that are spelt out in terms of a principle of *laissez-faire* suffer from the disability that that principle is itself practically vacuous. In civil society, the sphere of independence is constituted by a most complex structure of legal immunities, forms of property and personal and economic liberties – a structure whose specification is given to us by no general theory. The contours of the sphere of independence are not natural truths, but instead artefacts of law and convention, subject to the need for recurrent redefinition and often expressing a balance between competing interests and values. The ideal of *laissez-faire* is only a mirage, since it distracts us from the task of assessing our historical inheritance of laws and procedures and reforming it so as to promote the diffusion of power and initiative and thereby enhance the autonomy and dignity of individuals.

Theories of the minimum state, therefore, are worse than uninformative; they are virtually empty of content. Even if we grant them a rough-and-ready sense they are unrealisable. Government in Britain or the United States has never, even at its smallest, been the minimum state of classical liberal doctrine. We may regard the severely limited government that prevailed in the late eighteenth and early nineteenth centuries in Britain as embodying in many respects an ideal worthy of restoration. Nevertheless, present policy cannot be governed simply by the goal of restoring an earlier phase of more limited government. A century and more of interventionism has built up needs and expectations which must be addressed, and it is a mistake to suppose that every move from the status quo in the direction of earlier forms of limited government represents an unequivocal improvement. Again, developments wholly external to the growth of government – exogenous changes such as technological innovation and the emergence of a truly global market – render the project of returning to the limited state of early nineteenth-century Britain an exercise in anachronism.

We are on firmer ground if instead we take the status quo as our point of departure, and ask how government may best be constrained, given the history of the last two hundred years. This involves asking what might be the positive responsibilities of government. In the Hobbesian tradition, the primordial obligation of government is to make and keep peace, where this encompasses forging and maintaining in good repair the institutions of civil society whereby persons and communities with different and incompatible values and perspectives may coexist, without destructive conflict. It is evident that discharging this duty will unavoidably commit government to activities that go well beyond the provision of the public goods of national defence and law and order. It may (as I shall later maintain in greater detail) entail government's supplying families and communities with the means whereby their distinctive values and ways of life may be affirmed and renewed across the generations.

Again, the legal framework of a limited government cannot be (as it might be, if theories of the minimum state were credible) fixed and unalterable. As technology develops and social conditions change, the rules, conventions and practices which make up civil society – which specify the terms of contractual liberty, the character of property rights and the forms of market competition – are bound to need amendment and alteration. Yet again, the renewal of civil society demands more from government than patient attention to the rules of the game of the market. It requires concern for the health of the autonomous and intermediary institutions, such as trade unions, universities and professional organisations, which stand between the individual and the state. Wise legislators (if we had such) would have the responsibility of maintaining what Burke called 'a balanced constitution' by at once ensuring that none of these autonomous institutions becomes inordinate in its demands and at the same time assuring for them all a protected sphere of independence.

Finally, the conception of the minimum state neglects the crucial questions of membership and allegiance. Who is to be a subject of the minimum state, and how is its jurisdiction to be demarcated? And could a minimum state command the loyalty of its subjects in time of war? These are questions which classical liberal thought passes over or suppresses, but which are salient to any defensible conception of the modern state.[8]

THE LIMITATIONS OF CONSTITUTIONALISM

The insufficiency of the minimum state is patent. Far less obvious is the danger of relying on constitutionalism as a panacea for our ills. I do not mean by this that we cannot benefit by devising new constitutional conventions. On the contrary, I shall suggest that there may indeed be new constitutional devices which we might profitably adopt. The danger to which I refer is rather in supposing that we can at a single stroke cut government down to size by removing personal liberty, and especially the economic dimensions of personal liberty, from the realm of political contestation and embedding it in constitutional law. The ideal of curbing the political domain and enhancing the scope of law, in the belief that individual liberty might thereby be better secured, is a captivating one that has charmed many liberal thinkers. It is nevertheless a snare and a delusion for anyone who seeks to diminish the threat to liberty today.

That constitutional law, in and of itself, gives insubstantial protection to individual liberty, and fails when it is most needed, is clear enough when we consider recent history. The Constitution of the former USSR must be one of the most stupendous ever to be conceived, but it counted for little or nothing in the Soviet Union because of the lack of an independent judiciary and the overwhelming concentration of power in the Communist Party. The Soviet example should teach us that individual liberty depends less upon the terms or provisions of any constitution than upon the dispersion of power through autonomous institutions and society at large.

The Soviet example is, of course, an extreme one in that it refers to a totalitarian state which from its inception has been animated by the project of destroying or repressing the institutions of civil society. In Latin America and in post-colonial Africa, however, where totalitarian regimes have not been firmly established, there are many examples of an admirable constitution whose lifespan is limited by the brevity of the regime which gave it birth. This should teach us a second lesson: that the efficacy of a constitution depends critically upon the stability of the distribution of power which undergirds it. And that suggests a final and more comprehensive observation: that the efficacy of a constitution in protecting individual liberty depends not only on the distribution of economic and political power but also on the political culture of the people it is meant to safeguard. No constitution will thrive or even take root if the soil in which it is planted is that of a tyrannous or barbarous political culture.

In fact, we need not leave the English-speaking world to see the delusiveness of relying on constitutional provisions as the principal guardians of individual liberty. The paradigm case of the United States is deeply instructive in this regard. The American constitution was expressly designed to fragment governmental power, restrain majoritarian democracy and protect the necessary conditions of freedom and enterprise. Its early framers and theorists generated constitutionalist insights, which remain valuable today; above all, those of James Madison, who saw that no Bill of Rights could enumerate exhaustively the liberties of the individual (an insight embodied in the Ninth Amendment). Further, the Constitution provided an indispensable framework within which a country of immigrants could develop a national political culture. Its achievements in limiting government over a century and a half in America should not be underestimated. Over the past fifty years, however, it has proved a poor protection against inordinacy in government. Despite the manifest intentions of its framers, the American Constitution has in many important areas allowed worse invasions of individual liberty than have occurred in most other Western states. We need only think of the over-regulation of industry, especially of banking, finance and pharmaceuticals, of occupational licensure, of ill-conceived and overly restrictive environmentalist legislation, of the totalitarian powers of the Internal Revenue Service, of decades of protectionism and of the myriad attempts made by government, at both federal and state level, to enforce paternalist and moralist laws (of which Prohibition was only the most spectacularly farcical instance) to see that the Constitution has not prevented legislators from making significantly greater inroads into individual liberty in the United States than in most other Western countries.

The case is in fact worse than this. In the United States issues such as abortion, the interests of ethnic and cultural minorities and of women, which elsewhere are resolved by ordinary political reasoning and mutual accommodation, by legislation and the political arts, are treated as issues of constitutional law and of basic rights. The result of this legislation has not been the containment of the political realm but instead the politicisation of law. In consequence, questionable and often plainly unjustified policies of affirmative action, for example, which in other states are matters of legislation whose content is a matter of political debate, have in the United States become embedded in law at its highest and least alterable levels. Finally, the separation of powers which is a cornerstone of the American Constitution has progressively enfeebled the office of the Presidency and goes far to account for the débâcles of the Reagan and Bush administrations, in which the need to bargain with a refractory legislature inhibited the making of hard choices in many areas of policy, and above all in respect of the federal deficit. The economic pre-eminence of the United States in the post-war world was owed not to its Constitution but to the entrepreneurial genius of its people and to the individualist character of its culture. There are, doubtless, important reforms in the US Constitution which might be hoped to return it to the intentions of its framers, but such reforms have little relevance in Britain. In general, the experience of the United States gives no comfort to those in Britain (or anywhere else) who imagine that the adoption of a written constitution is the answer to the dilemmas generated by an over-mighty government.

If there were any reasonable doubt as to this conclusion, it would be dissipated by the evidence of the recent Canadian constitution, in which most of the fads and fallacies of our time – the elevation of minority interests to entrenched legal privileges, the canard of natural welfare rights and all the apparatus of affirmative action – have been carved in stone in the tablets of constitutional law. This is indeed the inexorable result of any uncritical recourse to constitutionalism at the present time: that it will freeze for perpetuity our current confusions. Nor is it at all likely that economic liberties would be effectively protected by a written constitution. If an economic bill of rights, which entrenched liberties of enterprise, contract, trade and property, were enacted in Britin, it would survive only so long as it was not challenged by a majority in Parliament. A conflict between the Commons, say, and whichever body interpreted or adjucated the terms of an economic bill of rights could only trigger a constitutional crisis in which the constitution as a whole, and thereby the stability of the entire political system, would likely be weakened. Once again, the experience of the United States, in which economic liberties have been progressively interpreted out of the Constitution by successive Supreme Court decisions, gives no comfort to those who believe economic freedoms can be effectively protected by constitutional entrenchment.

All of this is on the supposition that we are in a position to specify the personal and economic liberties which the constitution seeks to protect, which is far from being evident. Many issues of personal liberty, such as those raised by the legal control of immigration, of pornography and of narcotics, are matters of legitimate disagreement among reasonable people who are concerned with individual liberty. They are appropriately dealt with in detailed legislation which expresses a compromise between conflicting interests and ideals rather than by judicial interpretation of a fixed constitution. Again, many proposals for an economic bill of rights presuppose a liberal world order which no longer exists and will not be recreated in any foreseeable future. Proposals to entrench a constitutional right to free trade, for example, neglect the vital fact that trade between free economies and totalitarian states (such as all of the states in the former Soviet bloc) did not carry with it the mutual benefits of classical free trade but rather, by strengthening the economies of the communist states, harmed the cause of liberty. Thus, an economic bill of rights is a non-starter both in terms of domestic political life, in which powerful socialist movements would relentlessly contest it, and in international terms where it would need to be severely qualified in virtue of the rise of totalitarian states. And in the absence of these conditions it would probably be unnecessary.

The necessary conditions of individual freedom are, in truth, 'constitutional' only in the broadest sense of that term, the sense in which it is employed by Burke. They are delineated most concisely by Michael Oakeshott, when he writes:

> What, then, are the characteristics of our society in respect of which we consider ourselves to enjoy freedom and in default of which we would not be free in our sense of the word? But first, it must be observed that the freedom we enjoy is not composed of a number of independent characteristics of our society which in aggregate make up our liberty. Liberties, it is true, may be distinguished, and some may be more general or more settled and mature than others, but the freedom which the English libertarian knows and values lies in a coherence of mutually supporting liberties, each of which amplifies the whole and none of which stands alone. It springs neither from the separation of church or state, nor from the rule of law, nor from private property, nor from parliamentary government, nor from the writ of habeas corpus, nor from the independence of the judiciary, nor from any one of the thousand other devices and arrangements characteristic of our society, but from what each signifies and represents, namely, the absence from our society of overwhelming concentration of power.
>
> Similarly, the conduct of government in our society involves a sharing of power, not only between the recognised organs of government, but also between the Administration and the Opposition. In short, we consider ourselves to be free because no one in our society is allowed unlimited power – no leader, faction, party or 'class', no majority, no government, church, corporation, trade or professional association or trade union. The secret of its freedom is that it is composed of a multitude of organisations in the constitution of the best of which is reproduced that diffusion of power which is characteristic of the whole.[9]

Nothing in my criticism of constitutionalist illusion is intended to deny that there may be significant constitutional measures which could serve the cause of individual liberty in Britain today. Several examples could be cited, but I will confine myself to three. An amendment requiring that tax allowances be raised in line with inflation (of the sort promoted in Britain under the Rooker–Wise legislation)[10] may have considerable value in inhibiting the process whereby government pre-empts by stealth an ever greater proportion of the national income. Again, but more radically, we might envisage a legislative measure which would require government to balance its budget, a measure of the sort proposed in the United States by James Buchanan and others. Such a measure might have the effect, if it could be implemented, of partially restoring that tacit economic constitution, respected by Labour Ministers such as Philip Snowden, which it was the work of 'Keynesianism' (or rather, of Keynes's supposed disciples) to destroy.

A third measure is yet more radical, one requiring that government preserve a stable value in the currency. (I will return later to the question of how this might best be achieved: by the monetarist prescription of a fixed rule for monetary policy or the Hayekian proposal of monetary privatisation and currency competition.)

A fourth measure might be the incorporation into British law of the European Convention on Human Rights (to which Britain is, of course, already a signatory), a measure supported by the fact that the rights protected in the Convention are substantially those of classical liberal thought and practice and have proved helpful in curbing the over-mighty powers of trade unions and government bureaucracies.

I am far from underestimating the practical and the potential difficulties of implementing such constitutional measures in Britain. Nor do I intend to comment on the detailed content of such measures, a task beyond the author's competence. At this point, I stress only that measures of a 'constitutional' sort – constitutional in the sense that they aim to institute a framework of rules, conventions or procedures by which the policies of governments of any party are to be constrained – are not only a desirable but even an indispensable condition of reviving the project of limited government in Britain. No party at present is committed, clearly and unequivocally, to long-term policies of fiscal conservatism and monetary stability. Even if the present Government were so committed, it would be hard to rest content with a situation in which a single party has a monopoly on these concerns. There would therefore be no alternative to pressing on with the task of persuading the major parties that, whereas a fixed constitution or economic bill of rights has little or nothing to offer, everyone stands to benefit by forging and adhering to constitutional conventions which restrain the discretionary authority of government policy.

THE NEW HOBBESIAN DILEMMA

I do not underestimate the character of the transformation in existing political attitudes, policies and practices which is presupposed by the adoption of constitutional conventions of the sort that I have sketched. It involves a metamorphosis in the character of the modern state as it is found today in Britain and elsewhere, including the United States, that is little short of revolutionary. Consider the stark contrast between the state as Hobbes conceived of it and a modern state such as Britain. The state as Hobbes conceived of it had no resources of its own. Its duty in respect of property was exhausted when it had specified the rules for its acquisition and transfer and instituted procedures for arbitrating disputes about it. The Hobbesian state was not (as we have seen) a minimum state of the doctrinaire sort theorised in the writings of Spencer and Nozick and its task was not to protect an imaginary set of abstract (and contentless) natural rights. It had tasks above and beyond the provision of law and national defence, including charitable works and an early version of workfare,[11] but its interventions in economic life were strictly limited. Certainly the Hobbesian state is not conceived as itself an economic enterprise.

The contrast with a modern state could not be clearer. The modern British state, like the contemporary American state, and like practically every other modern state, owns vast assets (notwithstanding recent exercises in privatisation). At present levels of taxation and expenditure, something between a third and a half of national income is pre-empted by government. Furthermore, the modern British state, again like virtually every other modern state, operates a colossal apparatus of income transfers via progressive taxation, welfare payments, and a welter of tariffs and subsidies. As a result of its tremendous economic power, the modern British state continues to exercise an invasive influence on social life of a sort only comparable to that of the absolutist monarchies of early modern Europe. It is perhaps worth remarking that, in virtue of the current burden of taxation, government in Britain today expropriates more of the income and wealth of its subjects than did the lords of feudal times (who were often restricted to command over the labour of only one in three of their serfs).

The consequences of the growth of the state as an owner and controller of great assets, with a stake in every aspect of enterprise, are large indeed. In a context of mass democracy, it will almost invariably be in the interest of political élites to confer resources on existing and nascent interest groups rather than to reduce or abolish them, since the loss to concentrated and collusive groups will always be more politically significant than corresponding benefits to groups that are dispersed. In the modern British state, accordingly, government tends overwhelmingly to service private interests rather than protect the public interest. Contrary to the classical (and Hobbesian) theory of the state as the provider of public goods, the modern British state is first and foremost a supplier of private goods. Whereas in the Hobbesian conception government exists to supply the public good of civil peace, the modern British state exists primarily to satisfy the private preferences of collusive interest groups. In so doing, it has to a considerable degree defaulted on its classical functions of defending the realm, keeping the peace and renewing and repairing the institutions of civil society.

As government has waxed, so civil society has waned. This is the mutation in current circumstances that is identified in Hayek's *The Road to Serfdom*.[12] The result in contemporary Britain and America of the erosion of civil society by an expansionist state has been the eruption of a political struggle for resources. From being first and foremost an umpire which enforces the rules of the game of civil association, in Britain and America the state has become the most powerful weapon in an incessant competition for resources. Its power is sought by every interest and enterprise, partly because of the huge assets it already owns or controls, but also because no private or corporate asset is safe from invasion or confiscatory taxation. From being a contrivance whereby the peaceful coexistence of civil association is assured, the state has itself become an instrument of predation, whereby a political war of all against all is fought. Civil life soon comes to resemble the Hobbesian state of nature from which it was meant to deliver us. The Hobbesian state is the classical solution of the Prisoner's Dilemma faced by all in the state of nature: each must pre-emptively seek power over the rest, if only to defend himself or herself from attack. By providing a legal framework, coercively enforced, the Hobbesian state releases its subjects from destructive conflict into the peace and commodious living of civil society. In the modern state this order of things has been reversed. Individuals and enterprises are constrained to organise collusively so as to capture or colonise the interventionist state. As a result, productive energies are distracted into the struggle for influence in government. So is generated the new Hobbesian dilemma, in which subjects are constrained, often solely in self-defence, to expend their energies in capturing or colonising government institutions, in seeking influence over government policy, in order to protect or promote their interests against others – typically other producer groups – who are similarly constrained. The result is the legal war of all against all, with the Prisoner's Dilemma of the state of nature being reproduced in the context of an over-extended government and a weak civil society. The nemesis of this process, which we are mercifully far from confronting at present, can only be an impoverishment of civil society and the recreation of the state of nature by political means. The example of Peronist Argentina suggests that once this process has occurred, it is difficult, perhaps impossible, to reverse. In Britain, it is necessary to think only of the later years of the last Labour government to see that it would be complacent to suppose that we are immune from this new Hobbesian dilemma. Indeed, it is the burden of my argument that the present Government, contrary to its professed intentions, is abandoning the project of a limited state and, in arrogating to itself ever more discretionary powers, is creating the machinery through which a new political struggle for resources is bound to be fought. What is to be done?

The first and most essential step is the recognition that government activity should be confined to the production of public goods. In a Hobbesian perspective, the greatest of these is peace, but the pursuit of peace involves government in the provision of goods that go well beyond those comprehended in the maintenance of law and order. As I shall argue later, the concern by government for a civil society that is free from destructive conflict should lead it to a concern with the distribution (and not just the efficient production) of wealth, since – as we know all too well from the American experience – a society with a substantial propertyless underclass cannot reasonably be expected to be stable when the resentments of those with nothing are open to exploitation by radical movements. In addition to such involvements by government as are imposed upon it by its task of keeping the peace and superintending civil society, government may legitimately act to provide a variety of other public goods. Here I do not intend to specify as public only those goods which in the strict economic theory of the subject are indivisible and non-excludable, so that they are produced either by government or not at all, but instead any good which has weighty positive 'externalities'.

Universal literacy, for example, whatever disadvantages it may have, is a benefit to everyone in society, and government may legitimately act to promote it. Similarly, though more controversially, common cultural traditions provide the matrix without which the exercise by individuals of their autonomy becomes impoverished and attenuated, and government may act to promote the common culture by the support of the arts and by other measures. Here we may mention an important maxim, the first among several we shall invoke for the restraint of government:

> Government may act to provide a public good so long as the coercive aspect of ·such action is confined to its financing from taxation and the provision of the good by government does not tend to monopolise or dominate any market which may exist in that good.

As Hayek has well stated this maxim:

> In so far as government merely undertakes to supply services which otherwise would not be supplied at all (usually because it is not possible to confine the benefits to those prepared to pay for them), the only question which arises is whether the benefits are worth the cost. Of course, if the government claimed for itself the exclusive right to provide particular services, they would cease to be strictly non-coercive. In general, a free society demands not only that the government have a monopoly of coercion but that it have the monopoly only of coercion and that in all other respects it operate on the same terms as everybody else.[13]

Hayek's maxim, which echoes J.S. Mill's distinction between the 'authoritative' and 'non-authoritative' activities of government (according to which government may provide any public goods so long as the coercion involved is restricted to taxation), requires not only that the state claim no monopolistic power in respect of its provision of the good but also that its action should not dominate the market in it so as to swamp all private initiative in its provision. By this criterion, state support for the arts may be legitimate but the present near-monopoly in schooling is not. The maxim we have enumerated has a corollary which is also worth mentioning: that policy should be guided by the aim that government, aside no doubt from the core services of national defence and law enforcement, should, so far as is possible, always be constrained in its activities by market competition. As we shall see, this is a maxim with far-reaching and sometimes radical implications.

But what is the moral justification of relying so heavily on market competition? What, in other words, is the ethical argument for market freedom? In classical liberal writings, market freedom and its precondition, private property, are often defended negatively, as shields against coercion by other people or by a tyrannous state. This is, at best, only half of the story. The most fundamental argument for market freedom is in its contribution to individual well-being by positively enabling people to act in pursuit of their goals and to express their values and ideals. Unlike any collective decision-procedure, howsoever democratic, the market enables individuals to act to achieve their ends without the necessity of consulting their fellows, a procedure which often occasions social conflict, where it does not result in majoritarian tyranny. The market thus provides the positive freedom of autonomy and self-determination, and not only or primarily the negative freedom of non-interference. Where human values and goals are indefinitely various, and society harbours a diversity of cultural traditions and conceptions of the good life, market provision of most goods is a condition of peace, since each may act with his or her own resources to achieve the good without thereby depleting any collective resource. But the market not only allows practitioners of different traditions and proponents of different values to live together in peaceful co-existence, it also enables new values to appear and new minorities to form. As Hayek put it:

> action by collective agreement limited to measures where previous efforts have already created a common view, where opinion about what is desirable has become settled, and where the problem is that of choosing between possibilities already generally recognised, not that of discovering new possibilities. Public opinion, however, cannot decide in what direction efforts should be made to arouse public opinion, and neither government nor other existing organised groups should have the exclusive power to do so. But organised efforts have to be set in motion by a few individuals who possess the necessary resources themselves or who win the support of those that do; without such men, what are now the views of a small minority may never have a chance of being adopted by the majority.[14]

The ethical argument for the market is, therefore, not only that it allows practitioners of different traditions and values to live in peaceful co-existence, but also that it allows for innovation and novelty in thought and practice in a way that collective decisions cannot. This is to say that market freedom protects the very basic freedom to think new thoughts and try out new practices. At its most fundamental, the moral argument for the free market is one that appeals to its indispensable role in enabling people to implement their ideas and realise their goals. The language of 'enablement' is particularly apt, since it has lately been co-opted by critics of the market. Such critics do not (or will not) see that it is only the institutions of the market that accord full respect to human agency, while efforts to 'empower' people through government intervention typically turn them into passive and powerless consumers of impersonal bureaucracies.

Thus, the justification of the market is, in the end, as an indispensable condition of autonomy and self-determination. The claim that free markets best achieve prosperity, like the claim that markets allocate scarce resources most efficiently, is true but is not fundamental. Again, Adam Smith's famous observation that we rely on the self-interest, and not the benevolence, of the butcher for our provisions does not go to the bottom of things, despite its being indisputably correct. The case for the market is not that it allows for the motive of self-interest (since who supposes that motive to be absent when resources are subject to collective, political allocation?) but that it allows for the whole variety of human motives, in all of their complexity and mixtures. The defence of the market goes astray, accordingly, when it represents it as a means to aggregate social welfare. Instead, we should see the ethical standing of the market in its respect for human agency and its contribution to human autonomy.

In order to participate fully in the free market, people sometimes need resources which the market has not conferred on them. It is for this reason that a limited government, committed to the market economy, may and often ought to act to provide those with small resources with the wherewithal to make good use of market freedoms. When government so acts, it does so in accordance with the maxim that a necessary background condition of a stable market order is a wide diffusion of wealth and a reasonable measure of equality of opportunity. That this is no empty banality will become clear when we come to consider its implications for the tax treatment of savings and inheritance and the distributional aspects of voucher, loan and negative income tax schemes. However a limited government acts to confer resources and opportunities on those who have hitherto had few assets or options, it best prepares people for responsible life in a market economy by using the institutions of the market itself. It is for this reason that, when government acts to provide an under-produced public good or to correct distributional anomalies, it should do so, in most contexts, by providing purchasing power and not by the direct provision of goods or services. It thereby conforms to the maxim that markets are best reformed by the further development of markets.

A POLICY OF REFORM FOR MARKET AND GOVERNMENTAL INSTITUTIONS

> The practical moral of the failure of both the Reagan and Thatcher attempts to cut the public spending ratio is the futility of trying to roll back public expenditure without fundamental changes in the agenda of government.
>
> (Samuel Brittan)[15]

No set of legal or constitutional devices can by themselves restore limited government. The best prospect is in a range of measures which dismantle or restructure interventionist restrictions and policies and reshape the environment in which enterprise operates. The objective is so to strengthen the autonomous institutions of civil life that (as in nineteenth century Britain) the government is effectively constrained by the countervailing powers of independent social forces. I will consider the measures which seem to be appropriate under four heads: first, the monetary framework of a market economy; second, the privatisation of the welfare state; third, the role of local authorities; and last, but certainly not least, the legitimate distributional concerns and activities of a limited government in Britain, and its contribution to sustaining the moral and cultural preconditions of the market economy.

Monetary stability

I observed earlier that a vital obligation of the state (on which almost all modern states, including the present British government, have defaulted) is the maintenance of a stable currency. The crux of the present dilemma is that money is everywhere (even in states with a central bank having a measure of real independence) under the arbitrary control of governments which are subject to the vicissitudes of ephemeral political circumstances and governed by the vote motive. Given the costs and pains that are inseparable from a policy which genuinely aims at a zero inflation rate, it is inevitable that modern democratic government (except in Germany and Japan, where special historical factors have been important) should have a built-in inflationist bias.

The dilemma of a policy for stable money goes yet deeper than this. The unprecedented prosperity of the Liberal Era – the century between the Napoleonic Wars and the First World War – owed much to the stability provided by the impersonal and politically largely untouchable mechanism of the gold standard. Economic fluctuations occurred, but they were typically sharp and brief. Even with the demise of the gold standard between the Wars, post-war reconstruction brought about another guarantor of international monetary stability in the Bretton Woods system of fixed exchange rates. The breakdown of this system was predictable and unavoidable, given the very different inflation rates prevailing in the various Western economies, with Britain from the sixties onwards being the leader of the baleful process of currency debasement. A system of floating rates was then irresistible, but it has signally failed to satisfy the expectations of those who then championed it and it has fully justified the Cassandra-like warnings of Hayek, who always opposed it. Rates of exchange are now volatile to a degree which infects all business enterprise with a speculative psychology. Further, the ending of exchange controls (in itself an eminently desirable measure, and one of the high water-marks of British policy under the Thatcher administration) has made the control by government of the domestic money supply even more difficult. Currency management by target zones or other devices are at best temporary expedients.

The dilemma is indeed so difficult that Hayek has been driven to the extreme of advocating currency competition as the only effective way of disciplining government fiat money. His radical proposal[16] that the governmental monopoly on money issuance be ended and private money, subject to market disciplines, be allowed to emerge has several advantages over the monetarist prescription that the control of money by government be constrained by fixed rules.

Hayek's proposal will be regarded by mainstream opinion among economists and politicians, perhaps rightly, as in the realm of the politically impossible, but it will be the upshot of my argument that a lasting release from the uncertainty of endemic inflation is, in fact, to be expected only from radical measures of precisely the sort that appear at present to be politically impossible.

If by 'monetarism' we mean here the proposition that stable overall prices are a vital part of the framework of enterprise in a free society, then monetarism so understood has clear foundations in ordinary morality. Its justification is not in the economic growth that stable money ordinarily facilitates but in the moral hazards of inflation. (I set aside here the parallel dangers of deflation, since in the period from the end of the Second World War until the present, at any rate, the prospect of a general deflation has been far more remote than that of an endemic inflation.)

Chronic inflation has a corrosive impact on social and individual morality in a variety of ways. In the first place it results typically in a continuous redistribution of resources from civil society to government, since in most countries tax allowances are not subject to indexation against the rising price level, and taxpayers are therefore subject to the unremitting confiscatory pressure of fiscal drag. This is a process which undermines individual responsibility by making the real, post-tax income of the individual a function not of his or her efforts at prudence but of a vast impersonal process over which he or she can exercise little or no control.

Further, the impact of inflation varies radically, and often inequitably, across society. Those with substantial real assets in property or equities, for example, are usually able to protect themselves, while those dependent on fixed incomes are powerless, and the majority that relies on income from earnings is likely to be locked in constant conflict with employers. Debtors are rewarded and savers punished. Inflation thereby acts so as to effect an arbitrary and morally objectionable redistribution of resources across society. Again, the prospect of continuing inflation makes people reluctant to provide for their old age.

In an inflationary economy, people will look to government as the only power capable of protecting them from evils of which government itself is the chief cause. The result is an inescapable tendency towards further expansion in the size and interventionist activity of government. Last in the list of the moral hazards of inflation, is its corrupting effect on the ethics of contractual exchange. In an inflationary environment, we face not only the ordinary risks and uncertainties of market valuation but also the larger insecurity generated by currency debasement at unpredictable rates.

It is, perhaps, worth making once again the classical point that the success of inflationist policies depends crucially on the persistence of a pre-inflationary psychology – in short, on money illusion. Once people are cured by persistent doses of inflationary policy of their money illusion, and so come to index their expectations, the stimulating effect of monetary laxity on the economy begins to be lost. Inflationary policy is therefore self-limiting, and indeed self-defeating, in its effects over the medium run of a generation or so. It is not facetious to observe that the success of a 'Keynesian' policy of loose money depends on the existence of a majority of 'pre-Keynesian' people, which it is the effect of 'Keynesian' policy to destroy.

If human expectations under inflation soon come to be 'indexed', why not index contracts, so hoping to nullify the deleterious effects of inflation? Indexation of contracts, the inclusion of escalator clauses specifying the terms of exchange in real rather than nominal values, may offer some short-term protection to individuals, but it serves further to discoordinate relative prices and so make harder the task of the producer, entrepreneur and investor. In theory, it is true, perfect indexation of all prices would make relative prices transparent and would, in effect, simulate price stability. In practice, since not all prices will be indexed and the indices of inflation used will themselves be far from perfect, the effect of indexation is to distort further the real economy. Indexation is thus not even a second-best to stable money, which is the only way of avoiding the moral hazards of inflation.

The ultimate justification of 'monetarism' as the project for ending inflation is thus not in its contribution to economic growth but in the moral hazards of inflation. It is equity, and not the claims of general welfare, that is most immediately imperilled by chronic inflation. But what of monetarism as a prescription for policy? Understood as the morality of sound money, monetarism is unimpeachable. As a set of policy prescriptions, it is much more questionable. Essentially, mone-tarism as a project in policy-making holds that the object of stable prices is most likely to be achieved by government control of the money stock according to fixed and known rules. In Britain, this was the view embodied in the Medium-Term Financial Strategy, and in the United States, Milton Friedman, James Buchanan and others have urged that the Federal Reserve be constrained in its activity by strict rules regarding the quantity of money to be issued. In favour of monetarism as a policy prescription, it must be affirmed that the monetarist critique of the discretionary authority of central banks and governments over the money supply is thoroughly supported by evidence. Indeed, one of the strongest parts of the monetarist case is the claim that the discretionary action of central banks has been responsible for some of the most serious economic dislocations, such as the Great Depression, where it has been convincingly argued that an excessive reduction in the money stock triggered a decline in economic activity that turned recession into collapse.[17]

The monetarist solution of holding central banks to fixed rules faces difficulties, however, that may be insoluble. There is, first, an a priori point about the systematic elusiveness of money in a complex modern economy. As Hayck has always emphasised, 'money' in modern economies is not a single or a simple phenomenon but an attribute of many financial instruments and practices. Like other social objects, money is subjective; it is constituted by the beliefs and expectations that people have about it.

These rather recondite considerations perhaps had little practical significance for policy prior to the deregulation of financial institutions and could safely be ignored. In present circumstances, however, they have considerable practical force. The abolition of exchange controls, and the ever-increasing internationalisation of credit, have opened the British economy to flows of money that cannot be controlled by domestic monetary policy. Financial deregulation further deepens the problem. Now that building societies and other institutions act like banks in creating credit, money is, in effect, being generated by a host of institutions not subject to significant governmental control. This means that the difficulties in measuring and controlling the money supply, as theorised by Hayek, have in considerable measure become practical realities and make the monetarist solution increasingly unreal and anachronistic.

Monetarists (such as Congdon)[18] will object that these considerations fail to account for the comparative success of monetarist policy in Britain between 1979 and 1985. On this monetarist analysis, the rising trend in inflation since late 1985 is simply the result of a policy reversal in which monetary control was abandoned and laxity in the money supply allowed. Considered as an historical interpretation of the actual course of events, this monetarist analysis may well be sound. Using various measures of broad money, Congdon was himself able, uniquely, to predict the inflation of the past years. But, even if such measurement and prediction is achievable, it is more than doubtful whether control of the total money supply can be attained in current circumstances. On the analysis presented here, monetarist policy would have become increasingly unworkable after 1985 even if there had not been the policy reversal hypothesised by Congdon. In general, it seems that successful monetarist policy is incompatible with extensive financial deregulation, and can be revived only by reimposition of a corset of controls on financial institutions, including possibly exchange controls – a prospect that may be unrealisable and is probably undesirable.

There are, in addition to these difficulties, serious problems for monetarist policy of a political and constitutional sort. Even if the monetarist analysis of the period 1979–85 be correct, the fact would remain that monetary policies shifted at that time and the earlier policy was junked. In a public choice perspective, such policy reversals are inevitable in the context of a mass democracy in which governments are subject to the recurrent pressure of the vote motive and the collusive pressures of interest groups. As developed by the Virginia School, and especially by James Buchanan and Gordon Tullock,[19] the public choice perspective views the behaviour of politicians and bureaucrats as governed by the same imperatives as rule the consumer and producer in the market. In this economic interpretation of political life, it is to be expected that a monetarist anti-inflation strategy will not survive the long haul of political competition. There appears to be an insuperable political obstacle to monetarist policy, therefore, which is evidenced by the very policy reversal that Congdon and others maintain occurred in Britain in 1985. So what is to be done?

Within the Virginia School of Public Choice itself, it has been proposed that the monetary activities of government be constrained by strict rules. Thus, Buchanan and Brennan have suggested[20] the imposition of a regime of rules on the governmental monetary authority – the constitutionalisation of monetary policy, in effect. But this proposal confronts very powerful objections, stated concisely by Kevin Dowd in his Hobart Paper, *Private Money*:

> To begin with, such rules could easily destabilise the banking system still further. A classic example of a potentially destabilising rule would be the abolition of the central banks' lender-of-last-resort function whilst retaining the restrictions on the commercial banks' freedom to issue notes. Since these restrictions give rise to the apparent 'need' for a government lender of last resort, such a rule could leave the banking system exposed to a crisis it could not handle.[21]

Hayek has made a related point:

> As regards Professor Friedman's proposal of a legal limit on the rate at which a monopolistic issue of money was to be allowed to increase the quantity in

circulation, I can only say that I would not like to see what would happen if under such a provision it ever became known that the amount of cash in circulation was approaching the upper limit and therefore a need for increased liquidity could not be met.[22]

In support of this observation, Hayek cites Walter Bagehot's classic statement:

In a sensitive state of the English money market the near approach to the legal limit of reserve would be a sure incentive to panic; if one-third were fixed by law, the moment the banks were close to one-third alarm would begin and would run like magic.[23]

In this connection, it is fascinating to note that Bagehot himself favoured ideally a system of free banking, but regarded it as impracticable. As he put it in *Lombard Street*:

the natural system of banking is that of many banks keeping their own cash reserve, with the penalty of failure before them if they neglect it. I have shown that our system is that of a single bank keeping the whole reserve under no effectual penalty of failure. And yet I propose to retain that system, and only attempt to mend and palliate it. I can only reply that I propose to retain that system because I am quite sure that it is of no use proposing to alter it.... You might as well, or better, try to alter the English monarchy and substitute a republic, as to alter the present constitution of the English money market, founded on the Bank of England.[24]

Correct as Bagehot's judgement may have been when he made it, recent developments suggest that it has less plausibility now. One indication of this possibility is the recent conversion of the world's foremost monetarist, Milton Friedman, to a version of free banking. Friedman now advocates radical, non-monetarist measures: 'abolish the money-creating powers of the Federal Reserve, freeze the quality of high-powered money, and deregulate the financial system'.[25] Friedman's recent proposals are powerful reinforcements of the view that a monetary constitution confronts major obstacles in the United States.

A monetary constitution is in any case not a feasible remedy for the British problem of sound money. In Britain a monetary constitution could not be entrenched, given parliamentary sovereignty and the unfixed constitution. Further, as Dowd notes, the proposal of a monetary constitution has the disadvantage of retaining a considerable measure of government intervention (and, it may be added, all the classic disadvantages of monopoly). A return to more extensive and discretionary intervention by government in the money supply is a permanent possibility in Britain. The solution of privatising money by allowing for competition among concurrent currencies therefore deserves careful consideration despite its radically innovative aspects.

The limitations of monetarist policy, and the argument for currency competition as the best achievable constraint on government's monetary activities, were stated programmatically by Samuel Brittan in his Hobart Paper, *How to End the 'Monetarist' Controversy*:

> The defects of monetarism, in the narrow sense of the fixed rule for domestic money supply, are that it concedes too much power to official intervention, underrates the influence of competition in providing monetary substitutes, and takes official statistics far too much at their face value. 'Friedmanites' are often very good at analysing how controls and regulations in the economy generally will be avoided or will produce unintended effects quite different from those their sponsors desire. But too often they evince a touching faith in government in their own special sphere.
>
> The invention of new monetary instruments to replace old ones – and competition between currencies – is becoming more important as communications improve further and capital markets become even more closely linked. The abolition of exchange control in Britain in 1979 was bound to create complications for the measurements and control of the quantity of money, as the evolution of the Eurodollar market had already done for the USA.
>
> It is upside-down logic to suggest it was therefore wrong to abolish exchange control or reduce barriers between capital markets. The reluctance of people to hold a freely tradable worldwide currency which depreciates rapidly and erratically is a bigger long-run constraint on inflationary policies than monetary targets achieved by controls and manipulations which distort the meaning of the aggregates controlled.[26]

The implication of Brittan's analysis is that there is already a considerable measure of currency competition in the UK. A natural question then arises: why has inflation not continued to fall? What accounts for its resurgence in the late 1980s? One answer has to do with the deregulation of financial institutions. As monetarists have themselves observed, the entry of banks into the mortgage market may have triggered a housing-led inflation in which credit was expanded not only by the banks and the building societies but also by owner-occupiers taking out home equity loans on the strength of rising house prices. Another, and probably more fundamental, answer is to emphasise the radicalism of Hayek's proposal and the modest degree to which it has been approximated. As Peter Brimelow has observed:

> Hayek's proposal is particularly radical because it combines a number of distinct ideas that are already quite radical enough:
>
> 1   'Free banking'   Banks ought to be able to issue currency and create deposits (conceptually the same thing), choose their own reserve ratios and generally operate entirely without regulation.
> 2   Different denominations   Privately issued currencies need not be all denominated in the same unit: Citibank's Wristons and Chase Manhattan's Rockefellers would be traded against each other in a currency market just as the different national currencies are today.
> 3   Private fiat money   These private currencies need not necessarily be con-

vertible into gold or any underlying commodity, but would trade entirely on the word of the issuing bank that it would not debauch its money.[27]

In combining these three radical proposals, Hayek's scheme takes us into uncharted territory. None the less, the historical parallels we have at our disposal, such as the experiment in free banking in Scotland from 1728 to 1845, should encourage us to explore Hayek's suggestion. In the British case, implementing it would (as Dowd has made clear) involve abolishing the Bank of England, complete financial deregulation and the redefinition of the monetary standard in terms of a general commodity index. No country is at present prepared to countenance such proposals, involving as they do a massive relinquishment of government influence on the economy. Nevertheless, given the manifest failure of other policies, and the ingenuity of deregulated financial institutions in developing products to counteract governmental currency debasement, it may be that the privatisation of money is an idea whose time has come. If this is so, it will support the maxims enumerated at the start of this survey: that in present circumstances government is best constrained in most of its activities by market competition (rather than by a régime of rules which are typically honoured in the breach).

Currency competition would, it is reasonable to suppose, have many crucial advantages over current practice and over monetarist alternatives. Its chief recommendation is that it offers a promising, albeit a very radical, route to long-term stability in prices, and that it does so by harnessing those very processes of market competition which elsewhere have proved the most reliable guardians of general welfare. We see in the case for currency competition, accordingly, an instance of a paradox which may have more general applications: that the public good of price stability is best secured by private provision. We need not suppose that currency competition would have some of the results attributed to it by its supporters, such as a return to the gold standard, or an end to fractional-reserve banking, to see it as the most promising way of cutting the Gordian knot of government-created inflation. The present circumstance, which approximates Hayek's proposal in that it already evidences semi-free banking and the discipline of comparatively free currency markets, has probably prevented government-induced inflation from being worse than it might otherwise have been. In this present context, anti-inflation policy is best conducted by using the lever of interest rates. In the longer run, however, in which we approximate further the Hayekian régime, governmental control of interest rates is bound to diminish. As Hayek has described the highly desirable return of interest rates to control by market forces:

> With the central banks and the monopoly of the issue of money would, of course, disappear also the possibility of deliberately determining the rate of interest.... The whole idea that the rate of interest ought to be used as an instrument of policy is entirely mistaken, since only competition in a free market can take account of all the circumstances which ought to be taken account of in the determination of the rate of interest.[28]

The case for currency competition deserves the most serious consideration, if only because (in sharp contrast with monetarism) it does not expect government to succeed in producing the optimum amount of money, when it has signally failed in most other areas.

As I have argued, the necessary condition of free enterprise is not the minimum state but framework government. I have concentrated on the monetary framework because, perhaps more than anything else, it is indispensable to a stable market order. My conclusions have been that government can best secure stable money by privatising (or, at least demonopolising) it within a context of free banking. The contribution of limited government to stable money is that of defining the legal framework of free banking. Other aspects of the framework of enterprise are doubtless important – most notably, the legal power of trade unions, whose continued enjoyment of the legal immunities granted them in the 1906 Trade Disputes Act remains a distortion of contractual liberty. Equally, there may be significant areas for constructive reform in company law.

Again, privatisation policy raises important issues in those instances, regrettably so far the majority, where it has been principally a revenue measure and has not been accompanied by significant enhancements in competition. Yet again, the professions remain massively over-regulated, and any policy that favours market freedom must, sooner rather than later, confront the guild socialism of the established professions. I pass over these other topics, however, since I believe that none of them rivals in importance the need for stable money as a foundation for market freedom.

Reforming the welfare state

The term 'the welfare state' designates nothing definite. It embraces such disparate arrangements as state retirement pensions, maternity and disability benefits, the National Health Service, personal social services, municipal housing, education, and unemployment and social security benefits. The lack of any precise meaning of the term reflects an underlying lack of theoretical and moral content in the very conception of the welfare state and the historical fact that it has been shaped in its present form not by any genuine consensus on principles but by a succession of contingencies, of which war and the vote motive are the two main categories. To say this is to say (what is the plain truth) that the welfare state as we know it has no rationale, no animating principle and no genuine justification. It is not an adequate safety net, nor an instrument whereby the underclass is reintegrated into civil life, nor yet an effective machinery for redistribution, but virtually the contrary of each of these distinct institutions. The welfare state does not relieve poverty but institutionalises it. It does not emancipate the underclass but instead imprisons it in ghettos of dependency (such as municipal housing estates). It does not redistribute income from rich to poor but instead, for the most part, acts in accordance with Director's Law: it serves as a middle-class racket whereby income transfers are effected from rich and the poor to the majority in the middle. George Stigler has observed:

Government has coercive power which allows it to engage in acts (above all, the taking of resources) which could not be done by voluntary agreement of all the members of a society. Any portion of society which can secure control of the state's machinery will employ that machinery to improve its own position. Under a set of conditions... this dominant group will be the middle-income classes. Empirical investigation appears to establish that the necessary conditions for this law are created in the United States through farm policy, minimum wage laws, social security, public housing, public provision for higher education, tax exempt institutions, and 'welfare expenditures'.

Public expenditures are made primarily for the benefit of the middle classes, and financed with taxes which are borne in considerable part by the poor and the rich.[29]

The welfare state as we know it is a ruleless chaos of cross-subsidies about which there are only two general truths: that as things stand it is the affluent, leisured, verbally and socially skilled middle classes that do best out of it and that (because of the huge transaction costs, moral hazards and sheer waste associated with it) everyone, or nearly everyone, would probably be better off if the welfare state had never been invented.

It would nevertheless be the utmost folly to suppose that we can somehow simply abolish the welfare state, or to underestimate the massive difficulties in the way of any policy of its radical reform. It would be wrong to attempt simply to abolish the welfare state, not merely because the electoral imperatives of democratic government render that option politically impossible, but because fairness interdicts such a policy. Millions are now dependent on Government for all or a major part of their income because earlier unjust policies of inflationary financing and confiscatory taxation deprived them of the opportunity of providing for themselves. Any policy of radical reform by privatisation of the welfare state must face the fact that it will need at least a generation – and in all likelihood several generations – in which to diminish to an ineliminable minimum the burden of dependency fostered by earlier policies.

A utopian alternative: the negative income tax

We must beware, also, of simplistic alternatives to the present confusion. One of these, which has been much in favour among latter-day classical liberals, egalitarian social democrats, and market-oriented conservatives, is the universal negative or reverse income tax, whereby those with little or no income have it automatically supplemented by government up to a point of decent subsistence. The scheme has the immediate appeal of targeting the neediest and of apparent administrative elegance, but this appeal is entirely delusive. In the first place such a scheme would be a marked improvement on existing arrangements if, but only if, it replaced them altogether. In practice it could not do so, since replacing existing transfers entirely by a negative income tax would inexorably mean that the scheme would either be ruinously expensive or else involve politically costly, and conceivably inequitable, losses for some groups. In practice, one may confidently predict that the scheme would be tacked on to existing arrangements as a supplement to them and that the last state would therefore be worse than the first. Even if it could be introduced in all of its purity as a full alternative to prevailing institutions, the negative income tax scheme would soon be inflated beyond all recognition. The vote motive would generate a political competition for resources whereby the subsistence level would be progressively bid up, subject only to the constraint imposed by consequent tax rates. It is this practical certainty, rather than real but incidental problems to do with the choice of a tax unit (individuals or families? over what time period?) and with the administration of the scheme, that condemns the proposal.

The public choice analysis pioneered by the Virginia School suggests the overwhelming likelihood that the scheme would in practice rapidly degenerate into a vast, late twentieth-century Speenhamland system of outdoor poor relief.[30]

As Hutt has observed:

> If it were 'politically possible' for 'reverse income tax' to be accepted solely as a substitute for all other forms of electoral vote-buying, the outcome of such a substitution would be a magnificent achievement. It would mean the abandonment of kinds of control of men which curb freedom and are an affront to human dignity. It was largely because of this virtue of his proposal that Professor Friedman was inspired to put forward his scheme (in his great book, *Capitalism and Freedom*). Its adoption on his terms would be welcomed by all concerned about the survival of liberty in a world in which political power-seekers increasingly appease the intolerant. But it would not cease to be a means through which candidates for election would compete in generosity at the expense of taxpayers. And its supporters must openly avow this as a serious calculated risk.
>
> Professor Friedman has made no unjustified claims for his scheme. Yet it so resembles the notorious Speenhamland wage supplement of 1795 that it is impossible not to retain misgivings. The chief merit of the plan is one which he does not himself claim: that it exposes the vote-purchasing incentive for income transfers.[31]

This is not to say that some limited variations on a negative income tax may not be the least bad alternatives to many existing transfers. Old age pensions, child benefits and income support to one-parent families (where the absent parent cannot be made to shoulder any obligations) might all profitably be turned into limited and targeted reverse income tax schemes. Providing that they were not universal in scope, such schemes would have the virtues of maximum selectivity and (at least with marginal tax rates of no more than 50 per cent) of retaining a tolerable degree of incentive for the recipients. Unemployment assistance might also profitably be in the form of a 50 / 50 negative income tax, where (as I believe will often be the case) workfare schemes prove unworkable. Even in the case of disability assistance, where governments have been very niggardly rather than over-generous, there is a case for targeting resources by a limited negative income tax scheme. In all of these areas, reverse income tax schemes have the undoubted virtues of selectivity and (where relevant) of retaining incentives to productivity and, ultimately, independence.

As against the benefits, targeted negative income tax schemes carry significant hazards. They demand a great deal of detailed knowledge on the part of government bureaucracies, which is to say that they presuppose a large administrative apparatus capable of measuring accurately fluctuating incomes and assessing changing circumstances. Much more fundamentally, all such schemes of targeting run the risk of rewarding the imprudent. If targeting schemes are to allow for more generosity than is feasible under universal schemes, they thereby create an incentive to imprudence – most obviously in the case of targeted old age pensions. These same hazards apply to voucher schemes, targeted or universal.

Hazards of voucher schemes

In regard to primary and secondary education, a voucher scheme would undoubtedly have many advantages. The present system is riddled with inequities which cry out for remedy. It is inequitable that those who elect for private schooling should in effect have to pay twice. It is inequitable that the quality of state schooling should so often depend on the neighbourhood in which a family can afford to live. It is inequitable that the poorest, whose marginal tax rates are often the highest, should also receive the worst schooling. And it is both inequitable and socially divisive that religious communities and immigrant groups which, like the Muslim, Hindu and Jewish populations, seek a distinctive type of education for their children, should face a choice of paying for it out of taxed income or of engaging in conflict with head teachers or local authorities or other parents over the form and content of schooling. These inequities in the existing system are obvious and need no grand 'theory of justice' to be recognisable.

A voucher system for schools has hazards of its own, however. The introduction of a state subvention for private schooling could well weaken its independence. That this is no merely theoretical possibility is suggested by a moment's thought on what would happen if a voucher scheme were combined with current legislation for a national curriculum. The proposed national curriculum is in any case objectionable on various grounds. It over-emphasises the vocational dimension of education at the expense of its role as an initiation into a cultural inheritance. By centralising curricular choice to an extent hitherto unheard of, it concentrates authority further into the hands of educational bureaucrats, who will in practice be decisive in framing and implementing it. There is, no doubt, much in the Education Reform Act that is genuinely devolutionary in passing decision-making down to the level of the school. But the proposed national curriculum embodies an indefensible degree of centralisation which would not be curbed by the introduction of a voucher system and which enhances the dangers posed to the independence of the private sector in education attendant on any voucher scheme.

An alternative to vouchers: privatisation of schooling?

If the present bureaucratisation of schooling is to be challenged, it is necessary first of all to question the very principle of a national system of schooling. In this connection it is useful to recall the admonition of John Stuart Mill, uttered well over a century ago:

> A general State education is a mere contrivance for moulding people to be exactly like one another: and as the mould in which it casts them is that which pleases the predominant power in the government, whether this be a monarch, a priesthood, an aristocracy, or the majority of the existing generation; in proportion as it is efficient and successful, it establishes a despotism over the mind, leading by natural tendency to one over the body.
>
> An education established and controlled by the State should only exist, if it exist at all, as one among many competing experiments, carried on for the purpose of example and stimulus, to keep the others up to a certain standard of excellence. Unless, indeed, when society in general is in so backward a state that it could not or would not provide for itself any proper institutions of education unless the government undertook the task: then, indeed the government may, as the less of two great evils, take upon itself the business of schools and universities, as it may that of joint stock companies, when private enterprise, in a shape fitted for undertaking great works of industry, does not exist in the country.
>
> But in general, if the country contains a sufficient number of persons qualified to provide education under government auspices, the same persons would be able and willing to give an equally good education on the voluntary principle, under the assurance of remuneration afforded by a law rendering education compulsory, combined with State aid to those unable to defray the expense.[32]

Mill's argument suggests that the solution to the present difficulties lies in wholesale privatisation of the schooling system. Under a low-tax régime of the sort I shall later discuss, the vast majority of families could afford to pay for their children's education themselves with the role of a voucher scheme being confined to the supplementation of very low incomes. Because of the vast savings inherent in school privatisation, the resultant tax levels would be so low that tax deductibility for school fees would also be unnecessary. Like any other form of government funding to schooling, this arrangement carries with it dangers to the independence of schools since, at the very least, government must decide what counts as a school for the purposes of funding. Mill himself, however, proposed a way in which the danger of arbitrary governmental power over schools could be obviated:

> The instrument for enforcing the law could be no other than public examinations, extending to all children and beginning at an early age. An age might be fixed at which every child must be examined, to ascertain if he (or she) is able to read. If a child proves unable, the father, unless he has some sufficient ground of excuse, might be subjected to a moderate fine, to be worked out, if necessary, by his labour, and the child might be put to school at his expense.

Once in every year the examination should be renewed, with a gradually extending range of subjects, so as to make the universal acquisition, and what is more, retention, of a certain minimum of general knowledge virtually compulsory.

Beyond that minimum there should be voluntary examinations on all subjects, at which all who come up to a certain standard of proficiency might claim a certificate. To prevent the State from exercising, through these arrangements, an improper influence over opinion, the knowledge required for passing an examination (beyond the merely instrumental parts of knowledge, such as languages and their use) should, even in the higher classes of examinations, be confined to facts and positive science exclusively.[33]

In the present context in Britain, this would mean restricting the national curriculum to the 'core' subjects of English, Mathematics and Science. Such a reduced curriculum would surely be an entirely reasonable requirement for state funding. It would enable such schools as the Orthodox Jewish Yesodey Hatorah School in Stamford Hill, North London and the Islamic Zakaria Girls' School in Kirklees, Leeds to receive public funding, provided that their pupils performed adequately under a restricted national curriculum.

Here it is important to note, as a crucial part of school privatisation, that public funding need not, and should not, be restricted to vouchers for the neediest. It should also encompass (as advocated by Simon Upton, MP and others in the New Zealand National Party) a system of Merit Bursaries for the brightest. Such a scheme, which in the British context can be seen as an extension of the Assisted Places Scheme, embodies a sound meritocratic maxim, once institutionalised in the grammar schools: that educational provision be related to demonstrated ability. Such Merit Bursaries should be available to bright children from low-income families, in addition to whatever support is provided to them through low-cost loan schemes. Of course, private schools may opt out of both forms of government funding, if they so choose. But any school which wished to be granted this funding would have to conform to the 'core' national curriculum.

The Millian scheme conforms to two other important maxims, which ought to make the scheme commendable. The voucher scheme it incorporates is a targeted voucher scheme, with the bulk of the population benefiting from much lower taxes – a mix which best approximates the direct return of purchasing power to consumers. And it confers autonomy on families by giving them exit rather voice; that is to say, it enables them, in education as elsewhere, to vote with their feet by shopping around, rather than (as in the British Education Reform Act) seeking to enhance parental power by creating a costly and burdensome apparatus of democratic participation. Wholesale privatisation of the schooling system, therefore, with provision for the costs of families with slender means being defrayed under a limited voucher scheme, a system of Merit Bursaries for the bright who are also needy, and probably far greater flexibility in the school-leaving age, may be the best way forward.

Policy towards higher education

Present policy towards higher education is unacceptably *dirigiste* in a variety of ways. (Here I speak warily, since my own position as a university teacher rightly opens me to charges of special pleading.) Also, the *status quo ante* was hardly defensible, involving as it did a massive generational inequity in regard to aspiring entrants into university teaching and research. Once the unsustainable expansionism of the sixties had come to its inevitable end, British universities were bound to enter something akin to a stationary state. In such a state, existing staff with tenure had the privileges of *rentiers*, and newly qualified academics found few or no opportunities available to them.

Nevertheless, present policies are quite manifestly misconceived. The complete abolition of tenure is regrettable, since it is bound to discourage mobility within the system and to lower the quality of recruitment in subjects (such as philosophy and the humanities) which lack a significant external market. Loss of tenure following upon promotion or a lateral move into another institution is a massive disincentive against mobility, which is likely to freeze the system for a generation – a curious way of promoting flexibility in it. Furthermore, any blanket government policy on tenure is inconsistent with respect for autonomous institutions and the independence of civil society. Decisions as to whether to have tenure, and on what terms, are properly taken by universities themselves, not by governments.

Action on tenure is, however, far from being the worst aspect of current policy. The real disaster is the effective nationalisation of the entire system of universities and polytechnics, with the Minister of Education arrogating to himself huge discretionary powers over hitherto autonomous institutions, and the system as a whole being subject to a *dirigiste* policy animated by the conception of universities as instruments of economic growth. This is a development replete with ironies, since it is surely absurd that a Government which began by advocating its own withdrawal from economic life on the Hayekian ground that it inevitably lacks the information required to plan the economy should seek powers over universities so as to plan the growth of knowledge! It is yet more ironic that a commitment to civil society and autonomous institutions should be honoured by subjecting universities to the supposed requirements of economic growth. In this conception, the control of universities becomes an arm of industrial policy, and their character as institutions with their own *telos* is lost. It is obvious, further, that there is a danger to intellectual liberty in a situation in which departments can be closed at ministerial discretion. Whether ministerial judgement be based on an assessment of a subject's supposed contribution to economic growth, or on its inherent intellectual merits, it is entirely unacceptable that such decisions be within the discretionary authority of government.

What is to be done? A return to previous arrangements is out of the question. A 'marketisation' of university education, with grants being replaced by tuition and maintenance loans and the new University Funding Council being phased out, seems a solution far better in accord with the character of universities, with the protection of liberty and, for that matter, with the present Government's earlier project of restraining the arbitrary power of the state. It is true that, for the presently foreseeable future, most university funding would remain in government hands under a loan system. The pattern and content of university teaching and research would, however, be determined by individual choice rather than ministerial fiat. A further crucial reform is the according of full tax deductibility to gifts made to universities by individuals and firms – a reform which might be supposed to be an obvious one, given that British universities are expected by government to emulate American universities, which enjoy this privilege. It is to be hoped that some such proposal will gain support across the political spectrum, as the most feasible alternative to the present danger of a sort of mercantilism in the life of the mind.

Health care: the withering away of the NHS?

The standard objections to the NHS from the standpoint of individual liberty and consumer choice are familiar, and need little rehearsal here.[34] In essence, they amount to the observation that the NHS is by its nature a system of rationing, with a combination of finite resources and infinite demand generating an allocation of medical care by medical and bureaucratic fiat rather than by the preferences and choices of patients. We need not claim that the NHS embodies the worst possible system of delivery of medical care, since most others – the Soviet system, with its chaos and corruption, the unreformed American system, with its ruinous inflation of medical costs, and the complicated arrangements in continental Europe – carry with them equal, similar or yet more serious hazards. What is clear is that no country has yet devised a set of institutions for the delivery of medical care which protects equity and liberty. The NHS is subject to particular criticism in that the allocation of resources within it is constrained by bureaucratic rigidities and, because middle-class people are better equipped with leisure time and social skills to exploit it, the allocation of resources is often regressive, disfavouring the poor and unskilled. Current proposals for the reform of the NHS, as implemented by the present British government, are for the most part thoroughly objectionable, in that they encompass little more than the imposition of another tier of rationing on a pre-existent régime of rationing.

What is at the root of the widely perceived *malaise* of the NHS? The arguments of conventional health economists that 'health care is special' are specious, and have been effectively refuted elsewhere.[35] Such arguments presuppose what is undoubtedly everywhere, in varying degrees, a fact: a massive professional monopoly in health care, and a consequent diversion of the allocation of resources from patients to medical professionals, hospital managers and bureaucrats. My principal contention is that no policy of NHS reform can hope to succeed which does not aim, among other important objectives, to loosen the grip of professional monopoly on the supply of medical services.

A sound maxim in this area of policy is that basic medical care should be distributed in accordance with basic medical need. In the context of existing institutional provision, this means that any reform programme should safeguard the interests of those who are uninsurable privately, such as the very old, the disabled, the chronic sick, and so on. An evolutionary reform programme would allow all who wish to opt out of NHS coverage to do so, with insurance for those in the categories I have mentioned being underwritten by government. Within the NHS, policy might aim at the creation of internal markets, and at fostering the growth of such institutions as the HMO (Health Maintenance Organisation), which has been pioneered in the United States. We cannot prefigure the pattern of provision which would emerge if, in addition to such moves towards 'marketisation' within the NHS, consumers were enabled to exit from it and to recover the taxes they would otherwise have paid in its support. Most likely, a wide variety of forms of provision would spring up, especially if occupational licensure provisions were made more flexible, and professional monopoly was thereby diminished. In this scheme, the role of government would be confined to operating an NHS which would be likely to wither away, to underwriting the insurance of those who would otherwise be uninsured or underinsured, to enforcing a more liberal régime of licensure, and, in a limited exercise in paternalism, to requiring insurance from all for basic medical care, including provision against catastrophic illness.

The ultimate result of this evolutionary reform package could well be a situation wherein everyone is a private patient,[36] medical services are subject to individual choice and decision rather than institutional allocation, and the basic needs of the poor and those in high-risk medical categories are fully protected. Such an outcome can be envisaged, however, only if market competition and its precondition, a relaxation of professional monopoly in medical care, are allowed to work their effects both within the NHS and beyond.

Pensions: the case for voluntary Bismarckianism

Existing national insurance systems were meant (by Beveridge) to express a sort of Bismarckian conception, that of a universal self-insurance as a symbol of citizenship. But existing National Insurance contributions preserve the morally dubious fiction of compulsory self-insurance, when in fact they are actuarial nonsense and amount merely to income taxation by stealth. Both employees' and employers' national insurance contributions should be abolished in the interests of greater ethical clarity (and, in the case of employers' contributions, because they are a tax on jobs and so restrict employment opportunities). Their full integration into income taxation, whatever the administrative difficulties of such a reform, is eminently desirable.

A voluntarist version of the Bismarckian principle is that excellent American innovation, the Individual Retirement Account (IRA), whereby money set aside for old age is tax deductible. Combined with the removal of the tax immunities of pension funds, such a reform would restore to the individual responsibility for provision for old age. As I shall later argue, however, the need for IRAs could be obviated by an even more radical move to an Expenditure Tax, which exempts all savings from taxation. These are measures for the medium or longer term. In the present situation, perhaps the best that can be done for old people is to maintain pensions at a reasonable level, with disregards for income for the better-off and means-tested benefits to alleviate the lot of the poorest.

Unemployment and poverty

In discussing the heterogeneous range of policies and institutions that go under the head of 'the welfare state', I have thus far said little – save by way of comments on negative income tax schemes – about the problems of poverty and unemployment. The omission of any extended discussion of these was deliberate, inasmuch as I am confident that modern poverty, like modern unemployment, is a deep-seated problem that will not respond significantly to fine-tuning of welfare or unemployment benefits. It is vital, first of all, to grasp that most modern poverty, certainly that in Britain today, is a cultural rather than a merely economic phenomenon. This is to say that its origins are in family breakdown, poor education and the lack of human skills rather than in sheer stringency of resources. Certainly, there are many who are old or disabled or chronically sick, who can and should benefit from a more generous, and better targeted, allocation of government resources. But these groups do not make up the underclass which at present requires most urgent attention: that section of the society, comprising several millions of households, which is effectively outside of the market economy, or only peripherally involved in it. Two aspects of this 'underclass' are crucially relevant to any sensible policy in regard to it.

Firstly, it is important to note that the underclass is a highly differentiated and not at all a homogeneous category. It includes not only the long-term unemployed but also unskilled young people, impoverished pensioners, one-parent families, and diverse other groups.

Secondly, it is of the greatest moment to recognise that, for the most part, the existing underclass is an artefact of interventionist policy. Poverty among pensioners is, as we have already noted, a by-product of the inflation and over-taxation of earlier decades. Structural and long-term unemployment are consequences of rigidities in the economy that have been buttressed by government policies. Youth unemployment is, at least in part, a product of poor schooling, which fails to teach elementary skills of literacy and numeracy and which neglects to build up the human capital of the young. Much current poverty is tax-induced, in that the poor face higher marginal rates than any other group in society. And much unemployment is also tax-related, in that employers' national insurance payments and business rates are effectively taxes on jobs. In so far as it boosts house prices, the current tax relief available on mortgage interest on owner-occupied dwellings also fosters unemployment by making mobility harder. Much could be done to ease unemployment and poverty if these pernicious features of our present tax régime were done away with.

Yet the hard core of structural unemployment and of cross-generational poverty is unlikely to respond significantly to these necessary measures. What is to be done? Far-reaching reform in education of the sort already discussed, together with measures to promote a revival of the private rented market in housing, are likely to be indispensable parts of the solution to these deep-seated problems. Training vouchers, which enable the long-term unemployed (and others) to re-skill themselves for employment, could also be of considerable value. Most centrally, perhaps, measures designed to facilitate the accumulation of capital by those who have none or little are likely to do best over the longer run to promote the gradual disappearance of the underclass.

As to the welfare state as a whole, policy ought to aim to return provision to private hands under a régime of lower taxation and targeted voucher schemes. Such voucher schemes may and ought to have a redistributional aspect, as I shall later maintain. A reform package for the welfare state should recognise also that there will always be a need for some means-tested benefits, that a voluntarist version of Bismarckian self-insurance has considerable promise, and that (partly because of the costs of targeting) there is no reason why some benefits should not be universal. To acknowledge that in coping with poverty and unemployment a mix of measures is needed, involving unavoidable trade-offs among conflicting values, is to accept the pluralist insight, most profoundly expressed in the work of Isaiah Berlin,[37] that no single principle is adequate to morality or policy. No single measure can deal with the inheritance of earlier policy, whose consequences must now be confronted. The principal point that needs to be grasped by policy-makers at present is that it is the institutions of the current welfare state that constitute the chief impediments to curing the ills it was set up to prevent.

Local government and the role of intermediary institutions

In a Hobbesian limited state of the sort I have been commending, what is the proper role of local government? It should be clear at once that, if the national government is to be small as well as strong, there will be much that should be done by local authorities. Recent developments in local government in Britain have in many instances been vulnerable to the legitimate criticism that they exemplify a trend towards further centralisation. At the same time, local authorities have often performed worse in their respect for liberty than national government; they have been more invasive, less representative, more wasteful and more liable to capture by collusive interests and extremist groups. Sensible policy in this area would involve further reducing the size of local authorities, perhaps by reducing the various tiers of non-national government to a single tier of small, unitary, responsible local authorities. This would in effect be the opposite of devolution and federalism, whose advocates fail to perceive the dangers to liberty and economy in piling layer upon layer of government, with all their attendant bureaucracies (as in the United States).

The question of the proper mode of funding of local government is less fundamental than the question of its size and mode of representation. It might be funded by a poll tax, as was envisaged by the Thatcher government, by a local income tax, as advocated by many of the government's critics, or local taxation might be abolished altogether (as is virtually the case in France). In Britain, current legislation for a 'council tax' on domestic property that replaces the disastrous poll tax is nearly as misconceived as the poll tax itself was. A far better reform would be the abolition of local taxation itself, which would allow for vast administrative savings and (given that it amounts to less than an eighth of the revenue of local government) would do so at little further cost to local autonomy. Even in the last of these options, local government could still enjoy a real margin of financial autonomy by the operation of lotteries, by taking out loans, by the sale of their own assets which could then be reinvested for income and, most importantly, by the charging of user fees for its services. The unrepresentative character of many local authorities in recent times is likely to be diminished when, as under any of these options, there is a more direct connection between local expenditure and the costs of the local voter.

There is, in addition, a case for reconsidering the electoral system for local authorities, where plausibly a single transferable vote system would do much to restrain activist minorities, but such a proposal is beyond the scope of the present study. What is crucial is that, if local authorities were much smaller and far more numerous, they could compete far more effectively than hitherto for residents and businesses. Promoting competition among local authorities should be the guiding maxim for policy in this sphere.

Consideration of the place of local authorities in a limited government raises the vexed issue of the role of intermediary institutions in the kind of Hobbesian state I have advocated here. Is there a tension between the demand for a small, strong state as guardian of civil society and the independence of intermediary institutions which stand between the individual and that state? There is no necessary or inevitable tension between the two. A strong state is a necessary condition of civil peace: government must be strong enough to defy collusive interest groups, to confront and face down over-mighty sectional interests and to uphold the rule of law. Contrary to received ideas, a state whose functions are few and which is small in size is most likely to be a strong state, capable of curbing special interests. In this sense, a strong state is a precondition of the free market and so of a flourishing civil society.

There is no incompatibility between a strong state and the intermediary institutions which are the framework of civil life. Much recent discussion has been disabled by the assumption that intermediary institutions must be governmental (or quasi-governmental) institutions. This was not so in the nineteenth century, when civil society in Britain was at its most vital. It remains a legitimate concern about developments in Britain over the past decade that (as in the case of universities) government has attempted, with some success, to make intermediary institutions its servants. This unhappy trend can be reversed, in present circumstances, if at all, only by revitalising intermediary institutions on market lines. Here one may reasonably hope, for example, that an extension of the enterprise-zone policy into inner-city areas might revive local communities and their distinctive institutions. In addition, policy should aim at fostering community by endowing distinctive cultural traditions with enabling resources on the lines I shall sketch later.

The distributive role of government

A recent and powerful current in neo-liberal thought has sought to contest and overthrow the assumption that government ought to have as one of its primary concerns the distribution of goods in society. In its most incisive and compelling form, this is the argument advanced by Hayek in *The Mirage of Social Justice*.[38] Hayek's argument seems to have at least three prongs. There is first the claim that any viable market order presupposes and entails a large measure of economic inequality whose distribution is both unpredictable and uncontrollable. Secondly, there is the argument that distributive principles for important social and economic goods presuppose a value-consensus in the absence of which government intervention to implement such principles is bound to be perceived as arbitrary and coercive. Thirdly, there is the thesis that the slogan of social justice, being in itself vacuous, has in practice functioned, largely conservatively, as a legitimating formula for the protection of entrenched interest groups from the side-effects of economic change. The implicit moral of Hayek's analysis is that the concern by government with distributional issues is foolish and destructive and ought to be abandoned. On this view, government ought to confine itself to defining the rules of property and enforcing them, which together exhaust its responsibilities.

Hayek's argument against current popular and political uses of 'social justice' is devastating, recalling in its demystifying potency the critique of language of a contemporary of Hayek's Viennese youth, Karl Kraus.[39] It contains several powerful criticisms of current distributivist notions. There is, first, the epistemic insight that the actual dispersion of income in the market process cannot be predicted, or even known retrospectively in its entirety, by anyone. An impossible demand is made on the knowledge possessed by, or available to, government by patterned principles of justice in distribution, even John Rawls's elegant and, to many, intuitively appealing Difference Principle which requires that economic inequalities be only such as are needed to improve by the most the absolute position of the worst-off. Further, though this is a separate claim of Hayek's, the attempt to control incomes, in order to match some preferred pattern of merit, need or desert, is incompatible with the effective functioning of the market, which requires that prices be undistorted so as to act as signalling devices for individuals and enterprises. There is the second point, which I have myself elsewhere stressed,[40] that there is in present society little in the way of a consensus on basic needs which would enable us to rank them in weight when they come into practical competition with each other. And there is not much doubt that the rhetoric of social justice has further enfeebled government by providing a rationale for concessions to vociferous interest groups, and thereby deepening the new Hobbesian dilemma to which I have earlier alluded.

The idea that a limited government may safely or justifiably neglect questions of distribution is nevertheless a fatal one for policy. There is, to start with, a powerful argument in political prudence and collective self-interest for a concern with distribution. A liberal polity will not be stable, nor will its communal life be free of destructive conflict, so long as most people lack independent resources and an underclass languishes without assets or opportunities. Further, any exclusion from enjoyment of the benefits of property undermines its very *raison d'être*. Private property is justified not only or primarily as a shield against coercion by the state but also as a condition of autonomy and independence of one's fellows. Those who lack property and are denied the opportunity to acquire it may reasonably be expected to lack the dispositions appropriate to civil life and may well become its enemies. There is a final reason in justice for the view that all are entitled in a liberal civil association to an unfettered opportunity to acquire property. Existing distributions of assets are a product of historical accident rather than of any intelligible principle. Worse, they are plainly the result in part of manifest injustice – not least the injustice of earlier interventionist policies of confiscatory taxation and inflation. There can be no justification whatever for treating existing property distributions as sacrosanct or beyond reform. Nor are present policies without a clear impact on distribution: existing tax and welfare arrangements have a bearing on the distribution of goods – income, property and human capital – that is quite evidently non-neutral. Again, radical reform of the system of transfer payments, unlike privatisation policy, is sometimes a zero-sum affair: it benefits some at the expense of others.

For all of these reasons, distribution cannot avoid being on the agenda of limited government. Unless the underlying distribution of property entitlements is explicitly addressed by defenders of the market economy, they will properly be vulnerable to the socialist criticism that they are indifferent to the justice of the market order, and there will be constant demands for income redistribution. As James Buchanan has well put it:

> Libertarian critics of efforts to transfer incomes and wealth should concentrate their attacks on the unwarranted use of democratic decision-structures. An open society cannot survive if its government is viewed as an instrument for arbitrary transfers among its citizens. On the other hand, libertarians go too far and reduce the scope of their argument when they reject genuinely constitutional or framework arrangements that act to promote some rough equality in pre-market conditions and act so as to knock off the edges of post-market extremes.
>
> The libertarian may defend the distributive role of the competitive process on standard efficiency grounds, and he may, if he chooses, also develop ethical arguments in support of this rule. But this is not the same thing as defending the distributive results that might be observed in a market economy in which there is no attempt to adjust starting positions. The libertarian who fails to make the distinction between the two separate determinants of observed distributive results makes the same mistake as his socialist counterpart who attacks the market under essentially false pretences.[41]

Buchanan's statement in no way legitimates egalitarianism, or sanctions the imposition on society of any preferred or desirable pattern of distribution. Robert Nozick has shown that the attempt to impose a comprehensive overall distributional pattern on society involves constant governmental intervention, continuous invasion of individual liberty, and, ultimately, the prohibition of capitalist acts among consenting adults.[42] From this we may derive the maxim that respect for individual liberty entails the acceptance that there will be no overall pattern of distribution in society.

We may go further. Hayek has argued powerfully that acceptance of a market economy involves accepting a large and unpredictable measure of economic inequality. In addition, historical experience suggests that attempts to 'correct' market distributions of income and capital are costly, unsuccessful and counter-productive: they generate a black or parallel economy of untaxed services, flatten out incentives (especially for risky or speculative ventures), and freeze existing inequalities. These considerations suggest a further maxim, that a successful market economy requires that the overwhelming mass of goods and services be subject to market allocation.

Distributional policies which conform to should these maxims should seek to supplement market distributions rather than to 'correct' or thwart them. They should operate principally on the expenditure side, as with the Merit Bursaries and weighted vouchers and loans that I have discussed, or, when they work on the taxation side, they should seek to disperse wealth rather than transfer it to the state. Buchanan's statement, therefore, in no way supports the transfer of resources from civil society to government. Instead, it affirms that the legitimacy of the free market depends on a reasonable spread in endowments. What does this mean for policy? It has, I suggest, clear implications for policy towards savings and inheritance. At present, it is virtually impossible to accumulate significant capital from income, since money invested in a bank is effectively double-taxed. In order to remedy this situation, an Expenditure Tax should be instituted whereby all income that is saved or invested is tax exempt. The administrative difficulties of such a measure are familiar and formidable, but it is the most fundamental and radical step that could be taken to allow for the accumulation of capital by those who presently have none. If such a measure were adopted, the remaining tax privileges of owner-occupation and of pension funds could reasonably be terminated. These latter are at once hard to justify in terms of equity and serve to distort the pattern of investment. As James Meade has put the case against the present arrangements:

> A ... mistaken policy in the housing market is the exemption of owner-occupiers from taxation on the annual value of their houses. By no means all owner-occu-piers are poor. Consider rich Mr A. using stock exchange dividends to rent a house from rich Mr B. Mr A. will pay income tax at a high rate on his investment income and will pay rent to Mr B. out of the remainder of his tax-free income. Mr B. will then pay income tax at a high rate on the rent received from Mr A. This is as it should be; there are two rich men and two incomes from two important real capital assets, one from the profits of the companies whose shares are owned by Mr A., and one from the annual value of the house owned by Mr B. If now Mr A. hands over his shares to Mr B. and Mr B. hands over the house to Mr A. so that Mr A. is now an owner-occupier, according to present

arrangements no tax will be paid on the annual value of the house, though tax will, of course, still be payable on the investment income.

The undesirable results of this are fourfold: first, it is a way of giving tax exemption on a most important part of the real income of owner-occupiers provided they are rich enough to pay tax, an exemption which is the more important the richer the man concerned and the higher the rate of tax to which he is liable; second, it encourages the demand for housing by the rich, since this form of investment has so important a tax privilege, and thus diverts building resources and available land to the rich end of the market and drives up the price of houses and building land against the poorer end of the market; third, it greatly discourages the building of houses for letting as contrasted with building for owner-occupiers, although for many poorer families renting a dwelling is more feasible than purchasing a dwelling; and, fourth, by reducing in an important way the tax base, it means that the rates of taxation on the remaining sources of income must be so much the higher in order to raise total tax revenue which is needed on other budgetary grounds.[43]

There is a case, in addition, for reform of the current pattern of inheritance taxation so as to encourage the wider dispersion of wealth. What is needed is an Accessions Tax of the sort advocated by John Stuart Mill in his *Principles of Political Economy*,[44] that is to say, a tax on the recipient, rather than on the estate. Current inheritance taxation is both inequitable and economically damaging, harming small business and thwarting a reasonable cross-generational transmission of wealth. The advantages of such an Accessions Tax have been well-stated by James Meade:

> Such a tax would give the maximum incentive to a wealthy citizen to dispose of his property by spreading it widely among beneficiaries who have not them-selves received any substantial inheritances. At the extreme, a millionaire could avoid all duty on his estate if he split it up in many small bequests each of which went to someone who had not yet acquired any property from gifts or inherit-ances.[45]

The structure of a liberal system of taxation

It should be noted at this point that, although both Mill and Meade support a progressive Accessions Tax, they diverge on income taxation, with Meade but not Mill favouring progression there too. Here Mill is surely in the right. There is no ethical or economic case for progressivity in income taxation. It does not diminish economic inequality, and may indeed enhance it. As Hayek has noted:

> A ... paradoxical and socially grave effect of progressive taxation is that, though intended to reduce inequality, it in fact helps to perpetuate existing inequalities and eliminates the most important compensation for that inequality which is inevitable in a free-enterprise society. It used to be the redeeming feature of such a system that the rich were not a closed group and that the successful man

might in a comparatively short time acquire large resources. Today, however, the chances of rising into the class are probably already smaller in some countries, such as Great Britain, than they have been at any time since the beginning of the modern era. One significant effect of this is that the adminis-tration of more and more of the world's capital is coming under the control of men who, though they enjoy very large incomes and all the amenities that this secures, have never on their own account and at their personal risk controlled substantial property. Whether it is altogether a gain remains to be seen.

It is also true that the less possible it becomes for a man to acquire a new fortune, the more must the existing fortunes appear as privileges for which there is no justification. Policy is then certain to aim at taking these fortunes out of private hands, either by the slow process of heavy taxation of inheritance or by the quicker one of outright confiscation. A system based on private property and control of the means of production presupposes that such property and control can be acquired by any successful man. If this is made impossible, even the men who otherwise would have been the most eminent capitalists of the new generation are bound to become the enemies of the established rich.[46]

Proportional income taxation has the merit of avoiding the hazards diagnosed by Hayek. In addition, it has a clear intuitive appeal in that justice and proportionality are linked in ordinary thought and the rich man who has more to protect cannot complain if he is taxed proportionately more. The most important advantage of proportional income taxation, however, is that it separates taxation from the expenditure side of government. It indicates that, aside from inheritance taxation via an Accessions Duty, defensible redistributional measures should all be on the expenditure side.

It is only in regard to the Accessions Tax on inheritances that the case for progressivity is arguable. Plainly, the incentive to spread wealth the more widely, and thereby to diminish or altogether eliminate tax liability on the part of the recipient, is stronger if, given a generous exemption, larger inheritances are taxed progressively more highly. I shall not here attempt to specify either the level of exemption or the rate of progression, save to say that it is hard to conceive of any case for a rate on large inheritances higher than the current higher rate on income in Britain of 40 per cent. The proposal here is simply for a progressive Accessions Tax on inheritances (and analogous capital transfers) which is avoidable by the device of dispersing wealth more widely.

The argument for an Expenditure Tax has as a natural corollary that capital gains should be tax exempt. This means that, rather than achieving a level playing field among investment media by imposing capital gains tax on owner-occupied houses, the same objective should be achieved, instead, by abolishing capital gains tax altogether. In this case, removing the remaining tax immunities of owner-oc-cupation would mean merely removing tax relief on mortgage interest payments.

In the liberal tax régime envisaged, there would be no taxes on capital, aside from those imposed by the Accessions Duty. These latter would be eminently avoidable and need involve no significant transfer of capital from the private sphere to government. What of income taxation? Here a bold sweep of all allowances, as reportedly suggested by Frank Field, MP, should enable massive cuts in the proportional rate to be achieved. If, in addition to the abolition of personal allowances, we incorporate the huge savings resultant from school privatisation and from the abolition of child benefits, there is further scope for reductions. If, finally, VAT were to be extended at a rate of 15 per cent to items at present zero-rated, then it would be reasonable to aim at a flat-rate tax of 15 per cent on all income as an achievable goal, even given full integration of income taxation with the current national insurance system. This basic rate becomes the more feasible if we take into account a separate hypothecated Health Tax with an exit option for those who wish to insure themselves privately.

In addition to these measures, a legitimate goal of liberal policy should be the progressive reduction, and ultimate abolition, of corporation tax. As Bracewell-Milnes has persuasively argued:

> Corporation tax is a tax either on enterprise or on business structure or on business financing: it imposes double taxation either on corporations or on dividends or on both. As a tax on enterprise, it serves no economic purpose, since the taxable capacity of enterprise is nil. Double taxation of corporations or dividends is at variance with the liberal ideal of neutrality.[47]

The goal of liberal policy should be the abolition of corporation tax, with revenue being derived from proportional taxes on income (with savings tax exempt) and by a VAT on all goods and services. It is possible to go yet further. Given continued growth in the economy and static or declining public expenditure, there is no reason not to entertain an even more radical possibility, that of a liberal tax régime in which revenue is derived overwhelmingly from taxes on expenditure, with direct taxes being in the shape only of an avoidable Accessions Tax on capital and hypothecated income taxes with exit options. Such a régime may appear impossibly remote from current circumstances, but there is nothing utopian about it. If it could be achieved, it would render the Expenditure Tax redundant, and would confine tax relief to remission of VAT on charities and other desirable causes. For the foreseeable future, however, the goal of a 15 per cent flat-rate tax on income and a corresponding 15 per cent on all goods currently VAT-taxed, including those zero-rated, seems a sufficiently radical objective.

The liberal tax régime advocated here aims to promote individual liberty, personal independence, and the diffusion of capital. It aims to even out the many distortions created by present tax policy, but without making a fetish of tax neutrality. And it incorporates an explicit concern for distributional considerations, which figure also on the expenditure side of a liberal policy.

The redistributional dimensions of voucher and loan schemes

In discussing voucher schemes, I have argued that they should be selective or targeted rather than universal, with the vast majority of people benefiting from a low-tax régime. I want now to argue that there is a case for such limited income transfer schemes having a redistributional dimension. This is perhaps most evidently appropriate in respect of student loans, since the income of the student's family may well influence his or her decision on whether to go to university. For this reason, loans to students from low-income families can justifiably be made on terms that are easier than those to middle-class students. In doing this, government would honour a sound meritocratic principle and even out incentives across the various income groups. Vouchers for school education, analogously, ought to be generous for the poorest, since it is from the poverty of the human capital of the poor that their low incomes often arise.

Again, the limited negative income tax schemes I have advocated ought to take account of the fact that the disabled and chronically sick have often the poorest quality of life in our society and their income support should for that reason be at a higher level than for able-bodied persons. Provided cut-off rates for such redistributional measures were not in excess of 50 per cent, as with the limited negative income tax schemes argued for, there ought not to be overwhelming disincentive effects (where incentive effects are relevant at all).

Advocating such redistributional measures seeks to give practical effect to Buchanan's proposition regarding the fairness of the rules governing the game of the market and acknowledges the truth of Hayek's assertion that 'It is clearly possible to bring about considerable redistribution under a system of proportional taxation'.[48] Such measures can, I think, be defended for their own sake, by reference to sound principles concerning equality of opportunity. But they are also defensible by reference to the risks to the stability of the free market where attention is not given to its distributive aspects. Supporters of the free market who reject concern for distribution should be aware that they are, by their indifference to the distributive background and effects of the market economy, increasing the political risk that the free market will be attacked and conceivably suppressed as a result of socialist criticism of its apparent injustices.

Culture as a public good

One area of policy often neglected by market liberals is that relating to the cultural traditions whereby a market society sustains and reproduces itself. There is a tendency to suppose that, once taxes are lowered, culture can take care of itself. Certainly, the present tax régime makes private support for the arts, for example, expensive and difficult, and there is a clear case for reform of taxation so that it is far easier (as in the United States) for individuals and businesses to support cultural activity. If this were done, we would be conforming to the maxim that, where the goal is to encourage some kind of desirable development or activity which it is felt that the market underproduces, this is best achieved by tax relief rather than by direct subsidies, which inevitably concentrate discretionary authority in quasi-governmental organisations.

It is an open question, however, whether such tax reforms are by themselves sufficient to sustain the cultural heritage on which the free market ultimately depends. Market liberals, such as Samuel Brittan and Alan Peacock, have argued persuasively that deregulation of television should be accompanied by the institution of an Arts Council of the Air with a mandate to subsidise productions that the market would not of itself support.[49] Again, extending government aid (either directly, as under present arrangements, or via tax deductions or voucher schemes) to Muslim, Orthodox Jewish and Hindu schools is supported not only by considerations of equity but also as an enabling device whereby those cultural traditions can renew and reproduce themselves. Other examples could easily be found, but my general point is more important than any specific measures: that the stability of the market society depends crucially on a matrix of cultural traditions which at once legitimate it and find expression in it. As with the national curriculum, which fosters literacy in a common language, government may legitimately fund artistic activity so as to renew the common culture. A limited government has therefore a vital role in transmitting the values on which a market society depends. A limited government which rejects or is indifferent to the culture which underpins the market neglects one of the conditions of its own existence.

CONCLUSION: MARKET LIBERALISM AND THE FUTURE

Canst thou draw out leviathan with a hook? or his tongue with a cord which thou lettest down? Canst thou put an hook into his nose? or bore his jaw through with a thorn? Will he make many supplications unto thee? will he speak soft words unto thee? Will he make a covenant with thee? wilt thou take him for a servant for ever?

(Job 41: 1–4)

Free relations among free men – this precept of ordered anarchy can emerge as a principle when successfully renegotiated social contract puts 'mine and thine' in a newly defined structural arrangement and when the Leviathan that threatens is placed within new limits.

(James Buchanan)[50]

The argument for limited government is one that is addressed across the political spectrum. Market liberalism is a perspective that should be compelling for conservatives, who (like myself) affirm the foundation of market institutions in a historical inheritance of norms and traditions, and for social democrats, who seek to reform that inheritance by reference to general principles of equality.

By market liberalism I mean the proposition that the great bulk of economic activity is best conducted within the institutions of market capitalism in a régime of private property and contractual liberty. And by limited government I mean a form of government which restricts itself to setting the framework of market capitalism (a framework that encompasses, I have argued, policy which addresses the distributional and cultural preconditions of a stable market order).

The political debate between free-market conservatism and a market-oriented social democracy should focus on such issues as distribution, the scope and variety of public goods, and the best policy for supporting intermediary institutions and flourishing communal life. For this debate to occur and be fruitful, however, it is vital that market liberalism be accepted across the political spectrum as the only set of institutions which can in a modern society protect values of liberty, independence, equity and prosperity. This in turn presupposes that delusive visions such as market socialism be taken off the intellectual agenda. Social democrats should be encouraged in this move by the experience of the post-communist states, where there is growing recognition that 'market socialism' describes nothing that is defensible or achievable. They should listen to J. Kornai, one of the intellectual leaders of the Hungarian economic reform movement, when he says of the theorist of market socialism, Oskar Lange:

> Lange's model is based on erroneous assumptions regarding the 'planners'. The people at his Central Planning Board are reincarnations of Plato's philosophers, embodiments of unity, unselfishness and wisdom. They are satisfied with doing nothing else but strictly enforcing the 'Rule'... such an unworldly bureaucracy never existed in the past and will never exist in the future. Political bureaucracies have inner conflicts reflecting the divisions of society and the diverse pressures of various social groups. They pursue their own individual and group interests, including the interests of the specialised agency to which they belong. Power creates an irresistible temptation to make use of it. A bureaucrat must be interventionist because that is his role in society; it is dictated by his situation. What is not happening in Hungary with respect to detailed micro-regulation is not an accident. It is rather the predictable, self-evident result of the mere existence of a huge and powerful bureaucracy. An inherent tendency to recentralisation prevails.[51]

It is important to note that Kornai's incisive critique applies not only to the centralised market socialism advocated by Lange, in which government uses various devices to simulate market prices, but also to the market socialism of competing worker co-operatives that is currently fashionable in the West. This latter market socialism is unstable and unworkable for reasons closely analogous to those which condemn the Lange model as unfeasible. As the Yugoslav example has shown, self-managed worker co-operatives are risk-averse; tending slowly to consume capital rather than to invest in technological innovation, they produce structural unemployment because of their resistance to new entrants, and they cannot avoid involvement in a political competition for capital from the state investment banks. Where it is not a recipe for economic stagnation, market socialism is a mirage, an attempt to reap the benefits of market pricing without allowing for the market pricing of the most important productive factor, capital itself, and without permitting the necessary condition of free markets, which is a system of private property in which incentives and risks are decentralised in a régime of liberal ownership.

Western social democrats must recognise that, as well as incurring substantial costs in terms of economies of scale, underinvestment and structural unemployment, market socialism is inherently unstable. Both experience and theory suggest that it is bound to mutate in the potentially politically explosive direction of reinventing the central institutions of market capitalism, or else to return by the route of recentralisation to a socialist command economy. It would be a hopeful augury for Britain if, in future, debate were to focus on the cultural and moral preconditions of market liberalism, rather than on the question of whether market capitalism is to be accepted – a question which historical experience has in any case already decisively answered. Public discourse is now best addressed to the issue of the appropriate standards and measures for reform of market capitalism, not to delusive (or disastrous) alternatives to it. Indeed, the long-term survival of the free market in Britain depends ultimately on such an intellectual realignment within the major political parties, in which acceptance of market liberalism is at the heart of a new public consensus.

The argument for limited government and for the market economy is not in the end an economic argument. It is an ethical argument: that, in the conditions of a modern society, only market institutions can give practical realisation to the values of liberty and human dignity. The argument for the market is not that government be conceived of as an economic enterprise, but is instead the contrary, that only market institutions allow free individuals to opt into or out of enterprise. At present, when government – in Britain and elsewhere – speaks to us in the harsh accents of Bentham rather than the civilised tones of Hume, we face the danger of civil society being further weakened by the metamorphosis of the state itself into an enterprise association. It has been the argument of this chapter that only the reassertion of the project of a limited government with positive tasks can hope to protect us from the spectacle, tragic or farcical as it may turn out to be, of a *dirigiste* Behemoth, in whose wake nothing is left but a litter of ephemeral corporatist projects and the ruins of civil society.

2 A conservative disposition
Individualism, the free market and the common life

INTRODUCTION

It is said ... that conservatism in politics is the appropriate counterpart of a generally conservative disposition in respect of human conduct: to be reformist in business, in morals or in religion and to be conservative in politics is represented as being inconsistent. It is said that the conservative in politics is so by holding certain religious beliefs; a belief, for example, in a natural law to be gathered from human experience, and in a providential order reflecting a divine purpose in nature and in human history to which it is the duty of mankind to conform and departure from which spells injustice and calamity. Further, it is said that a disposition to be conservative in politics reflects what is called an 'organic' theory of human society, that it is tied up with a belief in the absolute value of human personality, and with a belief in the primordial propensity of human beings to sin. And the conservatism of an Englishman has even been connected with Royalism and Anglicanism.

Now setting aside the minor complaints one might be moved to make about this account of the situation, it seems to me to suffer from one large defect. It is true that many of these beliefs have been held by people disposed to be conservative in political activity, and it may be true that these people have also believed their disposition to be in some way confirmed by them, or even to be founded upon them; but, as I understand it, a disposition to be conservative in politics does not entail either that we should hold these beliefs to be true or even that we should suppose them to be true. Indeed, I do not think it is necessarily connected with any particular beliefs about the universe, about the world in general or about human conduct in general. What it is tied to is certain beliefs about the activity of governing and the instruments of government, and it is in terms of beliefs on these topics, and not on others, that it can be made to appear intelligible. And, to state my view briefly before elaborating it, what makes a conservative disposition in politics intelligible is nothing to do with a natural law or a providential order, nothing to do with morals or religion; it is the observation of our current manner of living combined with the belief (which from our point of view needs to be regarded as no more than an hypothesis) that governing is a specific and limited activity, namely the provision and custody of general rules of conduct, which are understood, not as plans for imposing substantive activities, but as instruments enabling people to pursue the activities of their own choice with the minimum frustration, and therefore something which it is appropriate to be conservative about.

(Michael Oakeshott)[1]

The common belief that there cannot be such a thing as a conservative political philosophy expresses a prejudice of rationalism which conservatives are not obliged to share. It embodies the primitive view that any political philosophy worth its salt must be articulated in a system of precepts that is universal in application, grounded in immutable principles, and capable of resolving any significant political dilemma. Whatever else it may be, a conservative political philosophy cannot be that. A central element of the conservative outlook is found in the sceptical denial that a political philosophy of that universal and rationalist sort can be anything other than an illusion. From this standpoint of scepticism, however, it does not follow that conservatism in politics cannot be given a coherent articulation, intelligible and acceptable to most who think of themselves as conservatives, and having a claim on the consideration of reasonable people who are not themselves conservatives.

As it has been articulated in the British tradition, in the writings of Hume and Oakeshott, Burke, Disraeli and Salisbury, Churchill and Thatcher, the most fundamental tenet of the conservative outlook on politics is the limited character of the role of government. For a conservative in the British tradition, political life is not a project of world improvement, or the reconstitution of human institutions on the pattern of any ideal model, but instead something much humbler. The office of government is to palliate the natural and unavoidable evils of human life, and to refrain from adding to them. Any government animated by a conservative outlook takes for granted the imperfectibility of human affairs. The political predicament of our species is not that of a creature of infinite possibilities that have throughout its history been inexplicably shackled. We are not, each of us, as our liberal culture encourages us to imagine, a limitless reservoir of possibilities, for whom the past is an irrelevance and the future an empty horizon. We are finite, mortal selves, burdened by the evils of our history and the miseries natural to the human condition, who achieve excellence and a measure of well-being only in so far as we accept the disciplines of civilisation. Conservatives acknowledge the imperfectibility of human life, not in virtue of subscribing to any metaphysical speculation, but as a result of ordinary experience and common observation. These were summarised by Thomas Hobbes, who, if he is not perhaps a conservative, nevertheless has an assured place in the Tory pantheon, when he famously observes that:

It is true, that certain living creatures, as Bees, and Ants, live sociably one with another, (which are therefore by *Aristotle* numbred amongst Politicall creatures;) and yet have no other direction, than their particular judgements and appetites; nor speech, whereby one of them can signifie to another, what he thinks expedient for the common benefit: and therefore some man may perhaps desire to know, why Man-kind cannot do the same. To which I answer,

First, that men are continually in competition for Honour and Dignity, which these creatures are not; and consequently amongst men there ariseth on that ground, Envy and Hatred, and finally Warre; but amongst these not so.

Secondly, that amongst these creatures, the Common good differeth not from the Private; and being by nature enclined to their private, they procure thereby the common benefit. But man, whose Joy consisteth in comparing himselfe with other men, can relish nothing but what is eminent.

Thirdly, that these creatures having not (as man) the use of reason, do not see, nor think they see any fault, in the administration of their common businesse: whereas amongst men, there are very many, that thinke themselves wiser, and abler to govern the Publique, better than the rest; and these strive to reforme and innovate, one this way, another that way; and thereby bring it into Distraction and Civill warre.

Fourthly, that these creatures, though they have some use of voice, in making knowne to one another their desires, and other affections; yet they want that art of words, by which some men can represent to others, that which is Good, in the likenesse of Evill; and Evill, in the likenesse of Good; and augment, or diminish the apparent greatnesse of Good and Evill; discontenting men, and troubling their Peace and their pleasure.

Fifthly, irrationall creatures cannot distinguish betweene *Injury and Damm-age*; and therefore as long as they be at ease, they are not offended with their fellowes: whereas Man is then most troublesome, when he is most at ease: for then it is that he loves to shew his Wisdome, and controule the Actions of them that governe the Common-wealth.

Lastly, the agreement of these creatures is Naturall; that of men, is by Covenant only, which is Artificiall: and therefore it is no wonder if there be somwhat else required (besides Covenant) to make their Agreement constant and lasting; which is a Common Power, to keep them in awe, and to direct their actions to the Common Benefit.[2]

On this Hobbesian view, political wisdom is the sad business of prescribing for ordinary mortals, not a mandate for adventures in infinite freedom. Accordingly, the primary task of a conservative government is not the pursuit of indefinite betterment, but the staving off of ever-present evils. It is, first and foremost, in the avoidance of civil strife, in the prevention or containment of war, in the mitigation of the arbitrariness of power through the institution of a rule of law, and in the provision of a sound currency that the achievements of a conservative government are properly to be measured.

Because conservatives deny the evanescence of imperfection, they reject the Procrustean politics of the utopian blueprint. They are rightly suspicious, more-over, not only of politics as the pursuit of perfection but also of the idea of history as a narrative of progress, with ourselves as its *telos*. As I understand it, the conservative outlook – at least as it is found within the European intellectual tradition of which British conservatism is an integral part – is deeply at odds with that sentimental religion of humanity, with its ruling superstitions of progress and of convergence on a universal civilisation, which is the secular creed of our times and which has largely succeeded in supplanting the traditional Western faiths. The growth of scientific knowledge, together with increased virtuosity in its applications, have given us conveniences – anaesthetic dentistry and flush lavatories are examples – whose place in the scheme of things is not to be despised. Scientific and technological advance has not, and cannot, diminish the realm of mystery and tragedy in which it is our lot to dwell.

This is to say that a conservative may be an agnostic, even (if that is his or her misfortune) an atheist, but never a humanist. By contrast with classical liberals and with American neo-conservatives, British Tories have not swallowed the canard that human life is open to indefinite improvement by judicious use of critical reason. For them, human reason is a weak reed, on which they must rely in daily life and in the formation of policies, but in which it is folly to have faith. Conservatives in the British and European traditions have been spared the hubris of those who make a religion of world-improvement. This is to say that, though they are committed to reform of institutions and practices that fail to serve human needs, they aim to do good in minute particulars, not in grand schemes. It is not that conservatives cannot be reformers, even at times radical reformers. Rather, the costs and advantages of reform need always to be weighed in detail, radical reform should go with the grain of the national character and tradition rather than against it, and conservatives should view with the deepest suspicion proposals for radical reform that are inspired by hubristic ideology rather than by evident necessity. Unlike the classical liberal world-view that has, regrettably, formed much of the thought of the New Right, conservatism is not a secular faith, a historical theodicy that aims to displace traditional faiths. On the contrary, conservatives seek to return religion to its proper sphere, and to divest political questions of the almost transcendent importance that they have acquired (by a return to public life of a religious sensibility that secular rationalism has subjected to an almost Freudian repression) in modern times. For this reason, conservatives are always friendly to the religious life in its proper sphere. At the same time, it is a cardinal point of my argument that people in Britain live in a culture that is in large part post-Christian and even post-religious, and in which a sceptical and secular conservatism is therefore appropriate. This is not at all to deny that Christianity is an enduring and precious part of British cultural inheritance, nor that the institution of an established Church has considerable advantages as an element in the unfixed and unwritten constitution. It is merely to observe the fateful fact that secularisation is in Britain far advanced and likely to be irreversible, so that the culture and traditions that bind people together cannot any longer be distinctively Christian or informed by any shared transcendental faith.

For a conservative, however, the waning of religious faith is not to be welcomed, even if it is conceived to be inevitable, because of the belief that

Civilisation is hooped together, brought
Under a rule, under the semblance of peace
By manifold illusion; but man's life is thought
And he, despite his terror, cannot cease
Ravening through century after century
Ravening, raging and uprooting that
   he may come
Into the desolation of reality.[3]

One of the tasks of conservative statecraft is to mitigate, so far as it can, the desolation of reality that overtakes human beings in a post-religious age that has grown too wise to swallow the shallow illusions of the Enlightenment. In this task, conservatives acknowledge that human beings may well have flourished better in ages, such as that of medieval Christendom, which had at the bottom of them an unquestioned transcendental faith. It will be one of my contentions in this chapter, at the same time, that sound conservative policy cannot be nostalgist in inspiration: once the cake of custom is broken, we must do our best with what is left. It cannot be baked anew. In practice, this means a policy which aims to infuse an irreducibly pluralist and self-critical society with the conservative virtues of coherence, self-confidence and stability. Nor should policy be informed by the triumphalist belief that government can secure the conditions for the successful pursuit of happiness. For a conservative in the sceptical tradition of Hobbes, Hume and Oakeshott, happiness is a matter of chance, and its pursuit is a profitless enterprise. People are better employed in struggling to reconcile themselves to their circumstances, on the whole, than in striving to alter them. The task of government is to bolster those institutions and forms of life which, if they cannot confer happiness, nevertheless enable the natural sorrows of human life to be endured in a meaningful and dignified fashion. In this respect, the British conservative tradition – and its Tory element in particular – has little in common with the Whiggish spirit which animates American neo-conservatism and libertarianism. It resembles far more the Augustinian vision that inspired the Founding Fathers.

It follows from what has so far been said that, though conservative government is limited government, it has nothing in common with the minimalist, *laissez-faire*, night-watchman state advocated by libertarian doctrinaires such as Herbert Spencer and Robert Nozick. A limited government has tasks that go well beyond keeping the peace – the vital Hobbesian task of staving off the nemesis of anarchy and civil strife in which commodious living is an impossibility. It has also a responsibility to tend fragile and precious traditions, to protect and shelter the vulnerable and defenceless, to enhance and enlarge opportunities for the disadvantaged, to promote the conservation and renewal of the natural and human environment and to assist in the renewal of civil society and the reproduction of the common culture without which pluralism and diversity become enmity and division. My argument in this chapter will be, therefore, firstly, that the role of government is other and larger than that specified in the libertarian dogmas of contemporary neo-liberalism. Contrary to neo-liberalism, a conservative government has good reason to concern itself with the well-being and virtue of its subjects, since if these are not promoted liberal civil society will decay and loyalty to the liberal state will tend to wane. Conservatives must therefore resist the pressure for the political disestablishment of morality that is the common coinage of liberalism in both its libertarian and its revisionist egalitarian varieties. But, secondly, this legitimate concern for the moral foundations of civil society cannot justify policies of social engineering aiming to revive a lost (and doubtless partly imaginary) moral solidarity among people. The project of restoring an organic national community, as currently advocated most perceptively by Roger Scruton,[4] is a distraction from serious policy-making in a society that is irreversibly pluralist, even if it has merit as an antidote to the lifeless abstractions of liberal doctrine. People today are not Victorians, nor even the folk portrayed by Ealing Studios, and serious policy must address them in all their intractable idiosyncracy.

In the third section of this chapter, I will consider the kinds of policy that seem appropriate for a conservative government in the present historical circumstance. The upshot of my reflections will be that the free market economy, which contemporary conservatives rightly see as the engine whereby a modern civil society reproduces itself, is not something free-standing, primordial or self-moving. It rests upon the foundations of a common culture of liberty and has as its supports the institutions of a strong state that tempers its excesses and shelters those – the very old, the disabled, the chronically sick, the educationally disadvantaged, for example – who may be without the resources, or skills, to prosper in it. The central thought of this chapter is that, whereas the institutions of the free market are indispensable conditions at once of liberty and prosperity in Britain and similar countries today, it is prudent to be sceptical of the radical libertarian ideology with which in recent political discourse they have come to be associated. The legitimacy of the free market in the political realm depends not only on its uninterrupted delivery of economic growth – something that, we are now reminded, cannot be always guaranteed – but also, and more importantly, on its being contained and sustained by the common allegiances nurtured by traditional Toryism, and tempered by a liberal social policy that is in harmony with the spirit of the age. Only in this way can conservative individualism have a political future.

THE LIMITS OF LIBERALISM

The argument that government should not concern itself with the virtue and well-being of its subjects, but only protect them from each other, is given a classic statement by J.S. Mill in his *On Liberty*.[5] There he makes a case for the view that individual liberty may rightly be restrained only when its exercise threatens harm to others. It follows that the coercive authority of law may never be invoked to protect people from themselves, or to promote the virtues. Mill's is a classic statement of the argument for the legal disestablishment of morality, which has found many echoes in later liberal theorists such as Hart, Dworkin and Rawls.

It is an argument that no conservative, and certainly no conservative individualist, can accept. The idea that one person may harm himself or herself without affecting others, that there is a sphere of self-regarding conduct which deserves absolute immunity from legal and social intervention, neglects the interdependency of human beings that is a central ingredient in any view of society that can be reasonably called conservative. We are not, in truth, Mill's sovereign selves, parading our individuality before an indifferent world: we are born in families, encumbered without our consent by obligations we cannot by voluntary choice renounce. If we harm ourselves, we harm those who care for us or who depend upon us. Government has a legitimate interest in protecting us from self-harm, if only because there are few such harms that are not also harms to others. Government may rightly concern itself, also, with the quality of the lives its subjects lead. Lives that are dominated by avoidable addictions, for example, are poorer than they need be; they result in the atrophy of the powers of choice on which responsibility depends; they are not examples of human flourishing. In the idiom of modern moral philosophy, government – and certainly conservative government – has good reason to undertake policies of paternalism and moralism, where these can expect a decent measure of success, and do not impose unreasonable burdens on the law. Conservatives have no reason to seek to privatise the good life.

In enacting policies that express concern for the virtue and well-being of the citizenry, and which do not merely protect people from one another, conservative governments accept (what is suppressed in liberal theory) that human individuality is not a natural fact but a cultural achievement, won with difficulty and easily lost. The matrix of human individuality is a cultural environment in which people are formed as choosers with responsibility for their actions. The formation of individual character cannot itself be a direct concern of government – it is rather the task of intermediary institutions, families, churches and voluntary associations. Nevertheless, government has an indefeasible obligation to tend and nurture those intermediary institutions. The society that a conservative individualist envisages is not one in which the solitary individual confronts the minimum state. Such a purely Hobbesian polity would likely command neither the allegiance nor the affection of its subjects. The limited government favoured by conservative individualists is one with a strong commitment to the intermediary institutions in which individuals are formed and in which for the most part their lives find meaning.

It is recognised, therefore, that a society held together solely by the impersonal nexus of market exchanges, as envisaged by Hayek[6] (whose insights into the failings of central planning have now been vindicated by events in the countries of the former Soviet bloc) and other neo-liberal thinkers, is at best a mirage, at worst a prescription for a return to the state of nature. Nor can any human society hope to approximate the Areopagitic and Socratic ideals of Mill or Popper[7] – the ideal of an open society of rational inquirers, united only in the activity of mutual criticism. It is more than doubtful whether such a society would be tolerable, even if it were achievable. For most people, the meaning of their lives is a local affair, and the examined life may turn out to be hardly worth living. Liberal ideologues, in the nescience of their rationalist conceit, suppose that they can answer the question posed by the greatest twentieth-century Tory poet: what are days for?

These ideologues have still to learn that, when local knowledge is squandered in incessant self-criticism, people realise that

> solving that question
> Brings the priest and the doctor
> In their long coats
> Running over the fields.

(Philip Larkin)[8]

Conservative individualists recognise that, before anything else, even before freedom, human beings need a home, a nest of institutions and a way of life they feel to be their own. Among conservatives, the practices of market exchange and of rational argument are familiar ingredients in, and even necessary conditions, of their way of life. They are not the whole of the way of life that they inherit, and they cannot hope to flourish, or in the end to survive, if the common culture of liberty and responsibility that supports and animates them is eroded in the pursuit of the mirage of the sovereign individual of liberal ideology.

What follows for policy from these reflections? In the first place, contrary to Mill's antinomian individualism, policies of legal prohibition may sometimes be justified in respect of activities that strike at the roots of individual responsibility and the common values that support civil society. Where, as in Britain, the legal prohibition of very addictive and highly dangerous drugs has been reasonably successful, there is every reason to resist libertarian demands for drug legalisation. It is only where, as is plausibly the case in the United States, the war against drugs is unwinnable and its costs insupportable, that the conservative individualist will endorse decriminalisation. Again, the conservative individualist will find unproblematic the proscription of pornography which involves violence or the exploitation of children or animals, though he or she may well have serious reservations about the large discretionary powers of the apparatus of censorship set up to control the video industry in Britain. The conservative individualist, unlike the Millian individualist, can have no objection to policies of legal prohibition of these sorts, where other measures are demonstrably ineffectual, and the activities proscribed pose a real threat to the values that sustain a liberal civil society.

It is in social policy, however, that the errors of unrestrained neo-liberalism are most egregious. Consider policy on poverty. There has been a tendency in neo-liberal thought to seek a technical fix for poverty in the appealing device of a universal negative income tax. Such policies neglect the heterogeneity of modern poverty, and suppress the distinctive causes of its most disturbing variant, the poverty of the underclass. It has been the great achievement of Milton Friedman to show that, at least over the longer run and in the last resort, inflation is always and everywhere a monetary phenomenon. Contrary to Friedman and his disciples, however, the poverty of the modern underclass is nowhere primarily a monetary phenomenon. It is instead a cultural phenomenon, caused by family breakdown, the depletion of human skills across the generations and the emergence of a dependency culture. No policy in regard to this species of poverty could be worse devised than the negative income tax, which supplements low incomes regardless of their causes, and thereby abrogates responsibility in the recipients. It also distracts the attention of policy-makers from those varieties of modern poverty which *are* occasioned primarily by lack of money: the poverty of the old who were prevented by inflation and confiscatory taxation from making provision for themselves, of the disabled, of the sick and of those whom catastrophe has struck.

There is a deeper lesson in the neo-liberal error about poverty. It is that social policy cannot be value-free or non-judgemental, and cannot be neutral with regard to the institutions that undergird the market economy. If, as is manifestly the case, much underclass poverty is a product of family breakdown, then policy must address the conditions of family stability – a large question that encompasses not only welfare benefits but also tax policy and divorce law. In all of these areas, sensible policy cannot and should not avoid giving legal recognition to specific forms of family life. The model animating policy ought never to be that of a society of strangers, bound together by a limitless diversity of contractual agreements. The concern which animates policy should instead be that of repairing and renewing, sustaining and supporting those inherited intermediary institutions which experience has shown are best capable of nurturing the responsible individuals who make up a free society. In framing policies to this end, it is necessary to beware, above all, the fixation on particular measures that has bedevilled neo-liberal thought. No policy is without costs and hazards, all necessitate trade-offs between legitimate interests and values, and none is a panacea. Schemes for targeting welfare benefits and other forms of selective provision have the cost of a cumbersome administrative apparatus and the hazard of generating disincentives for self-provision. In some instances – child benefit and basic pensions, perhaps – universal benefits *may* be the least undesirable forms of income support.

Voucher schemes, also, have important costs and dangers. Like all species of government provision of income, they are liable to inflation by the operation of political competition in the democratic market place: they have in this respect no advantage over direct provision of services by government. In some areas, such as schooling (where they may on balance offer the best solution to current problems), they carry with them the risk of blurring the distinction between the public and the private sectors, and effecting a covert socialisation of the latter in which it loses its present independence.

Again, in many countries, such as France, where (despite recent difficulties) state provision of schooling has been accompanied by the maintenance of traditional standards, experimenting with privatisation or a voucher scheme would be to disregard the deeper conservative wisdom expressed in the question, 'Why mend that which is not yet broken?' (This deeper conservative wisdom may be especially relevant to the post-communist societies, whose schooling systems – once free of communist deformation – are in general more traditionalist in character than Western schools and for that reason superior in performance. In such a context, privatisation – which in Britain and the United States is a counsel of despair about state schools – would be an absurd measure.) In many other areas, voucher schemes are simply unworkable, or else indefensible. Whereas voucher schemes may have a valuable role in community care for the elderly and the disabled, as I shall later suggest, they have little or no place in other areas of medical care, where people may be uninsurable and the resources they need not easily measurable.

Further, even where a voucher-based insurance scheme in medical care is feasible, experience shows that it issues in a ruinous inflation of medical costs. Is there any British conservative who wishes to import into the United Kingdom the pernicious American system, in which nearly forty million people lack any entitlement to medical care, and even the middle classes are bankrupted by catastrophic illness? For all of its imperfections, the National Health Service – preferably in its unreformed version – has a vital place in the common life in Britain as a provider of decent, basic medical care that is available to all, which any future Conservative government is bound to safeguard.[9] In these and some other areas of policy, it is reasonable to accept that direct provision by government may be the only viable option.

Voucher schemes have indeed a signal virtue – that of combining governmental provision with the market allocation of services. They are not for that reason perfect, costless or without hazards, and they are not a magic wand that will spirit away all ills. A conservative policy aiming to support the intermediary institutions, the common culture and the values that animate a free society, and to protect those in it who would otherwise be bereft of care, is bound to be pluralist in the measures it adopts. Certainly, no conservative policy-maker can afford the doctrinaire attachment to specific measures (such as the voucher and the negative income tax) that has been evident in much recent neo-liberal thought.

The spirit of conservative individualism can be seen to be far removed from the antinomian self-assertion that infuses *On Liberty* and which informs the more radical varieties of contemporary libertarianism. In the antinomian perspective, conventions are restraints on individuality, institutions (when they are recognised at all) are artefacts of agreements, traditions are burdens and habits symptoms of debility. Conservatives recognise, by contrast, that where conventions have fallen into desuetude and the authority of the past is denied, only a Hobbesian sovereign can keep the peace. It is an infallible sign of a genuinely free society, however, that in normal times peace is the mark of common life, and the powers of the Hobbesian sovereign are deployed chiefly against the outlaw – the terrorist or the criminal who has chosen to step outside of the circle of law and civility. This is to say that the transmission of freedom and individuality across the generations demands more than a framework of common rules. It presupposes a common culture – a shared culture of liberty and responsibility.

THE LIMITS OF COMMUNITY AND DIVERSITY IN A COMMON CULTURE: NOTES TOWARD THE DEFINITION OF A LIBERAL CIVIL SOCIETY

The individualism that is favoured by a conservative is, therefore, to be distinguished sharply from that sponsored by liberalism and libertarianism. In their different ways, these latter forms of individualism embody a romantic cult of self-assertion that is alien to the Tory sensibility and the British conservative tradition. Liberal individualism, in its political manifestations, impoverishes British culture by delegitimating its traditions and conventions by representing them all as constraints upon individual liberty, thereby obscuring their true role as necessary conditions of individuality and civil life. For conservatives, by contrast, the individualism that is prized is inherited as the patrimony of a common culture, which government may rightly act to reinforce.

At the same time, the historical circumstance of Britons today is not that of guardians of a common culture which they receive as a seamless garment. In society there is a prodigious diversity of histories, ethnicities, styles of life and views of the world. Since time immemorial, England itself has been an individualist culture,[10] whose individualism has owed much to its Christian heritage. For several centuries, the United Kingdom has been a composite state, encompassing four nations. In recent decades, this inherited diversity of national traditions has been enriched by large-scale immigration from Commonwealth countries – an immigration which has introduced into national life powerful currents of non-Christian religious belief and practice. Further developments in cultural diversity in Britain are to be expected as a result of the increasingly deep integration in a widening European community that encompasses many of the post-communist states. These aspects of the current circumstances make cultural diversity a brute historical fact with which any serious conservative outlook is bound to reckon.

The task of latter-day conservative government is not only to accept but to welcome this enhanced diversity, while seeking to buttress and undergird it with the rudiments of a common culture. Since the present historical circumstance is no longer that of a culture unified by a single religion, however fragmented, and since Britain has never in recent centuries been in a situation in which political allegiance and nationality are coextensive, the project of restoring an organic national community in Britain is vain, chimerical and perhaps harmful – if indeed such a community ever existed there. Like Spain, Britain is an artefact of the institution of monarchy, an institution which has the inestimable advantage that political allegiance is not dependent on nationality or ethnicity. Because Britain is a constitutional monarchy, not a national republic, and because of its imperial history, the country is in a better position than most to absorb the new elements of cultural diversity that recent decades have brought. The pursuit of a vision of nationhood that has no purchase on historical traditions can, for Britain, be only an aberration, a distraction from the task of sustaining the bonds which are shared and which in fact can hold the people together.

Because of British history and institutions, political and national allegiance for people in Britain today cannot be founded in ethnicity. It may, and should, invoke a shared sense of Britishness, where this means a sense of fair play, of equality before the law, and a spirit of toleration and compromise on matters about which people have deep differences. For people in Britain today, allegiance cannot express a deep community of shared values, since the communitarian ambition – the ambition of making political loyalty coterminous with membership of a single moral community – could not be more inappropriate. People are not, in the jargon of recent philosophy, 'radically situated selves'[11] persons whose identities are defined by membership of a single, all-inclusive community. They are members of many and sometimes conflicting communities: they are (in Fulke Greville's phrase) 'suckled on the milk of many nurses'. With such a plural inheritance, people cannot reasonably expect that political and national allegiance will express a deep culture of common values. It is to be hoped, nevertheless, that people have in common enough respect for the ruling ideas of a civil society – ideas of toleration, of responsibility and of equality under the rule of law – for diversity in society to be fruitful rather than an occasion for division.

What does all this mean for policy? In the first place, it suggests the wisdom of law having a minor, and often a merely regulatory role, in matters about which people deeply disagree. Consider, in this regard, the liberal reforms of the sixties, in which homosexuality was legalised, divorce and censorship relaxed, capital punishment abolished and abortion made freer. It is significant that, for all the charges of authoritarian moralism levelled against it, the Thatcher government (like its conservative predecessors and successor) has never sought to reverse these liberal reforms. In this it has, surely, been right. If there is a consensus on morality among conservatives, it is a liberal consensus that, where the interests of children are not concerned, adults may live as they choose, subject only to the law of the land as it applies to all. This is not to say that existing law may not profit from specific reforms, since, as recent proposals for the reform of the law on divorce suggest, the current legal environment may accord freedom to adults at the expense of the interests of dependent children. On the whole, however, the liberal reforms of the sixties ought to be accepted by conservatives, partly because they express an actually existing consensus on values. They are to be commended to conservative individualists, I suggest, because they also embody the good old liberal ideal of toleration – an ideal that has lately been occluded by obscurantist discourse about the rights of minority groups and cultures. It is in the nature of conservative thought and practice that it preserves its identity by absorbing other traditions, and in this case it does so by appropriating an old-fashioned liberal idea that has now entered deeply into common life.

Or consider policy toward the family. Here the principal danger to be avoided is that of revivalism – of attempting to restore a pattern of family life that economic change has radically altered, and whose legitimacy is no longer self-evident. 'Like prices in a free market', we are reminded by the greatest conservative thinker of our time, 'habits of moral conduct show no revolutionary changes because they are never at rest.'[12] Policy cannot sensibly be modelled on a form of family life which was common half a century ago, and which has now become that of, very nearly, a minority. It may, as I shall argue later, concern itself with irresponsibility in procreation and with the deleterious effects of unchosen single-parenthood. It cannot seek to impose any single pattern on the varieties of family life in society today. Some women choose the role of wife and mother for much or even all of their lives; many seek to combine motherhood with career; most, perhaps, alternate between work at home and work in the wider economy. Conservative government must be even-handed, and respect each of these choices. It makes itself absurd if, Canute-like, it seeks to stem the tide of social and moral change that floods inexorably from changes in the economy and in general outlook. Conservative policy cannot emulate the spurious liberal ideal of neutrality in respect of all forms of family life that meet some minimal requirement of rights-protection, since it recognises that there are forms of family life – particularly that of involuntary single-parenthood – which are injurious to children and to those who have to care for them. It must nevertheless respect and seek to sustain the legitimate diversity of forms of family life that spring from the responsible decisions that people make.

The question of the proper conservative policy toward the family suggests broader questions about education and about multiculturalism. The starting-point of reflection must be that, in present society, no-one can flourish who does not possess the basic skills of numeracy and literacy in the English language. The bottom line of governmental responsibility for schooling is not in providing institutions which are successful in inculcating these skills, but rather in defining and enforcing a national framework of assessment and achievement in respect of them. Whereas opinions may legitimately differ as to the best mode of provision, the duty of government to set and inspect national standards in schooling is beyond reasonable doubt. It may be true that, when British culture was far more homogeneous in its traditions and ways of life, curricular choice could be safely left to the tacit understandings of headteachers and staff. With the advent of mass immigration and other species of cultural diversity, a national curriculum, or something like it, is a manifest necessity. Current proposals are far from being the best that can be conceived in that, as Sheila Lawlor has shown,[13] they give insufficient priority to a core curriculum comprising English, Mathematics and Science. It is the inculcation of such skills of numeracy, literacy (in the English language) and scientific thinking that is the proper aim of any national curriculum.

There are clear implications for the issue of multiculturalism in this conclusion. Cultural minorities, such as the British Muslims, have an undeniable entitlement to government funding for their schools, if only on grounds of equity given the current practice in regard to Catholics and Jews. Along with every other school, however, a Muslim school ought to receive such subsidy only if it conforms to a streamlined national curriculum by teaching the basic skills to all of its pupils, both male and female. In Britain, it is taken for granted (even if the realities often fail to match this expectation) that opportunities for men and women, whether as children at school or later in life, be the same. The form of life that is inherited today, with all of its many variations, confers upon men and women the same responsibilities and opportunities. With regard to schooling, it follows from this that conservative governments cannot endorse, by subsidy or otherwise, schools that deny this equality of opportunity to the sexes. This is but one of the important limits on cultural diversity that any government which is committed to the protection of civil society is bound to impose.

It expresses a deeper, and less fashionable truth. Cultural minorities, whether indigenous or immigrant in origin, cannot expect public subsidy for aspects of their ways of life which flout the central norms of liberal civil society. They are entitled to protection from forms of discrimination which deny them full participation in the common life. They cannot justifiably claim privileges or immunities of the sort enshrined in policies of affirmative action and of group rights, which effectively shield them from the healthy pressures of the larger society. Although it is to be hoped that cultural minorities in Britain will retain many aspects of their traditions, including traditions of hard work and family stability in which many recent immigrants excel over the indigenous population, civil peace in the kingdom depends on their integration into the civil society that enables them to live in freedom. The lessons of states which have allowed unrestricted immigration of incompatible minorities or which have inherited profound ethnic divisions, are sobering and indeed ominous for liberals who indulge the dangerous fantasy that civil peace can be maintained solely by obedience to common rules. History and the news of the day suggest otherwise: that pluralism must be bounded by the norms and the common culture of civil society. Pluralism must have such limits, or else Beirut will be the likely fate.

The American experience, in which the courts (now virtually the only effective agents of policy-making in America) have been high-jacked by ethnic and other special interests, illustrates vividly the dangers of pluralist societies that only legalism holds together. It intimates the hard truth that a multiracial society, if it is to be peaceful and free, cannot also be radically multicultural. In particular, entry into civil society in Britain presupposes subscription to its norms, among which toleration, voluntary association and equality before the law are uppermost in importance. It must be made plain by any conservative government that cultural diversity cannot mean the subordination of women in state-funded schools, or (as in the Rushdie case) toleration of threats which endanger freedom of expression. The common culture to which people aspire is that culture of liberty which animates a civil society. This common culture may be reinforced by laws and policies which resist pluralism when pluralism threatens the norms of civil society itself. A civil society such as in Britain is entitled to assert its identity against those – be they recent immigrants or long-established indigenous groups – who challenge its central, defining practices of toleration and compromise. It is, indeed, these practices that set the limit to pluralism in Britain today.

The pursuit of a delusive organic community distracts from the humbler but indispensable task of filling out that thinner common culture of respect for civil society that presently enables people to co-exist in peace. Building up that common culture, in turn, effectively enfranchises all people as active citizens in a polity to which everyone can profess allegiance. A conservative policy, rightly conceived, is not one which seeks to renew old traditions by deliberate contrivance (which is, in Wittgenstein's lovely phrase, 'as if one tried to repair a broken spider's web with one's bare hands'); it is one which nurtures the common traditions that are currently shared, while respecting the variety of practices whereby they are held in common.

CONSERVATIVE INDIVIDUALISM, THE FREE MARKET AND THE COMMON LIFE

The preceding reflections may be regarded as offering provisional answers to the question, 'What must be true for the free market to be possible?'. The market, we have concluded, is not a self-sustaining order, but presupposes as its matrix a network of intermediary institutions animated by a culture of liberty. The political legitimacy of the free market depends on these institutions being in good repair and, where necessary, on their being tended and nurtured by government. The duties of government in according to the free market a political legitimacy that assists its reproduction across the generations go well beyond according intermediary institutions the space and resources they need. Conservative government has the responsibility of protecting and renewing the public environment without which the lifestyle of market individualism is squalid and impoverished. Conservative individualists, unlike their liberal and libertarian counterparts, recognise that the capacity for unfettered choice has little value when it must be exercised in a public space that – like many American cities – is filthy, desolate and dangerous. The exercise of free choice has most value when it occurs in a public space that is rich in options and amenities, and its value dwindles as that public space wanes. Free choice is worth little indeed if the life in which it issues is nasty, brutish and short, because the environment in which it is exercised approximates a state of nature. We do not want to walk the path of privatisation, if Detroit is at the end of it.

Everything suggests that it is possible to go further in extending the reach of the free market, if at the same time measures are devised to renew the physical and institutional environment that confers legitimacy on it. It is not my brief here to consider specific policies – a task in any case beyond my competence – but rather it is to explore the kinds of policies suggested by these concerns. In regard to poverty, I have already cautioned against the disastrously misconceived neo-liberal panacea of the universal negative income tax, which is objectionable both in effecting a further socialisation of income and in lumping together very different sorts of poverty. Without attempting to specify policy in any detail, what is most needed at present is a division within policy between measures which enable the vulnerable and defenceless who cannot expect to return to the economy as self-reliant producers nevertheless to live dignified and meaningful lives, and measures which assist and encourage the underclass of the families unemployed across several generations to reintegrate in the wider society. Policy in the first area – in respect of the mentally and physically disabled, the chronically sick and the old and frail – has under all recent governments been distinguished by its niggardliness, a lack of the sense of human solidarity, and by want of compassion. The shelving of the Griffiths Report,[14] the prospect of under-funding when it is at length implemented, and the low levels of benefits for those who care for dependents at home are aspects of policy in recent years which compound the neglect of community care for the most vulnerable and which are surely unacceptable to any humane conservatism, and certainly to any Tory. The evidence suggests that, in this area, the best policy is one which confers vouchers for community care on those who need it (or their guardians) – a measure which would widen choice for the consumer of such care and thereby avoid the paternalism of the otherwise admirable Griffiths Report (with its excessive reliance on bureaucratic assessment of individual needs). Voucher schemes in these areas will work, and work well, if and only if they are fully adequate to the needs of those concerned. Community care under conservative government should embody the values that its name suggests and should demonstrate the commitment of government to its most defenceless citizens.

Policy regarding to the underclass confronts difficult dilemmas which cannot be explored here. What is clear is that, in regard to the able-bodied, public assistance generates obligations, and the goal of such assistance should not be life-long pauperdom but speedy recovery of independence where this has been lost, and the inculcation of the skills of self-reliance where these are lacking. Training vouchers for the unemployed are one step in this direction. In general, a greater commitment of resources to the re-skilling of the unemployed, together with a willingness to reduce or withdraw benefit if retraining for genuine employment is not accepted, or to replace it by workfare, are elements of a workable policy aiming to reintegrate the underclass. Since, as we have seen, family breakdown appears to be a vital element in the creation of the underclass, recent measures introduced in Britain 'aiming to enforce paternal obligations on delinquent fathers of one-parent families', though not without their own difficulties, are essential ingredients in any policy agenda on reinforcing family responsibility. On the thorny and intractable issue of family benefit, there must be little that is new that can now usefully be said. What is clear is that the neo-liberal knee-jerk response of abolishing it altogether, and replacing it by a means-tested benefit, is to be rejected because of the costs and disincentives of targeting. At the same time, the existing benefit is massively wasteful and plainly inequitable. The proposal of David Willetts, MP, that child benefit be restricted to the first five years but substantially increased (and also made taxable), seems one that is eminently worthy of consideration, especially if (in order to guarantee even-handedness) it is combined with further aid (such as tax deductibility for child care) for those mothers who choose to work during their children's early years. In none of these areas of policy are there measures that avoid the necessity of trade-offs among conflicting values. There is in policy-making not only a scarcity of resources but also a moral scarcity (profoundly illuminated in Isaiah Berlin's most recent collection of essays)[15] that is endemic. It is important in tax and welfare policy to respect these trade-offs where they occur, and not make a fetish of the 'neutrality of the level playing field'.

With regard to education, it has already been argued that government has an indefeasible duty to equip children with the skills of numeracy and literacy without which they cannot hope to prosper in society. It is nevertheless important to beware of the danger that education becomes wholly or primarily vocational in purpose and content. In primary and secondary schools, the goal must be to initiate children into the history and principles of the civil society they will enter as adults, and to this end there is a case for courses in civic or political education. In higher education, the danger is that universities come to be regarded by government as little more than auxiliaries of economic policy. In education policy, as elsewhere, it ought to be a central maxim of conservative government that autonomous institutions have their own, internal ends and purposes and are not mere instruments of the ephemeral goals of the government of the day.

So far neglected here is an area of policy that is likely to loom ever larger in the years to come – that of the environment, natural and humanly constructed, in which we have to live. It must surely be clear that people in Britain do not want their cities to follow the American example and become places where people work furtively and in fear and then flee. The goal is, or ought to be, to renew cities in the British and European tradition as public spaces in which individuals and autonomous institutions live out their lives – and this cannot be done without significant injections of public money. Revitalising the cities will entail a reconsideration of the role of the private motor car in relation to public transport – a reassessment that will in any case soon be forced upon us by mounting evidence of its environmental hazards. The point will soon be reached when the dominant policy objective of post-war British governments (that of aligning the electoral and economic cycles so as to achieve re-election through uninterrupted economic growth) will be replaced by a new imperative in which the quality of life dominates, even though it cannot altogether supplant, the pursuit of economic growth. It will be wise to pursue, so far as possible, market solutions to the problems of the environment – road pricing for urban traffic congestion and a suitable tax regime for polluters. However, it will be foolish to suppose that market solutions alone will solve the environmental problems that now loom up as the chief threats to the quality of our lives and to those of our children. A Green agenda should come as a natural one for Tories, for whom the past is a patrimony not to be wantonly squandered; and in any case environmental policy is too important to be left to the Greens. The emerging Green agenda within British conservatism shows, more clearly than anywhere else, that a flourishing individualism cannot be envisaged save in the context of rich forms of common life which government has a positive responsibility to protect.

CONCLUSION

For over a decade, the policy agenda of British conservatism has been dominated by the goal of freeing up the market and according the market economy its rightful legitimacy. This policy orientation has had some impressive results and has produced a shift in the stance of government in regard to the market that is probably irreversible. There can be no return to the collusive corporatism of the sixties and seventies, with its legacy of stagnation and backwardness. Nor is the agenda of marketisation yet exhausted. There is much farther to go in extending market institutions into hitherto sacrosanct areas, in reducing taxation, inflation and government expenditure, and in privatising industries and services. There is a strong case for introducing market choice in many social and welfare services. In all of these areas, the achievements of the past decade will provide a sound base.

Yet it is, in all likelihood, only a reassertion of the traditional Tory concern for compassion and community in one nation that can hope to preserve the free market which the last decade of conservative government has achieved. Conservative policy which neglects or seems to neglect the needy and the vulnerable, or which is so committed to market freedoms that the human and natural environment in which markets operate is left to its own devices, will provoke a revulsion in which traditional Tory concerns for the health of the community are captured by egalitarians and collectivists. Accordingly, if this danger is to be averted, conservative policy presently needs a significant shift in orientation from concern with the market economy to concern with its social and cultural preconditions. Vital as the market is as an expression of individual freedom, it is only one dimension of society in which individuals make choices and exercise responsibility. People also live in families and belong to churches and other voluntary associations in which market exchange is inappropriate or peripheral. It is this cultural and institutional matrix of the market that conservative policy must now address. It must not be forgotten that, like any other human institution, the market is imperfect (and imperfectible). As the subtlest and least known critic of economic theory in our time has said of the idea of equilibrium in economics, 'It is an arresting triumph of the formal imagination. Beauty, clarity and unity are achieved by a set of axioms as economical as those of classical physical dynamics.' But, he asks, 'Can the real flux of history, personal and public, be approximately understood in terms of this conception? The contrast is such that we have difficulty in achieving any mental collation of the two ideas. Macbeth's despair expresses more nearly the impact of the torrent of events.'[16] These wise words should caution us against attributing to the market a perfection we have learnt not to ascribe to government. They should encourage us to recognise that, in certain areas of policy, exclusive reliance on market forces is a recipe for failure. We need only look to Germany and Japan for lessons in how, without resort to dubious corporatist strategies, market allocation may be supplemented – in science policy, for example – by the constructive engagement of government.

For a conservative, political life is a perpetual choice among necessary evils. Being an individualist, the conservative will have good reason to seek to devolve from government all those activities that are better done in markets, and so he will make a choice between the imperfections of markets and those of governments, in the hope that the resultant mixture will best promote freedom and community. On the view presented here, however, the conservative individualist will never concede hegemony to the institutions of the market. The market is made for humans, not humans for the market. The conservative individualist will deny that there can be long-term economic benefit in restricting free trade, for example, but will at the same time acknowledge that there may be reasons of military strategy, of the preservation of the common culture or the protection of the environment, which may defeat the ideal of unrestricted free trade. Even if, as with monetary policy, there may be good reasons for removing elements of the market from the political process – reasons that may support the institution of an independent central bank that is insulated from the democratic process and guided by clear policy objectives rather than by discretionary authority – conservatives must in general wish to preserve the primacy of the political order over the realm of the market.

Let us not suppose that an individualist form of life is the only one in which the human good can be realised. The lessons of history, and the present example of Japan, teach otherwise. However, for us individualism is a historical fate, which we may temper but cannot hope to overcome. The task of conservative policy is to tend the culture and institutions that are the matrix of individualism, so as to ensure that the individualist form of life does not so deplete its moral and cultural capital that it becomes (as Schumpeter feared it would)[17] a self-limiting episode. There is surely benefit to be gained from a study of that school of Tory pessimism, best exemplified in the writings of Lord Salisbury,[18] that viewed with foreboding the prospects in the longer term of freedom and excellence under a regime of democratic capitalism. At the same time much can be learned from Salisbury's great contemporary, Disraeli, who saw that conservative values could be preserved if their benefits were extended to ordinary people, and an obligation of concern for the poor accepted by those who had made a success of wealth creation. Indeed, one may safely predict that, unless these older Tory traditions are revived, the enterprise culture that has been so ardently fostered will turn out to be a shallow and an ephemeral affair. It is not, however, primarily in the revival of an older, patrician Toryism that can be rested any hope that conservative values will survive and prosper in the generations to come. That happy outcome will come about only if conservative governments are perceived to be committed to extending the advantages of freedom and independence to all. The measures introduced recently in Britain to foster a savings culture (by exempting small savings from taxation) are an admirable example of the judicious use of government to promote conservative values and secure loyalty to them among ordinary people. It is in extending the culture of choice and opportunity to the widest degree that the real prospects of conservatism, in Britain and elsewhere, are found. In the view presented here, the danger of market liberalism consuming itself is greatest if policy is allowed to be formed on the tacit supposition that the cultural preconditions of the market can safely be left to look after themselves.

For any conservative in the sceptical British tradition – a tradition which is shared with much of the rest of Europe, and which is exemplified in the writings of Montaigne and Charron, Savigny and Eotvos among others – there is in any case an incongruity in putting one's faith in any one remedy. It is a basic conviction, after all, that the human lot is imperfectible. The task of conservative government is primarily to concern itself with those cultural continuities to which the market is bound to be indifferent, but upon which its strength finally depends. The market is only as strong as the culture that underpins it – a culture of responsibility and choice-making that we must transmit to our children and they to theirs. Conservatism is not, like socialism or liberalism, a one-generation philosophy, but rather the opposite. For this reason it is necessary to repudiate firmly the neo-liberal metaphor of society as a contract, in which market exchange is primordial. If society is a contract, it is only in Edmund Burke's sense – a contract between the living, the dead and those that are yet unborn.

The Conservative Party in Britain, like conservative parties elsewhere, can never be solely or exclusively the party of capitalism – though it has no reason at all to be ashamed of its association with the desire of people to improve their standard of living and quality of life. Any conservative government, in Britain or elsewhere, must express not only the individual freedoms embodied in market capitalism but also the cultural identities that are renewed across the generations.

It is the most fundamental insight of conservatism, after all, that persons' identities cannot be matters of choice, but are conferred upon them by their unchosen histories, so that what is most essential about them is, in the end, what is most accidental.[19] The conservative vision is that people will come to value the privileges of choice all the more when they see how much in their lives must always remain unchosen.

The danger of the neo-liberalism that has lately come to dominate conservative thinking is the danger of utopianism – the belief or hope that the predicament in which people find themselves, in which goods are not always combinable and sometimes depend upon evils, and in which the elimination of one evil often discloses another, can somehow be transcended. This was the danger inherent in the domination of conservative thought by the ideology of the New Right – the dangerous delusion that contemporary problems could be conjured away, in their entirety and presumably forever, by the resurrection of the theorisings of the Manchester School of *laissez-faire* liberalism. At its deepest, this once-dominant strand in conservative thought expressed the thoroughly unconservative conviction that the crookednesses of practice could once and for all be straightened out by the application of a correct theory. The conservative politics of imperfection[20] amounts to a rejection of this seductive, dangerous and delusive view. It is for this reason that, for a conservative government, a sceptical turn of mind is indispensable. Above all, conservatives must recall the dangers of ideology, and the limits of theory: philosophy, if it is good, can do little more than effect prophylaxis against the virus of ideology, and then return us to the vicissitudes of practice; theories, at their best, can only remind us how little we know. It is this sceptical spirit that should inform the policies devised by conservatives, and which the greatest conservative philosopher of all evinced,[21] when he wrote:

> there are in England, in particular, many honest gentlemen, who being always employed in their domestic affairs, or amusing themselves in common recreations, have carried their thoughts very little beyond those objects, which are every day exposed to their senses. And indeed, of such as these I pretend not to make philosophers, nor do I expect them to be associates in these researches or auditors of these discoveries. They do well to keep themselves in their present situation; and instead of refining them into philosophers, I wish we could communicate to our founders of systems, a share of this gross earthy mixture, as an ingredient, which they commonly stand much in need of, and which would serve to temper those fiery particles, of which they are composed.[22]

3   The moral foundations of market institutions

INTRODUCTION

The argument of this chapter goes against the current of much recent political
thought and practice. It is that both libertarian and egalitarian doctrines are fatally
flawed and are therefore incapable of serving as fundamental political moralities.
The utopian models suggested by these doctrines – *laissez-faire* capitalism and
egalitarian socialism – are not only impractical but also, and more importantly,
philosophically indefensible. The position here advocated is instead one that has as
its central notions satiable basic needs, including that of autonomy, and the rich
diversity of options provided by a good community. It is not, as its critics will
undoubtedly claim, a muddled pragmatism of the middle ground: it is the only
principled position. It has the radical implication that supposedly principled views,
such as libertarianism and egalitarianism, are in fact highly indeterminate and
barely coherent. It implies, also, for reasons that will be explained, that distributional principles can never be fundamentally important, that the object of policy
cannot be the utilitarian one of maximising collective or aggregate welfare, that
political morality can never be based on rights, and that enablement or empowerment of those whose basic needs are not being met has its justification in the
necessary conditions of a community rich in inherently public goods rather than in
the supposed demands of justice.

The view presented here is that of a liberal market economy constrained (or
supplemented) by an enabling welfare state – in other words, a social market
economy, as understood in the Freiburg School of Eucken and Erhardt, freely
applied by the author to the current situation in Britain. This is a view that I would
hope could be found worthy of consideration both by liberal conservatives and by
liberal minded social democrats. I spell out the policy implications of this view in
the British context primarily, but it has implications for policy in other similar
countries by way of applications there of the philosophical perspective defended
herein, which I shall from time to time indicate.

It is a view which seeks to ground the ethical standing of market institutions in
their contribution to one of the vital ingredients of individual well-being in the
modern world, namely, autonomy. It differs from any classical liberal defence of
the market in valuing negative liberty, or freedom from coercion, not in itself but

as an element in autonomy. It further diverges from classical liberalism in holding that the very value that chiefly legitimates market institutions, autonomy, also mandates an enabling welfare state. The classical liberal minimum state is accordingly rejected even as an ideal. The conception of government animating this view is nevertheless that of limited government, inasmuch as the welfare proposals considered devolve as many activities on the institutions of civil society as can be appropriately discharged there and in respect of government are intended to conform to the principle of subsidiarity, with functions being devolved to the lowest feasible and desirable level of government.

The argument developed here diverges from the standard position of contemporary classical liberals in that it is avowedly an ethical argument and not an amoral appeal to the prosperity that market institutions deliver. This reflects the author's conviction that market institutions work well only where their practitioners accord them moral legitimacy – a point relevant especially in the emergent post-communist societies, where the ethical properties of market institutions are little understood and where an amoral defence of the market of the sort that is advocated by many contemporary liberal and libertarian economists only reinforces popular suspicion of it.

It diverges, therefore, from much standard argumentation on behalf of market institutions in resting its case, not on the contribution made to general or collective welfare by markets or on their embodying any imagined system of rights (such as rights to negative liberty), but on their contribution to individual well-being via their enabling individuals to live autonomously in a form of life containing valuable options furnished by a common stock of inherently public goods. The central conceptions of this account of the ethical foundation of market institutions – of a satiable basic need, of the value of autonomy and its precondition in a common culture containing a diversity of inherently public goods, together with the critique of egalitarianism and libertarianism – are all applications of arguments set out in Joseph Raz's *The Morality of Freedom*,[1] a seminal book which is at once the most important study in liberal philosophy since J.S. Mill's *On Liberty*[2] and the most powerful critique of the currently dominant schools of Anglo-American liberalism. Responsibility for these uses of Raz's arguments remains mine.

A feature of market institutions as enabling devices for individual autonomy that is not mentioned by Raz is their role in enabling agents to act autonomously on their own personal knowledge – knowledge that is typically tacit and practical in form. It is to this epistemic argument for market institutions, often neglected in economic literature but providing the most fundamental reason for the failures of socialist central planning and having serious implications for many distributionist and interventionist schemes, that we first turn.

THE EPISTEMIC ARGUMENT FOR THE MARKET

What explains the chaos, waste and poverty revealed by the Soviet *glasnost*? What accounts for the ruinous failure of socialist central planning, everywhere in the world? The commonest explanation advanced in Western scholarship involves the perversity of the structure of incentives under which socialist planners, managers and workers must live.[3] There is, no doubt, much force in this explanation. As the Virginia School of Public Choice[4] has taught us, the behaviour of bureaucrats and politicians can be theorised, to a considerable extent, in terms of the economic models used to explain human behaviour in market transactions. The incentive structure created by the Soviet system makes planners risk-averse, inclined to conceal malinvestments by pouring in good money after bad, and disinclined to pursue innovative strategies for which, if they fail, they may be disciplined. Equally, the Soviet manager has an incentive to comply with the quantitative production targets that he or she has been set, regardless of the quality of the products, and to fabricate statistics regarding output. The upshot of this perverse incentive structure can only be a largely chaotic economy, efficient mainly in its parallel sectors, which is successful (as in some sectors of military technology) only at massive and unnecessary cost. In the provision of items necessary for everyday life, the Soviet system cannot avoid being chronically inefficient, since it provides no linkage between consumer preferences and productive effort. Ignorance of these rudimentary truths has led generations of the Western Sovietological *nomenklatura* systematically to overrate performance and productivity in Soviet-type economic systems, with the real situation emerging only in the wake of the Soviet *glasnost* and German reunification. It is only now that it is understood in the West that the low productivity of ordinary workers in the Soviet bloc is to be accounted for by the absence of incentives to work, by antiquated plants, by the diversion of energy and enterprise into the parallel economy and by the endemic wastefulness of logistical and supply systems.

There can, therefore, be no doubt that the catastrophic failure of Soviet-style planning is in large part to be accounted for by the absence of the benign incentives provided by the disciplines of market competition and by the presence of incentives to mismanagement and malinvestment. The deeper explanation of the failure of socialist central planning is, however, not one that appeals to artificial distortion of incentives, but one that invokes instead insuperable limitations of human knowledge. At its simplest, this is expressed in the 'calculation argument', stated classically by L. von Mises and developed and enriched by Hayek.[5] The Misesian insight is that in any modern economy there will be billions of market exchanges and therefore billions of prices. In the production of any consumer good, for example, producers will need the guidance provided by the prices of many capital goods and these prices will typically be subject to constant change. Because resources and preferences are not static, the structure of relative prices will itself be in a state of constant change. Mises's argument is that, without market pricing of assets, their relative scarcities are unknowable, since simulating market pricing is a calculational impossibility in an economy where billions of market exchanges take place and pricing is in a state of dynamic flux. The limitation of human knowledge identified by Mises's argument is therefore a calculational limitation. For Mises there cannot be a socialist economy, since rational economic planning by individuals and enterprises is feasible only with the assistance of the information provided by market pricing. One might even say that, for Mises, a socialist system is not an economy at all, but an anti-economy.

It was the achievement of Hayek to deepen the Misesian argument and to show that the epistemological difficulty of central planning was far more than calculational. For Hayek, the market is not, primarily, an institution that allocates scarce resources to competing ends. He is concerned to show us that neither the resources available in the economy, nor the variety of uses to which they might be put, is known to anyone. The role of the market is to economise on the scarcest resource of all – human knowledge. The market is for Hayek an epistemic device, a discovery procedure for transmitting and indeed generating information that is dispersed throughout society. The epistemic impossibility of successful comprehensive central planning is not for Hayek, as it was for Mises, chiefly a calculational one; it is rather one that flows from the very nature of the knowledge possessed by economic agents. This knowledge, Hayek insists, is not only or mainly the propositional knowledge of basic facts that can easily be theorised or quantified; it is local knowledge of fleeting economic environments, often embodied in skills or practices or expressed in entrepreneurial insights. This is knowledge that by its very nature cannot be collected by a central planning board. Worse, it is knowledge that is squandered if, in the attempt to gather it centrally, market pricing is suppressed or distorted. The epistemic role of markets, accordingly, is to generate and to make available for general use information (transmitted via price signals) that is irretrievably scattered and cannot be subject to centralisation. The information embodied in market pricing, since it is not the property of any one market participant, is a sort of holistic knowledge of the whole society, a public patrimony that it is the fate of central planning to fritter away. It is this depletion of the stock of knowledge embodied in markets that explains the universal impoverishment of socialist systems.

The deepest and subtlest explanations of the epistemic failure of command economies do not come from the Austrian calculation argument of Mises or from its refinement as an argument about the character of knowledge in Hayek. The great achievement of these Austrian arguments was to show that market-simulating planning institutions (such as those proposed in the Lange–Lerner model) were unworkable in any realistically imaginable world because of the impossible demands they made on the knowledge of the planners. Instead, it is in the theorising of Michael Polanyi,[6] in the Polanyian work of Paul Craig Roberts,[7] and in the thought of G.L.S. Shackle[8] that the epistemic impossibilities of successful central planning are given their profoundest statement. Polanyi's argument against central planning of the economy is an application of his argument against the planning of science. In science, progress occurs by diverse scientists and laboratories pursuing divergent lines of inquiry, whose development is not laid down in advance. Each research programme, crucially, is developed in part by the application of that portion of the scientist's existing knowledge that is not theorised and may not be theorisable – the tacit knowledge which he or she possesses of the practice of science. Polanyi's argument against central planning of science is that, if it could be instituted, it would restrict the resources of further scientific advance to that which is contained in existing theories. It would thereby deny science the indispensable component of tacit knowledge, and so impoverish it. The central planning of science would, for these reasons, retard or even perhaps reverse the growth of scientific knowledge.

Polanyi puts to work in his critique of central economic planning the conception of tacit knowledge that is deployed in his attack on the central planning of scientific research. Tacit knowledge is that vast fund of practical, local and traditional knowledge that is embodied in dispositions and forms of life and expressed in flair and intuition, which can never be formulated in rules of scientific method, say, and of which our theoretical or articulated knowledge is only the visible tip. In Polanyi's account of it, the most important role of the market is that of a device for the transmission and utilisation of unarticulated, and sometimes inarticulatable, tacit and local knowledge. Attempts to collate and collect the tacit knowledge of millions of entrepreneurs and investors are bound to fail, if only because none of them can successfully articulate much of the tacit knowledge that he or she possesses. For this reason, computer simulation of market processes can never be very successful: market participants will always fail to program in that part of their tacit knowledge that is inarticulatable. This is to say that such knowledge exists only in use,[9] and is destroyed or depleted when given an articulation that is necessarily partial, abstract, incomplete and defective. The nub of Polanyi's argument against central economic planning is that it is an impossibility because human beings, when they act in markets as in all other areas of conduct, are always ignorant of much of what they know, and so always know more than they can ever say.

The other deep reason for the impossibility of successful central economic planning is found in the thought of G.L.S. Shackle and concerns the unknowability of the future and the subjectivity of expectations. If we have no formula, no algorithm, whereby we can predict or assess the likelihood of future events in the real world, if (in other words) there are singularities and novelties which defeat our inferences from past to future, then a central planning board will merely be wagering when it tries to assess likely future resources and prices. This is, in part, because economies are not self-contained systems, insulated from the rest of human life, in respect of which predictions may be made by way of formal models: they are parts of human life, only separable from the rest in abstraction, and constantly subject to the unpredictable changes wrought by political upheaval, war, fashion and innumerable other diverse causes. Even in the context of the market economy when it is narrowly conceived, we have a kaleidic world that changes suddenly and unpredictably, along with changes in subjective expectations. It is a characteristic feature of formal economic models that they suppress the openness of markets to exogenous factors and pass over the unknowability of the future. Economic rationalism has been devastatingly criticised by Shackle, when he writes:[10]

Rationalism, the belief that conduct can be understood as part of the determinate order and process of Nature, into which it is assimilated by virtue of the fact that men choose what is best for them in their circumstances, and their circumstances are laid down by Nature, is a paradox. For it claims to confer upon men freedom to choose, yet to be able to predict what they will choose. It speaks of *choice*, and what can this mean, except that a man is confronted with *rival available* actions? All the actions are available, but all except one are forbidden: forbidden by reasoning self-interest. By assuming that men pursue their desires by applying reason to their circumstances, the analyst can tell what their conduct will be, provided he can also assume that not only he, but they, are in possession of full knowledge of those circumstances? There are the actions of other men, freely chosen by them and constituting part of our individual's circumstances. How can men know each other's concurrent free choices? By pre-reconciliation in a general equilibrium. There is also the future. For the sake of pre-reconciliation of choices, and also for its own unfathomable possibilities, the future must be assumed away. Thus the value-construct describes free, pre-reconciled, determinate choices in a timeless system. It is an arresting triumph of the formal imagination. Beauty, clarity and unity are achieved by a set of axioms as economical as those of classical physical dynamics. Can the real flux of history, personal and public, be approximately understood in terms of this conception? The contrast is such that we have difficulty in achieving any mental collation of the two ideas. Macbeth's despair expresses more nearly the impact of the torrent of events....

The dissolution of belief in the value-theory account of economic affairs was an aspect of the dissolution of Victorian social and international stability. The depressions and business crises of Victorian times could be seen as occasional failures or aberrations of a basically orderly system. British troubles of the 1920s, and world troubles of the 1930s, made this difficult. But they did not overthrow in any lasting way the economist's vested interest in an analysable economic world. The trouble is that the world is not economic. It is political–economic, it is economic only subject to unappeasable greeds and rivalries and implacable enmities. A general *economic* explanation of economic affairs is an ambition which flies in the face of history and the observable contemporary scene. The economist's only hopeful objective is to provide an account of that shawl of loosely interknotted strands which waves in the wind of the other human influences, political contention, technological invention, explosion of population. He can seek to describe its modes of potential response to each fresh kaleidic shift of the environment, during the time till that shift is superseded by another. But he cannot tell what these shifts will be. Economic affairs are not self-contained or insulated, they cannot have a self-sufficient explanation.[11]

Shackle's argument has been restated by James Buchanan in the context of an appraisal of the work of one of Shackle's most prominent followers, Jack Wiseman:

Mises and Hayek had concentrated on the limits to the availability of knowledge to the central planning agency, by contrast with the knowledge that can be utilized by separate and independent market participants in their localized circumstances. Jack Wiseman's criticism went well beyond that of Mises and

Hayek, and for the first time, demonstrated that the problem was not one of dispersed knowledge *that did indeed exist*. The problem was the wholly different one imposed by the necessity that all choices be made in *time*, and, hence, under conditions of necessary uncertainty. If the future is unknowable, how can decision-makers, whether they be participants in a market or agents acting for the collectivity, be made accountable? How can any monitor check on the competence and the integrity of the chooser, other than through the observation of results? How, then, can we lay down a rule to be followed, in advance of the conditions to be encountered? Where is the collectivist equivalent of the bankruptcy court?

In Buchanan's restatement of it, the Shacklean argument against central economic planning invokes the non-existence of the knowledge which planners would need were they to be able to plan successfully. Like actors in a market, central planners are forever denied knowledge of the future. By comparison with market participants, however, planners will make larger errors – errors for which there is no elimination device such as bankruptcy in markets. Markets may, indeed, exhibit speculative manias and panics, as subjective expectations ebb and flow; they are not spared the fate of perpetual ignorance or un-knowledge (in Shackle's neologism) which is an inexorable consequence of our nature as time-bound creatures for whom the future can only be guesswork.[12] We are on safer ground, however, if in an irredeemably uncertain world we trust to the diverse expectations and plans of many market participants rather than to the monism of the plan, with its narrow and inevitably arbitrary expectations of the future. Shackle's argument is, in its way, a necessary complement to Polanyi's: we are always, according to Shackle, ignorant of what it is that we do not know, even as (according to Polanyi) we always know more than we can ever say. It is through these Polanyian and Shacklean insights that the epistemic impossibilities of central planning are best explained.

If central economic planning is an impossibility for these deeper epistemic reasons, what do we have in so-called command economies? It is the achievement of Paul Craig Roberts,[13] virtually alone, to have theorised in an illuminating way the realities of economic life under Soviet-style planning institutions. Roberts shows that such economies must in practice invariably be polycentric, with the plan reflecting, rather than dictating, the behaviour of managers, suppliers and workers. Since the planners inevitably lack the knowledge, tacit and articulated, necessary to any successful economic project, local managers must make their own local arrangements (with suppliers, and so forth), relying on their own local knowledge. Accordingly, the formal and the informal, the official and the parallel economies are at every point intimately and inextricably related, with the official economy achieving any degree of success only in virtue of its dependency on the institutions of the parallel economy. Quite apart from the unreliability and fictitious character of Soviet economic statistics, the gigantism of the Five Year Plans, for example, masked the permanent Soviet reality of polycentrism, in which the Plan functions chiefly as a summation, partly fictitious, of the activities of managers, who achieve as much as they do in virtue of their reliance on surviving market prices – in particular, historic, global and black market prices.

It is only in virtue of the immense resourcefulness of the Soviet peoples in devising and using these manifold informal economic institutions – in reinventing the market against the background of political institutions committed (at least until recently) to the suppression of commodity-production – that social and economic life in the Soviet Union has managed to renew itself at all. The failure of *perestroika*, indeed, arises from the fact that it encompasses both a partial dismantlement of the central planning institutions and an attack on one of the least inefficient parts of the economy – its parallel sector.

The epistemic argument for the market, most profoundly developed in the work of Polanyi and Roberts, provides a sound theoretical explanation of the systemic failures of socialist command economies everywhere. It shows why, even putting their rejection of consumer sovereignty on one side, the Soviet élites find achieving their own economic goals, including those relating to the Soviet military industrial complex, extraordinarily costly and difficult. It is indeed probably the case that the initial motivation of *glasnost* was in the realisation that, even in military technology, to which a massive proportion of GNP was being committed, the Soviet Union was in certain respects falling behind the West, and above all could not hope fully to replicate the American Strategic Defence Initiative.[14] Further, the Polanyian and Shacklean arguments demonstrate that, even if the Soviet leadership had been successful in creating a new *homo sovieticus*, who would not respond to the perverse incentive structure created by the planning institutions but would mechanically follow planning objectives, he would lack the knowledge needed to achieve the planners' goals. The Soviet system, or any modelled on it, thus reproduces on a vast scale all of the irrationalities prophetically foreseen by Tolstoy, when he criticised plans for a 'rational agriculture' in his novel, *War and Peace*.[15] From this point of view, we can represent socialist central planning as the reverse of the epistemic device of the market – as a device for depleting, wasting and finally destroying the tacit knowledge that is indispensable in economic life.

A number of caveats are worth making at this point. The epistemic argument for market institutions does not mean that, in the absence of a full-blown market economy, nothing of economic importance can be achieved. On the contrary, markets can be simulated or replicated, as they were in the Soviet Union when Stalin in 1939 created seventeen competing design bureaux for fighter aircraft, some of which were based in the *sharashka*, the special scientific institutes staffed by *Gulag* prisoners.[16] The sophistication of Soviet military technology, some of it known now to be far in advance of anything possessed in the West, shows that the idea that technological innovation requires economic or personal liberty is merely another liberal illusion.[17] Nor is it being asserted that in the consumer economy from whose chaos the strategic, military economy is largely insulated, nothing can be achieved by the planning institutions. Again, on the contrary, when (as in Czechoslovakia in the sixties) they have confined themselves to producing a few staple commodities, they have achieved a measure of success. What the epistemic argument does tell us is that, in the absence of an effective price mechanism that can only be provided by market institutions, there will inevitably be massive waste and malinvestment, with even the strategic military sector achieving what it does at the cost of something between 25 and 50 per cent of GNP being devoted to it (a percentage that has not changed since the events of August 1991). In short, the upshot of the epistemic argument is not that central planning institutions always fail, but that even their successes carry heavy and unnecessary human and economic costs. That socialist institutions everywhere generate poverty is to be explained partly by the epistemic argument, but partly also by the lack of incentives in the consumer economy. Taken together, the epistemic and the incentive arguments enable us to predict that central planning institutions will be wasteful and inefficient wherever they are set up, regardless of the cultural and economic environment in which they find themselves. The poverty of the Russians has, therefore, nothing to do with the alleged defects of the Slav work ethic: it has the same explanation – in the epistemic and incentive defects of central planning institutions – as the poverty of Cubans, Mongols and Balts.

Though they are distinct, the epistemic argument and the argument from incentives are complementary rather than competitive in their role as theoretical rationales for the market economy. They also have a common core. The incentive argument invokes the fact that planning institutions obstruct the individual in acting upon his or her projects and purposes, while the epistemic argument notes that they prevent the individual from using and benefiting from his or her own knowledge. In both cases, the planning institutions constrain or diminish the autonomy of individuals, partly by compelling them to act on purposes that are not their own, partly by depriving them of the opportunity to engage in projects animated by their own knowledge. The common feature of both arguments for the market is that they identify the detrimental impact of socialist central planning institutions on individual autonomy. This suggests that the epistemic device of the market has an ethical implication or presupposition that the market protects or enhances the autonomy of the individual. It has also a policy implication, to which I shall return later when I develop the case against market socialism. The policy implication of the epistemic argument, in its Austrian as well as its Polanyian and Shacklean forms, is that economic rationality demands not only market pricing of most factors of production but also (partly as a precondition of genuine market pricing) their private ownership. Why is this? The reason is to be found in the fact that individuals are most likely to be able to deploy their personal tacit knowledge when they are least constrained by collective decision-procedures in which this knowledge is diluted or lost. (This is, perhaps, especially true of that species of tacit knowledge which is expressed in entrepreneurial insight.) In order to be able to make the best of their personal fund of tacit knowledge, individuals need a domain in which they may act solely on their own judgment (and, of course, at their own risk). Such a domain is provided by private property in productive assets. (As I shall later argue, the institution of private or several property in a modern economy is likely to be embodied in the form of the capitalist corporation; but this need not always be so.) The epistemic and the incentive arguments come together in endorsing the institution of private property as a necessary condition of economic rationality. They also legitimate private property as a precondition of individual autonomy.

It may be objected, against the argument just developed, that much of modern business life is conducted via the bureaucratic structures of large corporations, in which individuals have little opportunity to act directly on their own initiative. Against this objection, one might respond that much innovation emerges from the small business sector, which thereby acts as a competitive constraint on the conservative tendencies of the larger firms. This would not, however, be the most fundamentally compelling response. The more powerful rejoinder would be an appeal to the body of theory developed by Alchian, Manne, Winter and Pelikan[18] on the contribution made to dynamic efficiency by the operation of the market for corporate control. In the somewhat evolutionary perspective developed by these writers, the market for corporate control, that is to say, the threat of takeover, acts as a filter device for the economic competence of managers. As Pelikan makes clear,[19] the economic competence of managers has as a crucial component their tacit knowledge of their business environments. The effect of the workings of the market for corporate control, at least to some degree, is selective pressure against less competent management, and the imposition of a competitive constraint on those that survive. Market competition for corporate control in this way replicates to some extent the individual's reliance on personal tacit knowledge by the entrepreneur acting directly on his or her own initiative.[20] Most fundamentally, however, the objection that modern corporations engage in large-scale, long-term planning neglects the evident fact that such corporations exist within, and are subject to the constraints of, a global competitive market. Bureaucratic planners in such corporations must heed the threat of actual and potential competitors in their strategies. If they do not (*pace* the Chrysler corporation) then they will fail. Unlike socialist planners, therefore, the planners of a modern corporation cannot (unless they acquire monopolistic governmental privileges) insulate themselves from market competition. It is this crucial distinction between the situations of corporate and socialist planners that defeats the objection to the argument considered above.

The epistemic and the incentive arguments for the market, especially when taken together, are overwhelming. They show us why and how prosperity in a modern economy can be achieved only through the medium of market institutions. These arguments are nevertheless deficient. As they stand, they are morally virtually empty, even if they have some ethical implications and presuppositions. They tell us that only the market can deliver the goods to us, but they leave moral criticism of the market economy unanswered. Critics of the market might accept all that has been argued here about the indispensable efficiencies of the market, and yet attack it on ethical grounds. They might argue that unfettered markets promote greed and envy, shatter communities, and debase cultural values. More radically, they might deny that markets promote individual autonomy, and maintain that we are constrained rather than emancipated by participating in markets. They might focus critically on the distributional effects and preconditions of market economies, holding that these necessitate or reproduce structural inequalities in

life-chances that are morally unacceptable. And, more simply but no less powerfully, they might draw our attention to the situation of those people, lacking in
skills or resources, whose plight prevents them from fully participating in the
market or enjoying many of its benefits. Such critics of the market might, in other
words, accept all of the criticisms that I have made of socialist planning institutions,
and yet deny that the market economy has any real ethical standing.[21] As the
argument I have developed goes so far, such critics could claim to occupy the high
moral ground, with the defender of the market appearing as a grubby pragmatist,
ready and willing to sacrifice important ethical values for the sake of mere material
prosperity. It remains to be seen if this potentially fatal weakness in the case for
the market can be remedied.

THE ILLUSIONS OF LIBERTARIANISM

The upshot of the epistemic argument for the market is that the socialist manager,
because he or she is denied the knowledge of relative scarcities given only by
market prices, is bound to fail to achieve the objectives set by the central planning
board, or to achieve them only at vast and unnecessary cost. This will be so,
whatever the objectives and motivations of the planners, and even if they have no
other reason for action than obedience to the plan. If the epistemic argument is
well-founded, even a population of socialist saints would be impoverished.

Socialist central planning invariably results in mass poverty, precisely because
of its adverse impact on human autonomy. It is, in truth, in its indispensable role
as one of the chief preconditions of the autonomy of the individual that the ethical
standing of the market lies. The free market enables individuals to act upon their
own goals and values, their objectives and their plans of life, without subordination
to any other individual or subjection to any collective decision procedure. It is from
its role as an enabling device for the protection and enhancement of human autonomy that the ethical justification of the market is ultimately derived. It is important
to distinguish this ethical justification of the market from two other defences, often
found in classical liberal and conservative writers. The first is the defence that,
under market institutions, economic growth is maximised, and with it the choices
available to individuals. This is a weak argument for several reasons. Though the
promotion of economic growth may be forced upon modern governments by the
pressures of political competition in mass democracies, economic growth, in and
of itself, has no ethical standing. Nor is it at all self-evident that economic growth,
as such, always enlarges or enhances choice-making.[22] It may or may not make a
contribution to that which in the end matters in ethics and politics, human well-
being. There is also an aggregative illusion in all of the quantitative measures used
in macro-economic theorising. These measures – of GNP or money supply, say –
may have limited, pragmatic uses for the purposes of policy, but they always
involve a simplification of and an abstraction from the human realities which
undermine any claim made on their behalf in ethical terms. The human reality is
that of distinct individuals, pursuing disparate and sometimes incommensurable
ends, whose satisfactions cannot be weighed or ranked on any single measure. The

theory of economic life of the classical economists, in which economics was conceived as a science of plutology, or wealth creation, rests on a communistic fiction in which it is supposed that resources and satisfactions are, in principle at least, knowable and measurable. It is the insight of the Austrian economists but also, and above all, of Shackle,[23] that, even under the institutions of an unhampered market, our aggregative assessments always contain elements of the conventional, the fictitious and the arbitrary. Artificial constructs of this kind cannot be supposed to possess any kind of ethical standing.

This is to state in other terms the classical objection to liberal utilitarianism.[24] In any of its many varieties, utilitarianism presupposes that an interpersonal comparison of utilities is a real possibility. On the view presented here, we can rarely, except in limiting cases, possess the knowledge required for such judgements. And this is not just in virtue of any remediable imperfection in our understanding, it is because of incommensurabilities among the various goods that go to make up human well-being.[25] In many cases, it is not possible even in principle to render the diverse ingredients of the good rationally comparable. For this reason, it is often impossible to make comparative utility assessments even within a single individual's life. It follows that any defence of the market, say, which stresses its role as a maximiser of utility, of desire-satisfaction or whatever, has fallen victim to a fallacy of conceptual realism.

This is, indeed, the ultimate argument against any political morality that claims to be utilitarian: that it has as its fundamental value, or maximand, a figment, general welfare, when the reality is that of distinct individuals pursuing incommensurable values. It is on this fallacy that liberal utilitarianism in all of its forms founders. More specifically, the defence of the market is, for this reason, best conducted not in terms of its contribution to an imaginary general or collective welfare, but instead by reference to its role in contributing to the well-being of the individual.

It is at this point that the defence of the market in ethical terms that is developed here diverges in a second way from the standard justification advanced by classical liberals and conservatives. Their arguments invariably focus on the role of the market as a shield against political coercion and on its contribution to the dispersal of power in society – in short, on its contribution to negative freedom.[26] This conventional classical liberal position is a dead-end for a variety of reasons. Let us at once set aside the sterile activity of linguistic or conceptual analysis, since it is evident that there is no consensus as to the meaning of freedom or liberty that could settle substantive questions in ethics and politics. (It may be worth noting that nothing important in Berlin's seminal defence of negative liberty turns on such semantic considerations.)[27] What interests us is not the uses in ordinary language of the terms 'liberty' or 'freedom', but instead the reasons why freedom or liberty itself is valuable. Here the weakness of the conventional classical liberal view is manifest. What, if anything, is intrinsically valuable about the negative freedom of absence of coercion?[28] If the answer is that it facilitates the satisfaction of wants, then the position that has thus emerged is one that will license abridgement of negative freedom whenever want-satisfaction is thereby increased. This does not seem a very principled line of defence of the free market.

The view that negative freedom is itself an intrinsic value fares little better. What is intrinsically valuable about it? The idea that negative freedom is a value that should be maximised or optimised in any case breaks down on the awkward fact that we have no agreed procedure for measuring or weighing on-balance freedom. Except in limiting cases, we find that judgements about 'the greatest freedom' are invariably controversial, in that they invoke rival conceptions of what is good and choiceworthy. This indeterminacy in the very notion of negative liberty spells ruin for the classical liberal project of stating a principle – Spencer's principle of Greatest Equal Freedom, say, or J.S. Mill's 'one very simple principle' about not restraining liberty save where harm to others is at issue – which can authoritatively guide thought and policy on the restraint of liberty. Because we cannot identify 'the greatest liberty', principles which speak of maximising it are empty. To talk, as classical liberals still do, of minimising coercion by maximising negative liberty, is merely to traffic in illusions. The objection to negative liberty, taken in and of itself, is that its content is radically indeterminate, just as its intrinsic value is negligible. For these reasons, it is highly implausible that any political morality can be defended that has at its foundation a supposed basic right or claim to negative liberty.

The value of negative liberty must therefore be theorised in terms of its contribution to something other than itself, which does possess intrinsic value. In truth, it seems clear that the chief value of negative liberty is in its contribution to the positive liberty of autonomy. By autonomy is meant the condition in which persons can be at least part authors of their lives, in that they have before them a range of worthwhile options, in respect of which their choices are not fettered by coercion and with regard to which they possess the capacities and resources presupposed by a reasonable measure of success in their self-chosen path among these options.

It is clear that autonomy is a complex status, not definable by reference to the presence or absence of any single condition. As Raz has put it, with a clarity and conciseness on which I cannot hope to improve:

> It is wrong to identify autonomy with a right against coercion, and to hold that right (i.e. the right against coercion) as defeating, because of the importance of personal autonomy, all, or almost all, other considerations. Many rights contribute to making autonomy possible, but no short list of concrete rights is sufficient for this purpose. The provision of many collective goods is constitutive of the very possibility of autonomy and it cannot be relegated to a subordinate role, compared with some alleged right against coercion, in the name of autonomy.[29]

Raz's insight here is of vital importance. The conditions under which a person enjoys a decent measure of autonomy are many and various, and cannot be covered by the umbrella of a single right. It is patently obvious that autonomy is far more than the mere absence of coercion by others, since it is self-evident that that condition may co-exist with a complete inability to achieve any important objective or purpose. This is a point of some considerable importance, as we shall see when we consider the case for an enabling welfare state.

The ethical standing of the market is its status as a necessary condition of one vital ingredient of human well-being, individual autonomy. Unlike any political procedure for the allocation of resources, free markets enable individuals to command goods and services on their terms, and to exit from forms of provision that displease them. The freedom of autonomous individuals in markets is not that of voice (having a role in collective decision-making), but typically that of exit.[30] In any collective decision-procedure, as Hayek has observed,[31] individuals will be constrained in their choices by the common or majority opinion of what is desirable, or even possible. By contrast with political institutions that require a policy binding on all, markets allow each person to go his or her own way, thus allowing an exfoliation of individuality and diversity. Markets are by their nature sensitive to differences among people, and hostile to the Procrustean conformism of the central plan.

It may be worth pausing at this stage of the argument to correct some common misconceptions of the moral standing of the market. It is a piece of conventional wisdom about the market that it promotes or depends upon egoism, and therefore discriminates against altruism and sympathy. This common prejudice neglects several important features of market institutions, and of the realistic alternatives to them. It is often associated with the primitive misconception that human behaviour in collective or political institutions is less likely to be egoistic than altruistic – a belief for which there is no evidence whatever. Both common sense observation and the theorisings of the Virginia Public Choice School suggest that human beings in political contexts are animated by the same motives that dominate market exchanges. There is this difference, however, that whereas market exchanges are voluntaristic transactions which typically benefit all parties to them, political transactions are often zero-sum or even negative-sum exchanges in which what is gained by one is lost by another. This Smithian insight about the mutual advantageousness of voluntary exchange leads to another: that the motives which animate market exchange are mixed, and need not be (and usually are not) purely egoistic. When a businessman seeks to make a profit, his motive may be to enrich himself or his family; but it may also be to endow a university chair. When a consumer seeks the lowest price for a product, his motive may be to economise on expense so as to build up his own fortune; but the consumer may be acting on behalf of a charitable organisation and may be seeking the lowest prices in order to promote its good works to a greater extent. There is, in truth, no uniformity, but rather considerable diversity, in the motives that animate people as they enter into market exchanges.

The prejudice that markets promote egoism, while collective procedures facilitate altruism, is, if anything, the reverse of the truth. As anyone familiar with life in former Soviet lands knows all too well, the reality of everyday existence there is one of incessant mutual predation and necessitous bargaining. The caricature of *laissez-faire* capitalism in which all relationships are turned into market exchanges applies far better to the socialist societies than to any market economy. The reason for this is that many goods – such as housing or education, and now perhaps even food – which in market economies are generally available to all are, in socialist societies, positional goods which are acquired through the Party or its subsidiary networks. The competition for positional goods is, by its very nature, a zero-sum conflict, since a positional good is one that cannot be possessed or consumed by all. In socialist systems, access even to the goods essential to daily living depends to a considerable extent on possession of the supreme and paradigm positional good, that of power. It is a virtue of the market economy that in it access to most goods depends solely on ability and willingness to pay for them.

Conventional academic wisdom about the market has also gone astray in neglecting the virtues that market systems inculcate or demand in people. These encompass not only honesty and diligence but also sensitivity to the needs and preferences of others. In predatory Soviet-style systems, the virtues that are at a premium are the Hobbesian ones, appropriate to his hypothetical state of nature, of force and fraud, coercion and deception. By contrast, the virtues elicited in market economies are those of the autonomous person – the person (in Feinberg's excellent account)[32] who is self-possessed, who has a distinct self-identity or individuality, who is authentic and self-directed, and whose life is to some significant degree a matter of self-creation. These autonomy-dependent virtues may not be characteristic of all market systems, since East Asian Confucian-inspired market orders may function perfectly well without many of them, but they animate all of the market systems whose inheritance is, like the British, an individualist moral culture.

Market systems of the kind in Britain, therefore, depend upon and reward autonomy-based virtues. They are far from being amoral instruments of wealth-creation. Nor is the autonomy they foster the bohemian, antinomian or nihilistic autonomy which some have found in J.S. Mill's *On Liberty*, and which has been devastatingly criticised by Lomasky.[33] The autonomy to which I refer here may exist to some extent, and may indeed flourish, in cultures (such as those of East Asia) which are not individualist in their moral inheritance. There, as in Britain, market exchange occurs among persons responsible for their choices in voluntary transactions. In these cultures, voluntaristic human agency is pervasive, even if Western ideals of autonomy are not prized, and it is arguable that, in a broader sense of autonomy in which it encompasses the ascription to persons of responsibility, autonomy animates even those market systems which are not based on individualism. Indeed, even in a culture from which autonomy were absent, if such be conceivable, the market economy would remain as an expression of voluntary human agency without which no modern society can successfully reproduce itself. The autonomy fostered by market orders is, therefore, that of independence and responsibility, not that of the free-floating sovereign self, or the rootless author of the *acte gratuite*.

Autonomy-based market systems are therefore fully compatible with tradition and community, since autonomous men and women will typically emerge from strong and stable communities and will remain embedded in them. In general, the twentieth century decimation and destruction of communities has been the work, principally, not of markets but of governments, from the genocidal terror of the Chinese communist government in Tibet to the desolation wreaked on working-class communities in Britain by municipal projects of urban renewal. All of the evidence suggests that, left to their own devices, people will in free markets renew their traditions and communities rather than desert or destroy them. In promoting autonomy and enabling its exercise, the market also and necessarily promotes and rewards virtues of a sort required by a voluntarist culture.

In invoking their role as enabling devices for human autonomy in order to explain the ethical standing of markets, it is important to be clear as to what is not here being claimed. It is not claimed that autonomy is an essential ingredient in any good life, nor even that the best human life will of necessity be an autonomous one. Perhaps, when comparing autonomous with non-autonomous forms of life, non-autonomous ones may emerge sometimes as superior forms of human flourishing. (Compare the forms of life of medieval Christendom, or of Japan in the Edo period, with those of the contemporary American inner city.) Or perhaps we are here in a realm of incommensurables. At any rate, the claim being made here is not that autonomy is a universal good, but that it is an essential element in any good life that can be lived by us. No inhabitant of a modern pluralistic, mobile and discursive society can fare well without at least a modicum of the capacities and resources needed for autonomy.[34] Most modern societies are such, in other words, that the constitutive ingredients of autonomy – the capacity for rational deliberation and choice, the absence of coercion by others and the possession of the resources needed for a life that is at least partly self-directed – are among our most vital interests. They are, indeed, vital ingredients in our well-being as a whole.

Autonomy is not, therefore, a necessary element in human flourishing *tout court*. It is an essential element of the good life for people situated in our historical context as inheritors of a particular, individualist form of life. The conditions constitutive of, and demanded by, autonomy are therefore not universal human rights, but conditions that are to a considerable degree culture-specific. Nor are they the same for all members even of our own culture. As Raz has observed in the passage already quoted, there is an essential indeterminacy in any account of the rights that support autonomy, since no complete or exhaustive list of them can be made. Nevertheless, we can clearly see that the conditions necessary for the autonomy of a disabled person, say, may well require the possession and exercise of claims which the able-bodied may not legitimately have. To say this is only to make the commonsense points that circumstances alter cases and that the conditions of autonomy may vary across persons, or, for that matter, may alter over time, during a single person's life. The content of the conditions that contributed to the autonomy of a person with Alzheimer's Disease may well differ from those that contribute to his or her autonomy before the illness struck, since the kinds and degree of autonomy achievable by the person may well now have altered, and the place of autonomy in the interests vital to his or her well-being may also have changed.

The conditions that enter into and support individual autonomy will be subject to considerable variation. Even among the modernist societies in which autonomy is a vital ingredient in human well-being, there are divergent conditions and inheritances, different resource levels and forms of political and moral culture and of economic and social life, which mean that the detailed pattern of rights promoting autonomy will vary significantly. The content of the conditions promoting autonomy has, therefore, an ineliminable dimension that is cultural and conventional. But, within these broader variations, the content of autonomy rights (as we may term them) will also vary according to the categories of the persons concerned – their abilities or disabilities, their position in the human life cycle, their resources, their needs, and so on. With respect to autonomy, it is not remotely plausible to suppose that its conditions can be specified in any fixed and highly determinate set of basic right entitlements or liberties. To suppose that this is possible is to fall prey to the legalist illusion that animates much recent theorising, especially that of Rawls,[35] and which is a perpetual temptation for liberal thought.[36]

Because the classical liberal idea that our liberties, negative and positive, can be specified once and for all in a highly determinate fashion is a mere illusion, I shall reject the idea that the conditions which support and ground autonomy can or should be theorised as rights. While criticising the standard neo-liberal arguments against positive or welfare rights, I shall maintain that the preconditions of autonomy are too complex, too variable and too diverse to be captured in the legalist discourse of rights. They encompass, among other things, a broad diversity of institutions aiming to provide the conditions of autonomous action, as well as a rich and deep common culture containing choiceworthy options and forms of life. In theorising autonomy as the primary animating value of market institutions and of a liberal civil society, we should (as I shall argue) resist the rigidity of the legalist discourse of rights; and instead acknowledge the dependency of autonomous thought and actions on a whole range of institutions, conventions and forms of life whose structure and content eludes the purblind perspectives of rights theory.

Several caveats may be worth mentioning. It is not being argued that the institutions of the market have any unique role in promoting and enhancing individual autonomy. That value is also promoted in voluntary associations – families, churches and many other forms of life – in which market exchange is peripheral. The claim is not that market institutions alone promote autonomy in society, but rather that in their absence people will be denied autonomy in a vital part of their lives – the economic dimension in which they act as consumers and producers. Indeed, far more is needed for reasonably autonomous persons than the market economy; in particular, as I shall argue, a system of welfare institutions which guarantees the resource conditions of autonomy to all, and a rich public culture and forms of common life which offer people a wide array of worthwhile options.

Nor is it at any point in the argument assumed that the institutions of the market are given to us once and for all, or that they will be everywhere the same. On the view presented here – a view inspired by the social market theory of the Freiburg School – the market is not a natural datum but (like every other human institution) an artefact, and an extremely complex artefact at that. We must not suppose, as the delusive perspectives of *laissez-faire* philosophy encourage us to do, that the free market is what remains after all control and regulation has been abolished. The forms of property, and of contractual liberty, which go to make up the market are themselves legal artefacts, human constructs that human design may amend or reform. The idea, common among latter-day classical liberals, of the market as a spontaneous order may be illuminating in so far as it generates insight into the ways in which unplanned market exchanges may coordinate human activities better than any plan; but it is profoundly misleading if it suggests that the institutional framework of the market process is given to us as a natural fact, or can be deduced from any simple theory. There will, in fact, be considerable variation, across countries and over time, in the forms of property, the varieties and limits of contractual liberty and the kinds of competition which the institutions of the market encompass. The view of the market that is to be rejected, accordingly, is that (common in the United States) which theorises its institutions as flowing from some underlying structure of rights. On the contrary view developed here, market institutions, like rights themselves, are social artefacts whose justification is in their contribution to individual well-being. If, as I have argued, markets are to be justified in that fashion and, in particular, by reference to their contribution to autonomy, then it follows that they may also be reformed or redesigned when their contribution to that interest is compromised. That this is no merely formal or abstract point will be seen when I consider how government policy may complement and inform the market process.

Thirdly, and finally, it is not here claimed that it is in their contribution to autonomy that the sole or exclusive justification of market institutions is to be found. Such a claim would be wholly contrary to the Berlinian value-pluralism that animates the argument here advanced. Rather, the argument is that it is the contribution made to autonomy by market institutions that gives them their deepest and most neglected justification for us. Doubtless market institutions promote many other good things but it is their role as enabling devices for autonomy that is focused upon here, partly in response to the inadequacies of the standard liberal defence of them in terms of their contribution to negative liberty. The argument is, therefore, that it is in their contribution to autonomous thought and action that the primary value of market institutions lies.

It is evident that the defence of the market as an enabling institution for individual autonomy has important implications for the matrix of claims which people possess when they enter the market economy. If, as I have argued, the morally unsatisfactory value of negative freedom cannot account for the ethical standing of the market, then it is plausible to suppose that the entitlements or claims which people possess as they enter the market cannot coherently be restricted to those which grant them immunity from coercion by others. They will also be positive claims that guarantee a decent array of worthwhile options and which confer upon people entitlements to resources. At this point, a crucial feature of the logic of the ethical defence of the market becomes apparent. This is that the argument which justifies free markets as enabling devices for autonomous choices also, and inexorably, justifies the institution of an enabling welfare state, where this is among the conditions of autonomous choice and action. Before we set out the purposes and policies of such a state, however, it is worth examining why two common alternatives to the social market model advanced here, egalitarianism and market socialism, are indefensible and should be removed from the intellectual and political agenda.

THE MIRAGE OF EGALITARIANISM

The enabling welfare state to be advocated later in this chapter is meant to guarantee far more than the subsistence claims acknowledged in classical liberal thought. The welfare claims defended in the argument go well beyond subsistence claims, since they are claims to the satisfaction of basic needs, including that in autonomy. In defending and advocating such an enabling welfare state, I have rejected as rationally indefensible and morally superficial the libertarian view that the scope of a limited government is confined to the sphere of passive rights to negative liberty.

In rejecting this conventional libertarian position, am I not occupying an unstable middle ground between libertarian and egalitarian positions? In particular, why do I stop short of accepting equality of well-being, say, or of the value of autonomy, as a legitimate goal of policy? It is the burden of Raymond Plant's argument[37] that a commitment to egalitarianism is necessitated by any liberal position which aims, as mine does, to empower or enable people in the satisfaction of their basic needs. Plant's argument seems to have two prongs, one normative, the other empirical. The normative one is the appeal to a principle requiring that people's well-being, or the value of their liberty, be equalised. The empirical argument is the thesis that, if the goal is the empowerment of the needy and if power is a positional good, then guaranteeing basic need-satisfaction will often generate zero-sum exchanges in which a rule of equality would seem to be the only fair distributional principle.

Neither of these arguments shows the rationality of egalitarianism or addresses its most serious difficulties. The normative principle neglects the satiability of most basic needs, including those connected with autonomy, and has the flaws (later to be explored) of all distributional principles that are designed to have a foundational role in a political morality. If most basic needs are indeed satiable, as I have argued, then the welfare claims that they generate can be met completely and without remainder. More specifically, Plant's argument is defective in that it follows the early Rawls in conceiving liberty as a variable that can indefinitely be maximised. On the account of autonomy given here, this is a mistake. Autonomy is best theorised as a basic need that is satiable. Though the level at which its satiation occurs may vary across and even within societies, there is nothing in the nature of things which prevents us from specifying the conditions under which the basic need of autonomy has been satisfied. Consider again the instructive example of the severely disabled person. If, let us say, we consider two people with the same, severe disability, where one is a millionaire and lives in the Ritz Hotel and the other lacks resources and is provided for by disability benefits, but where both persons enjoy the conditions necessary for a dignified, meaningful and autonomous life, then in my view the difference in the level of resource-provision of the two disabled persons has no moral significance. If both have good lives, why should the difference between them in terms of wealth concern us at all?

The answer given by Plant – an answer which invokes some principle regarding the equalisation of human well-being or the value of liberty – begs the question and has deep difficulties. It is not shown why justice demands equality in any of its forms. The suggestion is counter-intuitive, given that it neglects considerations of desert as well as of need. Again, no principle of equality is stated by Plant, save perhaps the principle demanding equal value of liberty. It is unclear that this is a workable principle, given the difficulties associated with the making of interpersonal utility comparisons: if there are incommensurabilities as between the goods of different persons, then these incommensurabilities will be just as much an impediment to an egalitarian deontic morality as they are to a consequentialist ethic. (If there are incommensurabilities among liberties and among the values they possess for their holders, how can we ever know that the value of liberty has been equalised? Is it supposed that we can construct a libertarian calculus?) Alternative egalitarian principles that do not demand or depend upon such utility assessment fare no better. The demand for equalisation of resources, if it could be given any definite content, would prove counter-intuitive because it fails to give weight to handicap.

Rawls's famous Difference, or Maximin Principle, which affirms that only that degree of inequality is just which elevates the position of the worst-off to the highest level possible, is indeterminate as to the degree of inequality it sanctions and makes impossible demands on the knowledge of policy-makers. (Again, how could anyone ever know when the level of the worst-off had been maximised?) And Dworkin's principle of equal concern and respect is hopelessly indeterminate, its content being given by the ephemera of American academic conventional wisdom rather than by any form of principled reasoning.

The empirical side of Plant's argument depends on claims about the operation of markets that are highly controversial and on a view of empowerment that is misconceived. Market exchanges are very rarely zero-sum transactions in which one person gains what the other loses. Indeed, it is precisely the character of market exchange as a transaction which is typically positive-sum, and so advantageous to both parties, that distinguishes it from most forms of political resource allocation. Plant has provided us with no empirical evidence that shows, or even suggests, that market provision of services typically renders them positional goods.

It seems, in fact, that Plant's argument rests on a conceptual fallacy rather than upon theory or evidence. It is true that political power is a positional good and can be nothing else. It is for this reason that, in societies where resource allocation is highly politicised, goods that are not positional in market economies often become markedly so. In the communist regimes, for example, goods such as housing, medical care, education and even food, which in the West are not significantly positional, become highly positional because access to them is mediated by the institutions of the Party and its corrupt and exploitative *nomenklatura*. In other words, the allocation of goods via political power is bound to enhance their positionality, or to render them positional when they were not so before, in virtue of the fact that access to the political power of the Party cannot in its nature be equally distributed. For this reason, the positionality of the good of political power tells against the political allocation of resources and speaks in favour of their allocation by markets.

The conceptual fallacy in Plant's argument is in assimilating the empowerment of the poor and the needy to the model of political power. Empowerment, or better, enablement, as I understand it, means conferring on such people the opportunities and the resources they need to live autonomously. It is thoroughly unclear, and Plant gives us no reason to suppose, that the enablement of any one person necessarily or even commonly entails the disablement of any other. How do welfare benefits for the disabled, perhaps framed in terms of voucher schemes, limit or disempower the able-bodied? In general, such schemes will have the effect of enhancing autonomy in the population, without incurring any significant cost in the heteronomy of others. Because it is a satiable good, autonomy – the basis of many of the welfare benefits that are defended here – is rarely, if ever, a positional good. Plant's argument seems to invoke, not any scarcity or conflict in the real world, but instead a conceptual claim that has no leverage on policies that aim to empower or enable people to act autonomously in markets. It leaves unanswered the crucial question: if, in the real world, positional goods are rarer and less important for individual well-being than Plant supposes, what does that portend for Plant's commitment to equality? Would it (in other words) make sense to be an egalitarian in a world (if such there could be) without positional goods? It is the confusion of empirical and conceptual claims that prevents Plant's argument from addressing these hard questions.

Plant's egalitarianism depends crucially on this conceptual error, and its conflated empirical claims, and has few arguments at its disposal without it. It remains to look at the flaws, and indeed the incoherencies, of all forms of egalitarianism, flaws which are not unique to egalitarianism but which affect any political morality that is supposed to be distributionist at its foundation. Let us consider the flaws, first, of egalitarianism. It has many implications (whatever specific egalitarian principle is under consideration) that are absurd or offensive. As Raz has noted,[38] egalitarian principles are indifferent between achieving equality through taking away from those who have and giving to those who have not. Further, the only intrinsic goods and evils that egalitarian principles recognise are relational ones. As Raz observes, decisively:

> If they [egalitarian principles] constitute the entire foundation of morality then the happiness of a person does not matter except if there are other happy people. Nor is there any reason to avoid harming or hurting a person except on the ground that there are others who are unharmed and unhurt. The absurdity of this view is seen by the fact that we have reason to care about inequalities in the distribution of *goods* and *ills*, that is, of what is of value or disvalue for independent reasons. There is no reason to care about inequalities in the

distribution of grains of sand, unless there is some other reason to wish to have or to avoid sand.[39]

Relational goods, or the principles that regulate them, accordingly, are never what ultimately matters in morality. It is, in any case, bizarre to suppose that a purely relational property could have intrinsic value. Moreover, egalitarianism, like other forms of distributionism, has a corrupting effect on our thought, since it distracts us from concern with what alone matters in political morality, namely, the well-being of individuals. As Raz has again put it:

> What makes us care about various inequalities is not the inequality but the concern identified by the underlying principle. It is the hunger of the hungry, the need of the needy, the suffering of the ill, and so on. The fact that they are worse off in the relevant respect than their neighbours is relevant. But it is relevant not as an independent evil of inequality. Its relevance is in showing that their hunger is greater, their need more pressing, their suffering more hurtful, and therefore our concern for the hungry, the needy, the suffering and not our concern for equality makes us give them priority.
>
> Our concern for the suffering, the unhappy, the unfulfilled is greater the greater their suffering or unhappiness. We have no reason to stop and ask whether the gap between the unhappy person and the rest of humanity is great to justify or to quantify our concern for him. His suffering or unhappiness matter in themselves, and the greater they are the more they matter.[40]

Egalitarian political moralities have other absurd and offensive features. Consider the question of natural endowments – the abilities and talents we receive via the genetic lottery. It has never been explained satisfactorily by egalitarians why these should not be subject to redistribution. If one person is blind and another fully sighted, why not transfer one eye from the sighted to the blind person, so that both are then partially sighted? If, as seems obvious, the natural talents of people are sometimes decisive for their well-being, ought we not (on egalitarian principles) to tax those of superior natural abilities, so as to achieve a level playing field in society? The standard, conventional answer to these pertinent questions is that the pursuit of equality is reasonably constrained by other values, such as individual liberty and respect for human personality, which policies of redistribution of bodily parts, say, would violate. Common, indeed ubiquitous, as this response is, it is extremely feeble. Policies which forcibly redistribute estates that have been in the hands of families for generations may have as injurious an impact on the liberties and personalities of the family members as any hypothetical policy for the redistribution of bodily parts might be expected to have. There is nothing in egalitarian morality that can in principle rule out the horribly dystopian society envisaged in L.P. Hartley's novel, *Facial Justice*,[41] in which the beautiful and the ugly are subject to mandatory facial surgery with the aim of assimilating them to the average or mediocrity in personal appearance.

Nor is it clear why financial assets, say, acquired in the lottery of the market or in the family lottery of inheritance, should have any different moral status from those acquired via the genetic lottery. Either both are liable to redistribution or neither. On the view presented here, there is no defensible principle for the redistribution of either type of asset. The welfare benefits defended are defended, not by reference to any distributional principle, but instead by appeal to the well-being of their holders. When we institute welfare benefits for the congenitally handicapped, we are not seeking to compensate them for bad luck in the genetic lottery. (How would such compensation be calculated, anyway?) We are aiming to protect and promote their well-being. No distributional principle is at stake in these or similar policies. Egalitarian moralities which make distribution fundamental not only incur all of the absurdities identified by Raz but also obscure the real reasons why we help the unfortunate.

Egalitarian moralities also soon come up against an awkward institution, the family. As Hayek and Nozick, among others, have noted,[42] the good fortune of being born into a happy, civilised family is one that may prove decisive as to one's life chances. Quite apart from any question as to the propriety of inheritance of financial assets, the institution of the family is bound to confer very different inheritances of cultural or human capital on different children. It will also play a decisive role in sending them out into the world happy or sad, alert or insensitive, confident or hesitant. Whereas good (and, in part, state-funded) schooling ought to have as one of its aims the goal of enabling every child to make the best of his or her abilities, it cannot wholly undo whatever harm families may have already done. For this reason, egalitarian morality cannot be other than hostile to the institution of the family – a point which Plato (no egalitarian himself) recognised, but which most egalitarian theorising has since suppressed. Egalitarians who are sufficiently intrepid as to entertain an assault on the family might care to scrutinise the evidence regarding the early socialist kibbutzim in Israel, which uniformly failed.[43] Egalitarianism suffers from the disadvantage of making impossible (as well as morally unacceptable) demands on us.

The proposal advanced here is that, rather than concern ourselves with any distributional principle, egalitarian or otherwise, which is conceived as foundational in political morality, we treat as foundational satiable basic human needs. These are human needs which are basic inasmuch as the satisfaction is a precondition of a worthwhile human life and which are satiable in that (unlike the pursuit of pleasure or power, say) their content can be fully met. The proposal is that guaranteeing the satisfaction of these needs – by an enabling welfare state, where the institutions of civil society cannot do so – is a fundamental principle of the same political morality, aimed at promoting autonomy, that grounds market institutions. Identifying basic needs and specifying resource levels for their provision is, on this account, a matter for rational public discourse, just like discourse about the allocation of resources for law and order and national defence in that it has an aspect of essential indeterminacy (but not, therefore, of arbitrariness). Like market institutions, an enabling welfare state dedicated to the satisfaction of basic needs is justified neither by its function as a maximiser of aggregate or collective welfare nor by any theory of rights or of justice, but instead by its contribution to human well-being, and in particular to that vital ingredient in human well-being that we have specified as autonomy. As will later emerge, the truth that the enabling welfare state is justified by its impact on the individual human good is important, since it distinguishes it from any conception of the welfare state that is distributionist, rights-based or justice-orientated. In this view, the welfare state is an enabling device for autonomy, different only in structure from market institutions; and, like market institutions, it facilitates not only the exercise of individual autonomy but also the renewal of a voluntarist community. These are points to which I shall return.

Unlike, say, the classical utilitarian principle of maximising pleasure, principles mandating the satiation of basic needs have the property of being diminishing, and they can always in principle be met completely. However much pleasure one has had, one can always have more; but once a basic need has been met, there is no reason for further action. Utilitarianism in morals and politics is to be rejected, among other reasons, because of the limitless and inexhaustible demands it puts upon us. Egalitarianism, along with other forms of distributionism, is to be rejected because it falsely attributes intrinsic value to relational properties that have none in themselves. It is a cardinal point in my argument, therefore, that the basic principles of political morality can be neither aggregative (having to do with collective or general welfare) nor distributive (having to do with comparative standing). They are instead, all of them, diminishing principles, having as their subject matter individual human well-being and the satisfaction of basic needs in respect of vital interests central to well-being.

Political morality – at least one that is in any sense liberal – can therefore be neither consequentialist nor distributionist in its foundation. That does not mean that it cannot be sensitive to consequences and distributions. Indeed, the diminishing principles that mandate satisfaction of basic needs arc themselves both consequence-sensitive and distribution-sensitive. They give guidance when resource-scarcity prevents the full satiation of the needs of all. They guide us to relieve the greater suffering rather than the lesser, to give medicine to those who would otherwise die rather than food to those who (though suffering from malnutrition) will survive, and so on. It may even be that a version of Rawls's Difference Principle, which enjoins that we ought to give priority to bettering the lot of the worst-off, should be adopted as a ruling maxim in social policy. If so, however, it would be as a rough rule of thumb, not as a matter of principle, and it would not arise from any distributionist concern. It would recognise (as Rawls does not) that the worst-off are a very heterogeneous bunch, not a single group, and that they have very different needs. And it would have no concern (as Rawls does) with lowering the maximum in society: its concern would solely be with the worst-off. It would thereby diverge radically from any fundamentalist egalitarian standpoint, even as it assigned priority to the needs of the neediest, and so was distribution-sensitive. The very principles that mandate satisfaction of basic needs enjoin us to satisfy the most urgent needs when all cannot be fully satiated. They thereby deviate from the straight maximising objective of utilitarian ethics – even if, on occasion, when resources are scarce and satiable needs commensurable, policy may unavoidably and rightly have a utilitarian dimension. They are for these reasons consequence-sensitive (but not consequentialist) principles.

Similarly, these principles will take note of distributions in so far as these are relevant to the project of satisfying basic needs. A policy of paying nursing home fees for all who need such care, regardless of their income or capital or other resources, would be massively wasteful and would yield a level of care that would be unacceptably low. Accordingly, it is reasonable to target such benefits, as at present in Britain, to those whose income or capital is nonexistent, small or exhausted (I leave aside here the precise mix of criteria that ought to be invoked to assess needs for targeting purposes – should it count capital or the income from capital, or some compound of the two? – as not being material to the substance of my argument.) Such a policy of targeting the disability welfare benefits of the sorts under consideration at this point is inherent in our concern for the efficacy of the right itself. Although they are not distributionist, the principles underlying welfare rights are in this way distribution-sensitive.

The importance of distribution is always contingent or subsidiary, never primordial or fundamental. What is objectionable in egalitarianism is what is wrong with every form of distributionism: its fixation on relational qualities that have no moral status. As Hayek has noted,[44] the very concern to impose a pattern on distribution is illiberal, in that it can only distort the constantly changing patterns produced by free individual choices. Governments may be concerned about distribution, and may have policies to affect it which aim to discourage excessive concentrations of wealth and to encourage its wide dispersal. These will be policies motivated not by justice but by other values, such as communal harmony and the enlargement of opportunity.

Distributionism has corrupted our thought by focusing not on individuals in themselves but on their relative positions. It has introduced into thought and practice a corrosive spirit of comparison which has obscured our perception of what is truly good and bad in human lives. Recent liberal thought has been fettered by the distributionist dogma that justice is the first virtue of social institutions. This may be so, but only in the Millian sense that it protects certain utilities, interests or goods that are vital to a worthwhile human life.[45] A fully worthwhile human life can be lived, as has been recognised at least since Aristotle, only in a community that is itself rich, sound and harmonious in its practices. The virtue of justice – in a society, an economy or a polity – is never primordial, in that it always presupposes, as one of its necessary conditions, a host of other virtues in a common form of life. When justice is conceived, as it often is in recent liberal and libertarian ideology, as a virtue appropriate to those who have nothing else in common, it is being theorised as a virtue for a society of strangers that, in real historical practice, would be unlikely to last much longer than a generation. In real historical terms, justice in human institutions always depends on the resources of a common life, and it is weakened as these are depleted. Justice is a virtue of common procedures – the virtue of fairness – not of substantive outcomes. We may rightly concern ourselves with the endowments that people have when they enter the market; but, when we do so, we do not invoke the imaginary claims of social justice, but rather the preconditions of individual well-being and of a stable and harmonious community.[46] The bottom line in political morality is thus never justice or rights, but instead the individual well-being which they protect and the common form of life in which it is realised.

Egalitarian distributionism is, from a point of view that is genuinely liberal, perhaps one of the worst forms of distributionism. In practice, it often amounts to little more than the 'anti-social envy'[47] that Mill presciently condemned among his contemporaries. Again, the rhetoric of social justice in which egalitarian demands are framed often serves merely to give a moral rationale to entrenched interests. In real political life, it is not the submerged and defenceless elements of the population – the disabled, the chronically sick, or the long-term unemployed, for example – who are the focus of attention of those who speak of social justice. It is instead the professional and middle classes, who already do best from the welfare state. The egalitarian rhetoric of social justice thereby has, in actual political practice, the perverse functions of curbing healthy alterations in relative incomes in society and of distracting attention from the lot of the truly unfortunate. Worst, egalitarianism suppresses the vital truth that, if the really unfortunate amoungst us are to be assisted by redistribution, it will have to be by a redistribution from the affluent majority, and not from the rich minority (whose wealth would be insufficient to the task, even if it could be transferred without loss). The real effect of egalitarianism in political life in Western democracies, accordingly, is to generate pernicious illusions about the potential benefits of redistribution from the rich, while doing nothing to enhance the opportunities of the disadvantaged, or to alleviate the lot of the needy.

Because it neglects merits and deserts, egalitarianism is especially inimical to liberty and responsibility. It dissociates the rewards people receive from their actions, and so nullifies the moral importance of their actions. Note that, by recognising the importance of merit and desert, we are not thereby arguing that the distribution of resources in society as a whole should correspond to these moral values. As Hayek has noted, people's merits and deserts are difficult to know, except in very limited contexts, and are surely unknowable by governments. Again, even if merit and desert were knowable, allocating resources according to them would have massive disincentive effects and a devastating impact on the self-esteem of those judged undeserving or unmeritorious.[48] For many reasons, of which the epistemic problem is the most important and least appreciated, the ideal of allocating resources across the whole of society according to such moral criteria is a foolish one. The objection to egalitarianism depends, not on such a distributionist ideal, but on the complete severance of rewards from personal conduct which egalitarianism would effect. As Hayek has put it, the market is akin to poker, a game of skill and chance.[49] The objection to egalitarianism is that, in removing the elements of both skill and chance from the allocation of resources in society, it would destroy market institutions. Or, to put the point the other way around: accepting market institutions involves accepting an unpredictable dispersion of rewards that is only partly connected with anyone's merits or deserts. It is this partial or imperfect connection that egalitarianism would destroy.

Proposals for the equalisation of resources among people fail to recognise, where they do not actively suppress, the vital truth that virtually all of the resources and wealth in a modern society are the result of human action, not manna from heaven. The egalitarian idea that production and distribution are radically separable activities, first advanced by J.S. Mill,[50] expresses the extraordinary delusion that human actions will proceed as before, even when their outcomes have been thoroughly distorted by a distributional programme on egalitarian lines. In truth, an egalitarian regime in which rewards bear no relation to human action would be one in which (if it could be achieved) human responsibility had been altogether extinguished. In practice, egalitarian policies invariably generate a corrupt, ineffi-cient and often exploitative parallel economy, in which human responsibility survives only in a compromised and degraded form. Ultimately, it is the logic of egalitarianism to collectivise responsibility for individual actions and thereby to destroy it.

Finally, as de Jouvencl points out in his unjustly neglected study,[51] the political result of distributionism in its egalitarian variety is to effect an ever-greater socialisation of income. It is one of the many ironies of egalitarianism that, in aiming to reduce the economic inequalities thrown up in market economies, it should create vast inequalities in political power, which (as in the communist regimes) soon reproduce themselves as economic inequalities often greater than those in market societies.[52] History and experience teach us that, incoherent as it is in philosophical terms, egalitarianism has in practice the signal inconvenience of being self-defeating.

Egalitarianism lacks philosophical credibility and, in practical terms, is felled by the same epistemic and incentive problems that defeat socialist central planning. Let us see if market socialism can escape these results of our argument so far.

THE BLIND ALLEY OF MARKET SOCIALISM

The argument so far has been that, whereas unconstrained libertarian capitalism cannot be justified by moral arguments, egalitarianism is in no stronger a position. The principled position appears to be that which grounds the market economy in its contribution to autonomy as a vital ingredient in individual well-being and which (as I shall next argue in greater detail) invokes precisely the same value to ground an enabling welfare state. It might be argued, however, that the defence of the market economy so far developed does not justify market capitalism, since it is acceptable to market socialists. By market socialism is meant here, not the simulation of market pricing by central planning institutions theorised in the Lange–Lerner model and devastatingly criticised by Hayek,[53] but instead the model of an economic system in which the private ownership of the means of production has been abolished and replaced by a system of communal or collective ownership by worker-cooperatives which stand to each other in relations of market competition. Market socialism so conceived, and as advocated most ably in Britain by David Miller,[54] is to be distinguished not only from the simulated markets of the Lange–Lerner model but also from the 'competitive syndicalism' of J.S. Mill and from egalitarian social democracy. It differs from Millian competitive syndicalism in that the worker-cooperatives that Mill envisaged as ultimately supplanting capitalist firms were to be voluntarily instituted and were conceived as forms of producer cooperation in which the shares of individual workers were individually owned, and could therefore freely be alienated, by them.[55] In the model theorised by Miller and other market socialists, the collective ownership of productive assets by the worker-cooperative precludes individual workers selling off their shares, or, at the very least, it prohibits the reinvestment of such shares in other worker-cooperatives of which the worker is not a member. The constitutive feature of market socialism in this model is, accordingly, in the fusion of job-holding with capital ownership, and, in consequence, in the prohibition of wage-labour and of a market in workers' assets in their cooperatives. Market socialism on this model is, finally, to be distinguished from Swedish-style egalitarian social democracy, in which an extensive redistributionist and welfarist apparatus was superimposed (with considerable damage to incentives) on classical capitalist economic institutions.

It is evident that, in the model so presented, there is market pricing of all or most assets, including labour, but not of capital. Although market socialist schemes come in a variety of forms, it is a feature of all of them that capital is allocated to the worker-cooperatives by state investment banks, not by private investors, institutional or personal. It is at this point that objections to worker-cooperatives on Austrian and Virginian lines emerge. As we noted earlier, it is a fundamental objection to central planning that the planners will in the absence of market pricing inevitably lack the knowledge of relative scarcities needed for rational resource-allocation. It is for this reason that centrally planned economic systems are endemically wasteful and riddled with malinvestments and other allocative inefficiencies. The question now arises: if market pricing is a precondition of rationality in the allocation of all other assets and resources, why is not the same true of capital? In other words, without a capital market, how can the state investment banks know what are the most productive uses of the investment capital at their disposal? This is, it is worth reminding ourselves, an epistemic argument against market socialism that depends in no way on any assumptions regarding the motives or the incentives of the state investment bankers. The argument is merely a further application, in a very important specific context, of the epistemic case against central planning. Its policy implication is a radical one, undercutting a constitutive feature of market socialism in all of its varieties. The policy implication is that there be a market in capital, which is to say, private or several ownership of capital. At this point, we are at least half-way towards the reinvention of one of the key institutions of market capitalism, or at least of the institution of a free market in private or several property in the means of production, which market socialism sought to suppress.

Though the epistemic argument is the deepest and most fundamental one against socialism in all of its forms, including market socialism, it needs to be supplemented by the incentive argument as theorised in the Virginia School of Public Choice. The incentive argument applies, in the first instance, to the state investment banks themselves. Since they lack the information for the rational allocation of capital, by what criteria or procedures will they distribute it? Why, in particular, should they not be highly risk-averse and conservative of their capital assets? If the answer is that there ought to be a plurality of such banks, competing with each other as profitable enterprises, then, once again, we are now well down the path toward reinventing a central institution of private property and the free market. This will be especially so, if, in order to give the various banks an incentive to pursue profits, an element of the profit accrues to the state investment bankers themselves. This is tantamount to a partial reinstitution of private banking and is unlikely to be a stable institutional arrangement.

The second level at which incentive arguments apply is at the level of the worker-cooperative itself. Existing worker-cooperatives will have an incentive to engage in a political competition for capital from the state investment banks. In this competition, it is virtually inevitable that existing, well-established worker-cooperatives will have a structural advantage over those that are new and speculative – and, above all, over those that are at present just a gleam in an entrepreneurial eye. It is to be expected, for this reason, that the allocation of capital under market socialist institutions will replicate the disabling inefficiencies of straightforward central planning institutions: it will favour entrenched producer groups, exhibit a high degree of risk aversion, and a tendency to seek to conceal malinvestments. In none of these respects is market socialism a significant improvement on socialism as theorised and practised in the terms of a command economy.

The structure of worker-cooperatives will also generate perverse incentives within them. Since job-holding and capital-ownership are fused, there will be an incentive for the worker-cooperatives to limit entry to the enterprise – in practice, often to relatives – since every extra worker dilutes the share of the rest in the enterprise's capital. Moreover, there will be an incentive slowly to consume the capital of the enterprise, rather than to invest it in risky research and development schemes, for example, since the enterprise always has the option of replenishing its capital fund by turning for help to the state investment bank. It is difficult to envisage a workable set of institutions that would prevent this upshot, since the only one we know for a surety that prevents, or inhibits, this tendency to slow capital-consumption is the traditional sanction of bankruptcy. Were this to be introduced, we would be yet further down the slippery slope towards the full-scale reinvention of the institutions of private property and the free market. In fact, the policy implication for the worker-cooperative enterprise of the incentive argument is that its dynamic efficiency is likely to be enhanced, only if worker-cooperators are fully liable to the risks of a policy of stagnation. This, in turn, will be so, only if worker-cooperators have the freedom to exit from the enterprise, taking with them their share of the capital assets. At this point, however, we are witnessing the reinvention of private property in the means of production – albeit in one of its least developed forms, that of the private family firm. If we have gone this far, under the compulsion provided by the perverse incentives of a system of worker-cooperatives, it is unclear why we should not go the whole way, and allow fully alienable and marketable private ownership of the means of production.

The shortcomings of market socialism that are derivable from its theoretical model are fully corroborated by the evidences of the Yugoslav experiment, now manifestly at an end.[56] This is a system that has exhibited massive structural unemployment, technological stagnation, a chaotic political auction of capital and recurrent episodes of authoritarian intervention by the central government to prevent or redirect the abuses of the worker-cooperatives. All of the empirical evidence supports what the theoretical model itself implies, that market socialism is an unhappy half-way house between socialist central planning and the key institutions of market capitalism. Economically highly inefficient, it is likely to be politically transitional, sustainable only under conditions of less than complete democratic political practice. Once again, the Yugoslav experience confirms this, disclosing that, as the communist state disintegrates to be replaced by varieties of popular democracy (and of popular authoritarianism), market socialism will vanish down the memory hole of history, unremembered and unlamented by the workers who have been subject to its inefficiencies and inequities.

It remains to consider what are the positive arguments for market socialism, given its considerable theoretical and practical failings. We may, I think, justly set aside arguments from exploitation and alienation as distinctive or peculiar features of capitalist institutions. Either these arguments invoke conceptions of exploitation and alienation that derive from classical Marxism or they rest upon empirical claims about the actual circumstances and preferences of workers. It is an unambiguous result of recent philosophical inquiry, including that of the school of analytical Marxism,[57] that classical Marxist conceptions of alienation and exploitation are indefensible, depending as they do on untenable doctrines such as the labour theory of value and a Hegelian account of human nature that is not translatable in ordinary empirical terms. On the other hand, if we look instead at the empirical realities of the lives of workers – their bargaining power *vis-à-vis* their employers, their attitudes to the jobs, and so forth – nothing whatever supports the view that the sense of estrangement or exploitation is reduced under socialist institutions. If anything, the opposite appears to be the case. Nor does it matter much whether the institutions are those of centralist command-style socialism or those of market socialist worker-cooperatives. Under the latter, the institutions and practices of self-management are diluted by the inevitable emergence of managerial élites and curtailed by frequent episodes of authoritarian intervention (in investment and hiring policy, for example) by central government. There is not a shred of empirical evidence that most workers prefer self-managed worker-cooperatives to capitalist corporations, or that they would not choose to exit from the former to the latter if they had the choice.

A complex counter-argument to that sketched above has been developed by David Miller.[58] Miller's argument is exceptional in acknowledging the problems of under-investment which are generated by the incentive structure of worker-co-operatives and in accepting that there is little, if any, real evidence of widespread demand for producer cooperatives or even for employee participation. However,

Miller seeks to explain these observed facts, or at least to resist their normative force and implications, by invoking the idea that worker-cooperatives in a predominantly capitalist environment find themselves in a Prisoner's Dilemma whereby they cannot flourish competitively, or, in the end and for the most part, even survive. The problem of under-investment alone, which worker-cooperatives face, condemns most of them to extinction. More subtly, but according to Miller no less pervasively and effectively, a capitalist economic environment will bias workers' preferences to income-maximisation as distinct from other, unobtainable goals (such as job-satisfaction or workplace participation). The upshot of Miller's argument is that a minimalist state in which most assets are embodied in capitalist institutions is not, as Nozick claimed it to be, neutral with respect to the form of productive enterprise in which its citizens elect to engage. Instead, because the intending worker-cooperators are in a Prisoner's Dilemma which condemns most of their projects to extinction in a capitalist environment, we must say that they are discriminated against in the circumstances that Miller and Nozick have specified. The result of Miller's argument, as he himself candidly acknowledges, is that if worker-cooperation or market socialism is ever to come about, it can only do so if the state intervenes and (in Nozick's famous expression) forbids capitalist acts among consenting adults.[59]

Miller's ingenious argument fails. It is true, as he says, that worker-cooperatives will on the whole fare badly in a capitalist environment. On this point market socialists and market liberals have no reason for disagreement. But does this failure show the non-neutrality of the legal framework of a liberal state? Or suggest that worker-cooperatives, or the ideal of worker-cooperation, has been discriminated against? It does not, for at least three reasons. Firstly, the neutrality of the liberal state is bound to be limited.[60] No liberal state can afford to legitimate, or to tolerate, practices (such as slavery, serfdom or enforced marriage) that violate the central norms of a liberal civil society. It is open to the critic of worker-cooperation to maintain that a system of worker-cooperatives of the sort Miller advocates violates the legitimate freedom of the worker who, after due consideration, decides that he or she wishes to work for a capitalist corporation. What justifies the coercive interdiction of the worker's choice? Why is the conscription of the unwilling worker into a worker-cooperative (or his or her marginalisation into self-employment or public service) more justifiable than his or her impressment into serfdom? As Gaus has well put it:

> Worker managed market socialist firms certainly can reward workers differentially, recognizing the differential claims to the fruits of labour, but market socialism in effect expropriates the earnings of workers invested in their firms. If, as Mill said, one has a claim to the fruits of his abstinence, market socialism tends systematically to ignore this. Workers who have heavily invested, especially older workers, have no exclusionary rights to these funds, entirely losing them on leaving the firm.[61]

The effect of market socialism on workers is, in short, to imprison them in their worker-cooperatives, where they may be subject to exploitative interference by central government. It is difficult to see what advantage such an arrangement has (from the point of view of the worker) over the more straightforward and transparent exploitation of workers' labour practised in socialist command economies.

A second objection to Miller's argument is that it accords an undefended privilege to the ideal of worker-cooperatives. It is true, as I have already observed, that capitalist economies tend to drive out worker-cooperatives. But they also tend to drive out other forms of productive enterprise that embody ideals that are incompatible with those of market socialism. The small corner shop is as threatened by capitalist competition as the worker-cooperative. The family firm, especially when it is also small, does not often last for many generations. Capitalist economies make life difficult for those with the ideal of productive enterprise harboured by early, pioneering capitalist managers and free-wheeling entrepreneurs. Is the liberal state (within which capitalist institutions are dominant) thereby discriminatory, or non-neutral with regard to these other ideals of productive life? If not, Miller needs to explain why its adverse impact on worker-cooperatives amounts to discriminatory non-neutrality when its undermining impact on such other ideals is discounted. It is difficult to avoid the conclusion that, the moral appeal of market socialism appearing self-evident to Miller, he proceeds to project it on to workers, who in practice care nothing for it, or who resist it because of its clear disadvantages for them.

The third point follows naturally from the first two. If Miller has any good reason to accord a privileged position to the ideal of worker-cooperation, it must be that he supposes there to be a submerged preference in its favour among the workers. It is hard to see why he supposes this. It is true, as he says,[62] that there is some evidence, albeit rather inconclusive, pointing to a preference among workers for somewhat greater participation in managerial decision-making. This is far from constituting a considered judgement in favour of a fundamental change in economic systems. On the one hand, evidence from progressive capitalist enterprises (such as Volvo) suggests that much of this dissatisfaction can be met within the context of capitalist institutions. On the other hand, there are good reasons for supposing that, even if (contrary to all available indicators) there were a significant, submerged body of worker opinion in favour of a shift to worker-cooperatives, it would dwindle or vanish once the economic costs of such a shift became evident to workers.

The costs would be massive, and would come in various forms, some of them recognised by Miller himself. Large economies of scale would have to be sacrificed if the economy were to be broken down into small, participatory units. The benefits of the international division of labour would be compromised to the extent that such a fragmentation occurred within a nation-state. (Would there be market socialism in one country? Would transnational corporations be forbidden to operate upon market socialist soil, or to invest in worker-cooperatives?)[63] The costs of production in a market socialist system would, almost inevitably, be higher than in capitalist corporations, and so the resultant prices would be higher, too. Would a nation-state that had opted for market socialism protect its worker-cooperatives, by tariffs and subsidies, against competition from foreign capitalist corporations?

If so, reduced living standards would very likely follow. The evidence is that, for these reasons and because of endemic under-investment, worker-cooperatives would under-perform capitalist corporations even where the latter had in a particular nation been rendered illegal. The prospect for a nation-state that adopts market socialism is that of falling living standards and of increasing isolation from the global economy. It is difficult to see this as a prospect that workers will welcome, or as one they are prepared to accept as the price for an ideal that few of them even avow or prize.

In world-historical terms, market socialism is in any case an anachronism. If in Western societies there is an absence of any political force in its favour, in the post-communist countries it has been abandoned and rejected, both by workers and by the ruling élites, as a utopian third way between market capitalism and socialist planning. In the former Soviet bloc, when market socialism is not treated with indifference, it is rejected with derision. It is hard not to endorse de Jasay's verdict that

> non-private ownership is a core requirement of market socialism, and genuine markets must somehow prove to be compatible with it. It is the pivotal place of this doctrine that really differentiates market socialism from the bankrupt doctrine of orthodox and, as I would insist, genuine socialism, as well as from the *ad hoc* compromises of social democracy.[64]

Theoretically indefensible, market socialist institutions are in practice systemically unstable, tending to revert to central planning or to mutate into something resembling market capitalism. Wherever political democracy is instituted, the tendency to the latter is virtually irresistible.

Having been removed by the force of events from the agenda of history, it is high time that market socialism be struck off the agenda of policy. At most, the real spectrum of political discourse now extends from unconstrained libertarian capitalism to egalitarian social democracy, with both ends of the spectrum accepting the core institutions of private property and free markets in most productive assets. Market socialism is little more than a distraction from this emergent consensus.

Nothing said so far is meant to imply that existing capitalist institutions are to be endorsed in their current forms, which are a product of historical accident and may well be appropriate subjects of reform. As a long tradition of liberal thought has always stressed, the corporation as we know it is an artefact of law, a legal fiction whose powers and immunities are open to criticism, reform, and amendment.[65] Again, the form of unencumbered property rights that Honore identifies as liberal ownership[66] is in the real world of law almost a limiting case with the law allowing a variety of forms of variously encumbered property rights. Yet again, the pattern of contractual liberties and immunities which characterises current Western capitalist institutions is not necessary or inevitable, but may be inappropriate in many contexts, and in need of reform even as it stands in the West. Finally, and perhaps most importantly, there is no convincing reason to suppose that the model of the Western capitalist corporation will be the most appropriate one in the emergent post-communist societies or that it should be copied every-where in the world. A policy of privatisation on the Western model presupposes, in most of these societies, and especially in Russia, a law of property and a tradition of legal corporate personality which either never existed or else has been compre-hensively destroyed. It may be that, as James Buchanan has argued in a seminal paper, what is needed in Russia is not the transposition there of Western capitalist institutions but instead a radical deconcentration of economic power,[67] in which private property and market exchange are reinstituted at village, cooperative and municipal levels. (Freeing up the parallel economy, alongside deconcentration of the state sector, is likely to be another necessary measure.) If this is so, then an agrarian capitalism of cooperatives, together with something akin to Millian competitive syndicalism in industry (incorporating the vital freedom of the worker to exit from the cooperative with his or her capital, which market socialism denies), may well be a far better prospect for the reinstitution of a market economy in Russia than the (probably futile) attempt to import the standard institutions of Western capitalism. Again, the Western, and particularly the American project of forcing liberalisation on a Western model upon Japanese economic institutions may well be thoroughly misconceived, neglecting the embeddedness of Japanese economic life in a uniquely distinctive and highly resilient culture. To recognise this is to acknowledge that, whereas market socialism is an unworkable absurdity, free markets can be combined with a variety of forms of ownership, and do not flourish only within the institutions of Western corporate capitalism.

In any modern state, forms of property rights will be pluralistic and diverse, fitting badly with any single theory or doctrine. In any modern Western state, no doubt, the dominant form of economic enterprise will be the capitalist corporation. It, too, however, comes in a variety of shapes and may properly be the subject of reform (by the encouragement of employee share-holding, and other devices, for example). With all of these qualifications and variations, it is in the acceptance of the core institutions of the market economy – the institutions of private property and voluntary exchange – rather than in the deluded pursuit of the mirage of market socialism – a mirage long dispelled in the post-communist lands – that progress, intellectual, economic and political, is to be found.

AN ENABLING WELFARE STATE

It has been the argument so far that market institutions are best defended as enabling devices for individual autonomy. The argument now being advanced is that the same considerations of individual autonomy which justify market institu-tions over real-world alternatives mandate the institution of an enabling welfare state which confers on people a variety of claims to goods, services and resources. Before proceeding with the substantive argument for the institution of such a welfare state, it may be worth briefly setting out in the most general terms the structure and content of such a welfare state. It would aim to provide a guarantee of the resources and opportunities required for the autonomous pursuit of the good life, where these are not provided or are under-provided by the institutions of civil society – by the spontaneously formed groupings of family, neighbourhood and community, by private self-provision and by charitable agencies. The argument here is that, having given full scope to these elements of civil life, there remains in any modern state such as Britain an indispensable and vital role for government in the funding (but not always, or most desirably, the provision) of welfare benefits, aimed at the satisfaction of basic needs. The structure of an enabling welfare state will inevitably by pluralist, because of the complexity of human needs and the environment of incentives which welfare institutions (like market institutions) create. It would encompass: universal provision, as with the National Health Service and, perhaps, the basic state retirement pension; benefits aimed at reintegrating, or integrating for the first time, people into the market economy and civil life, which should typically carry with them correlative obligations; and a variety of benefits for those incapable of full productive life in the economy, such as the disabled, which do not carry with them correlative obligations but are targeted with reference to the recipients' capital and income, and which, in having the status of entitlements (subject to the relevant criteria), are akin to welfare rights. The justification of this pluralist mix of welfare policies and institutions is the same as that of market institutions: the promotion of individual well-being and, more particularly, of autonomous choice among the worthwhile options provided by a rich and deep community. It is in these terms, and not in the terms of justice or rights, that the enabling welfare state is to be defended.

It is important that the rejection of a rights-based defence of the welfare state, which is advanced here, should not be confused with the objections to welfare rights that are part of the received conventional wisdom of latter-day classical liberals. These objections are well summarised by Norman Barry.[68] Welfare rights, unlike the traditional negative, passive liberal rights against coercion and force, demand more than the non-interference of others for their protection: they impose obligations on others to act to supply goods and services. Further, welfare rights are extremely sensitive to resource-scarcity and conflicts among them can easily arise: welfare rights therefore do not possess the property of non-conflictability or compossibility[69] held by negative rights against aggression. As a related point, welfare rights are highly indeterminate, their content being under-determined by any easily ascertainable body of hard empirical fact. (Is it a matter of objective or empirical fact, the critic of welfare rights asks, what are a person's medical needs?) For this last reason, welfare rights are not easily justiciable. And, since they presuppose a level of wealth that is historically rare, they cannot claim the property of universality that is usually associated with basic rights. In view of the fact that welfare rights do not possess the properties of nonconflictability and consequent peremptoriness or non-overridability that are possessed by negative rights, nor the determinacy of content and universality that are commonly attributed to the classical liberal negative rights against aggression, the critic of welfare rights concludes that there is a deep moral asymmetry between negative rights and welfare rights, such that the latter are not really rights at all but at best perhaps ideals or expressions of benevolence.

None of these arguments has any significant force. Negative rights, like welfare rights, impose obligations on others and make demands on resources in any real world in which rights are not afforded protection, by the enforcement of sanctions for their violation. A minimum state, concerned solely with national defence and the enforcement of the criminal and civil law, might still be enormously large, devouring up much of the wealth of society.[70] Not only does the protection of negative rights demand the appropriation by the state of scarce resources, it is also true that there may be competition and conflict among negative rights in their claims upon resources. Switching police manpower from street patrols to anti-terrorist activities may save lives but result in an increase in muggings. Negative rights are no more compossible in the real world, that is, no less likely to conflict with each other, than are welfare rights. Again, the obligations imposed by negative rights are not always those of forbearance. Jury service and military conscription, as well as the obligation to pay taxes to support even the minimum state, are all positive actions, constraining the negative liberty and appropriating some of the resources of the citizen. Finally, all rights are conditional: rights to life or liberty may be withdrawn, overridden, or forfeited by imprisonment or capital punishment if their holder's conduct justifies such abridgment. In all of these respects, negative rights and welfare rights enjoy full moral parity.

The classical liberal defence of negative rights, like its defence of negative liberty, depends upon a number of disabling illusions. Consider the claim that specifying the content of welfare rights comes up against problems of determinacy. Is this not also, and equally, the case with specifying the content of negative rights? No one who knows anything of the legal history and jurisprudence of the supposed rights to property, to privacy or to freedom of information can suppose that their content is easily determined, or that conflicts among them can be arbitrated simply. The easy justiciability of negative rights is merely a seductive mirage, generated not by anything in the real world of law but by a theory that is insulated from the uncertainties, indeterminacies and endemic hard cases with which real law abounds. The universality of negative rights is no less delusive. They sometimes compete with each other, such that not all can be protected, and their content is often significantly culture-specific. (What counts as rape in other cultures and other jurisdictions? What murder?) There may be something akin to the minimum content of natural law, theorised by H.L.A. Hart,[71] but it is doubtful in the extreme if this can be given a content statable in a determinate list of universal negative rights.

We may, therefore, dismiss these commonplace objections to the discourse of welfare rights, and proceed to consider the true objections to the discourse of rights in general. At this point it is well that a few remarks are made on the very notion of a right. As Raz has shown,[72] rights are never fundamental or primordial in political discourse or political morality. Claims about rights are intermediary or conclusionary claims about the relations between the interests central to the well-being of persons and the obligations generated upon others by these interests. There is, therefore, an ineradicable open texture (not avoidable in other theories) about the discourse of rights, whether negative or positive. The content or contours of any alleged right are shaped by our judgements of the vital interests, or the conditions of well-being, of the persons under consideration. This is to say that, in political and in moral philosophy, the good is always prior to the right: we make judgements about the rights that people have, only on the basis of our judgements of the interests central to their well-being. The project of a purely deontic theory of rights – that is to say, one which appeals only to principles of justice or the right, and which does not invoke any particular conception of the good life – is bound to founder, as it does in Kant and Gewirth, in the no man's land between content-lessness and foundationlessness. All of the content that rights may have and all of their ethical weight derives, in short, from their contribution to vital human interests.

The dependency of rights on their contribution to individual well-being gives the clue as to the true limitations of rights discourse in respect to government and the welfare state. In the first place, the conditions of well-being are too diverse, too subtle and too variable to be captured in the thin and rigid discourse of rights. Individual well-being depends on a host of conditions, including decent cultural traditions and rich forms of common life, which the theory of rights cannot address nor the practice of rights guarantee. Autonomy, as a vital ingredient in well-being, cannot be guaranteed by any structure of rights, since it too depends on a matrix of cultural traditions and of communal life which rights cannot assure. Although, as I shall argue, there are classes of welfare benefit that ought to have the status of entitlements if they are to promote or respect autonomy, and so are akin to welfare rights, the goal of enhancing autonomy demands a pluralist mixture of institutions and policies that cannot be squeezed into the Procrustean contours of rights theory.

There are other, no less fundamental objections to the discourse of rights in its application both to government in general and to the welfare state. The discourse of rights is in its nature universalistic and monolithic. If there are any rights at all, it would seem that they must be universal and immutable, possessed by everyone, once and for all. The implication of Raz's analysis, however, is that rights are variable and mutable, their scope and content waxing and waning as the conditions of individual well-being change. On the view advanced here, the discourse of rights is reducible to that of individual well-being, and is for that reason redundant. Moreover, the discourse of rights has the danger that it suggests that the best governmental and welfare initiatives and policies are (at least in principle) always the same. The view presented here, on the contrary, is that the conditions of human well-being are many and various, that they change and have only a few common elements (such as the importance of autonomy to human well-being in most modern societies). If the conditions of well-being are complex and variable in this way, it would seem folly to try to compress them into any structure of rights.

The conditions of human well-being are, therefore, highly complex and change-able; but they may also be conflicting and competitive in their claims and in their demands on resources. This enables us to state yet another objection to the discourse of rights. The legalist discourse and practice of rights is peremptory and does not allow the trade-offs and compromises that are the stuff of political (and moral) life. When rights come into conflict with each other, they cannot be balanced: one must be overridden, or even extinguished, by the other. The theory and practice of rights conceals the fact, otherwise self-evident, that political life, like moral life, is a choice among necessary evils, as well as among uncombinable goods. It also acts as a recipe for intractable conflict among rival ideals and interests. The treatment of abortion as a matter of fundamental constitutional right, rather than of legislative policy and political compromise, makes of that issue an insoluble dilemma, hostile to civil peace. If rights are eliminated from political discourse, then a settlement can sometimes be reached on such issues which is stable because it is perceived as fair, even if no party to it is wholly satisfied with it. The effect of rights-discourse is to render political conflicts non-negotiable.

Nothing thus far advanced here is meant to suggest that rights have no place at all in political life. An institution such as the European Convention on Human Rights may be worth incorporating into British law as a summary of the various practices and procedures in which important civil liberties are embodied. It is as a conventional abridgement of the practices of civil society, however, and not as a statement of fundamental rights, that such institutions should figure in political life. The hegemony of the discourse of rights in political life has among its consequences a culture of endemic legalism and the political corruption of law, as in the United States. Rather than attempting to fix political discourse within the illusory constraints of legalism, we are on firmer ground if we direct political discourse towards the conditions of individual well-being, the content of basic needs and the depth and limits of the common culture, and the inherently public goods that it contains.

The use of the rhetoric of right in the context of welfare institutions, though it has leverage in some important areas of policy, is in general inappropriate. It inclines us to form welfare policy and institutions on the model of a theory of justice, with all its distributionist and universalist preoccupations, whereas the animating values of an enabling welfare state should be values of autonomy, human solidarity and community. A society in which there is an abandoned underclass, in which the frail and the ill are left to their own devices and lack organised assistance, governmental as well as private, is ignoble, unlovely and graceless, whether or not it violates any specifiable precept of justice. A society in which the poor lack dignity, in which those whom catastrophe has struck are left to their own devices, is not worth living in, regardless of whether or not it exemplifies the virtue of justice that is the shibboleth of recent liberal political philosophy. And, if the unfortunate can be helped and a harmonious community preserved only at the cost of minor injustice, then so much the worse for justice.

In truth, the liberal claim for justice that it is the first and supreme virtue of social institutions is a piece of hubris. Justice is a far humbler affair, an artefact of the common life, a remedial virtue in which unfairnesses are corrected, and it is essentially procedural in character. Justice designates a set of reciprocities whereby we achieve a *modus vivendi*, not an ideal specified in terms of rigorist principles. It is true of some welfare benefits, I shall maintain, that they should be entrenched in entitlements governed by rules, and it is in general true that discretionary allocation of benefits will be perceived as arbitrary, so that considerations of fairness will arise in the first case and will tell against the latter. The model for an enabling welfare state is not, however, any theory of justice, if there can indeed be such a thing, but instead the preconditions of individual autonomy and rich community, with all of their variations over time and across cultures. There is no one set of policies, no one structure of institutions, in which an enabling welfare state is best embodied. There is instead a diversity of local settlements, never final and always provisional, in which conflicting claims are given a temporary reconciliation, and the values of autonomy and community are accorded a more or less complete embodiment and expression. The enabling state is defended, accordingly, not as a dictate of justice (whatever that may be), but as a precondition of the good life.

At this point in the argument we need to return to the notion of a basic need, and to put to work Raz's seminal exploration[73] of the satiability of most basic needs. A basic need, as I shall understand it, is one whose satisfaction is essential to the possibility of a worthwhile life, and whose frustration renders impossible the living of a good life. For us, at least, autonomy is a basic need, whose deprivation curtails our prospects of a good life. Basic needs encompass needs whose satisfaction contributes to or enhances autonomy, such as needs for food, housing, medical care, education and so forth. As I have noted, the satisfaction of these basic needs may be demanded as a condition of a worthwhile life, even if the life that is then lived fails to be very autonomous (as in the case of the Alzheimer's patient, say). This suggests that the claim to the satisfaction of a basic need may be over-determined in its justification on the ground that any welfare claim may promote several vital interests at the same time, including that upon which I mostly focus, the vital interest in autonomy.

The claim that is being advanced here is that an enabling welfare state provides for the satisfaction of basic needs. This claim must at once be qualified in a variety of ways. In a liberal civil society, it is, or ought to be, taken for granted that, for most people most of the time, the satisfaction of basic needs is a matter of personal responsibility. There is no persuasive ethical justification for the massive, over-extended welfare states of most modern societies, which often involve perverse redistributions to the middle classes (a process which is, however, not at all easy to reverse under democratic institutions). The welfare state being defended here, though more sensitive to the needs of the worst-off, is more restrictive than most that exist in contemporary states.

Further, it is intended to come into operation when the resources of civil society are exhausted or inadequate. Much welfare provision will always occur in the context of spontaneously occurring social groups – families, neighbourhoods, churches, friendships, and so on. Again, much that is presently done by governmental agencies could be devolved to private self-provision. Finally, charitable agencies will always have an important role to play in welfare provision. In each of these three areas, the vitality of civil society could be strengthened by the extension of existing tax reliefs to families and other similar groups, to voluntary schemes for self-provision, and to charities. Such extension and development of tax deductibility would go against the neo-liberal dogma of the neutrality of the 'level playing field' in tax policy, but that is no fault in it. At the same time, it would be the height of folly to suppose that such desirable measures could circumvent the necessity of government funding and (in some instances) government provision of welfare benefits.

Schemes involving government activity in the area of welfare are many and various. They may have different objectives, even where they are promoting the same values. Such schemes fall into three categories which it is important to distinguish. The first are welfare schemes which aim to return to the productive economy people who for one reason or another have fallen out of it, but who possess or can acquire the skills and capacities to become active, self-reliant participants in the market economy. These are claims, for example, to unemployment benefits, to retraining schemes, to remedial education and so forth. These are welfare benefits whose aim is to promote the autonomy of members of underclass groups by returning them to and reintegrating them into the market economy. It is a point of cardinal importance that these welfare benefits always carry with them obligations: to engage in workfare, or to accept reasonable employment once re-skilled, for example. In Britain, policy on unemployment is almost the worst imaginable, with stagnant pools of the long-term unemployed living by eking out their low benefits, without having in most cases any real prospect of genuine re-skilling. Policy-makers in Britain could with profit study labour policy in Sweden, where very generous assistance in re-skilling is given but has attached to it an obligation to accept employment in the areas for which the person has been retrained. One consequence of this – one neglected by American and British neo-liberal and neo-conservative theorists, who argue that welfare institutions always generate dependency – is that Sweden (whatever its other problems may be, and whatever may have caused the political changes of late 1991) has no underclass, or as yet only a small one, of the multi-generationally unemployed.

In British society, having a job is for most people a basic need, if only because for most people involuntary long-term unemployment deals a severe blow to self-esteem. A welfare entitlement to re-skilling, whenever this is feasible, together with the complementary obligations, is for this reason one element in the matrix of welfare policies that promote autonomy. In Britain, literacy and numeracy are necessary conditions of almost any kind of autonomous life, so that access to education is also a welfare right. We have here an instance of the second class of welfare benefits, those designed to prepare people for the status of autonomous individuals in a liberal civil society. How this welfare benefit to education is to be embodied is a matter for reasonable debate. I have elsewhere speculated in Millian terms[74] that a privatised schooling system, with targeted vouchers and merit bursaries for the needy, might be the best system to this end, but in the present context it is the principle of education as a valid welfare claim rather than the institutional means for guaranteeing it (which will greatly vary according to circumstances) that is most important to establish.

What of health care? In which category of welfare benefit does it fall? Here we need to distinguish among different categories of health care, and the various means whereby it might be provided. In respect of catastrophic and chronic serious illness, and of most forms of disability, especially in its more severe forms, we have a clearly distinct third form of welfare benefit, which (unlike the first) does not carry with it concomitant obligations. When their capital is exhausted or their incomes are low, people falling into this category have a welfare claim to whatever services are needed to enable them to lead a life that is as autonomous, as dignified and as meaningful as that of able-bodied persons, in so far as this is achievable. Incentive considerations are largely irrelevant here. Such persons possess welfare claims with no corresponding duties. Policy in this area has been particularly poor in Britain, and may well get even worse. As I have elsewhere argued, a voucher-based scheme for community care[75] seems particularly appropriate in that it combines a guarantee of public provision with individual choice of its forms made in competitive free markets. This is a point to which I shall return later in general terms.

It is here that Raz's observations on the satiability of most basic needs are relevant. Raz illuminates a fundamental property of basic needs, as distinct from wants or preferences, when he notes that most of them, in principle, are capable of complete satiation. The needs of the disabled, or of the illiterate, though sometimes perhaps expensive to meet, can usually be met completely, that is to say, to the point at which they can lead reasonably autonomous lives. The crucial conceptual distinction is made by Raz[76] when he notes that happiness is a satiable value, whereas pleasure is not. A person with a happy life need have no reason to seek to improve that life, whereas someone devoted to pleasure always has reason to seek more pleasure. Most basic needs have the property of satiability, which means that, once they are met, the content of the welfare claim which guarantees their satisfaction is exhausted.

Medical care generates peculiarly difficult problems, not only for the thesis advocated here but for all views, in that by no means all medical needs are fully satiable. Whereas those of the disabled are usually fully satiable, those connected with the process of ageing, or with illnesses which are terminal but which can (with an ever worsening quality of life) be indefinitely staved-off, sometimes are not. The problem of basic needs that are non-satiable is a hard one for any theory, or, at least, for any theory that is unprepared to consider the legitimacy of euthanasia. This is not a problem on which I can hope to say anything useful in this context, though I am sure that Dutch policy on euthanasia merits careful study, as does the admirable American legal innovation, the Living Will (which mandates withdrawal of life-support systems under certain conditions).

Against the thesis that welfare benefits are valid claims to the satisfaction of basic needs, it will doubtless be objected that the scope and content of any basic need is disputable and perhaps arbitrary. More subtly, it may be objected[77] that basic needs may be incommensurable, in that satisfying them yields no overall measure of need satisfaction. In response to these objections, it must be accepted that at least those basic needs not having to do with biological survival will have a significant cultural or conventional dimension. The basic needs of a Kalahari bushman will not be the same as those of a young urban professional. It is hard to see, however, how this evident variability in the content of basic needs across cultures and societies renders them altogether subjective. In any particular society, reasoned public discourse can occur as to the content of basic needs, which invokes the shared norms and common life of the society. Such discourse will never achieve the precise objectivity of the natural sciences, but that will be an objection to it only for those (and there are many) who have forgotten (or never known) Aristotle's wise dictum that we should only expect in any subject the kind and degree of precision of which it is capable.

The objection that the scope and content of basic needs is disputable, and the implication that the satiability of basic needs is therefore delusive, presupposes that the indeterminacies in the account of basic needs are remedied, or avoided, in other theories. It is difficult to see what sustains this illusion. The indeterminacy that afflicts discourse about basic needs is merely an instance of the pervasive indeterminacy that haunts moral and political discourse. It is not a defect of the theory, but rather a fact of life. The favourite policy measures of latter-day classical liberals – the negative income tax and voucher schemes, for example – themselves confront precisely the same indeterminacies. What should be the size of a school voucher, and how (and by whom) is this to be determined? What level of income is to be specified as the minimum in a negative income tax scheme, and how can such a specification avoid invoking contestable value-judgements about the level of subsistence? Or, to turn to the functions of the so-called minimum state, to what level of police protection are citizens entitled, and by what formula is this to be decided? It is evident that classical liberal principles and proposals are beset by all of the indeterminacies that afflict my own. This is a point not without practical significance, as I shall show when I come to consider the case of a government that sought to implement the ideas sketched here about an enabling welfare state.

The deeper objection concerns the commensurability of basic needs. Among medical needs, can the preservation of life be ranked against the alleviation of pain? And how are medical needs to be weighed against educational or intellectual needs? It would seem that such judgements could be made, if at all, only by invoking a thick and comprehensive conception of the good life about which there is no consensus. Distribution according to basic needs would then be arbitrary, in that it would impose on all a conception of the good life that was only one of several, possibly incommensurable conceptions harboured in society. What can be said against this claim? An answer can be found, I believe, in the fact that the content of a basic need is subject to partial self-definition by the agent. A person may have basic medical needs which require residence in a nursing home, but the detailed mixture of goods and services may again be determined by the person him/herself. Equally, a person may have a basic need for literacy, but the form in which this is satisfied – the mode of teaching and learning – may be decided by the person him/herself. This is especially so, if the guarantee of the basic need comes in the form of a voucher which the person may spend on a range of services. Vouchers are in this sense a species of welfare benefit that is akin to a positive right.

Nor is the incommensurability of basic needs an obstacle to their satiability. As Raz has observed, satiability does not mean that there is a point which is reached by all who get to the point of satiation (in the alleviation of hunger, the satisfaction of needs, or in happiness, etc.) such that they are all at precisely the same level in the relevant respect. All it implies is that there is no possibility of improving the positions they reached. That condition is satisfied by complete incommensurability of happiness once a certain level of it is reached.[78]

If we allow, as in voucher schemes, a partial self-definition of basic needs, then these may be satiated, even if the needs concerned are not commensurable. Difficulties arise, so far as I can see, only in areas of policy where basic needs are not satiable, or where there is radical resource-scarcity in respect of satiable basic needs. In these areas, voucher schemes may be neither appropriate nor workable. This illustrates a central aspect of my argument: that all welfare policies and institutions, like all other policies and institutions, have costs, hazards and other imperfections. For this reason, no single measure can conceivably be adequate to our concerns, and all will have side-effects that are regrettable.

It is worth saying something as to the institutional and policy framework of an enabling welfare state, with particular reference to issues of universality versus selectivity, and entitlement versus discretion in welfare benefits. Let us take, first, the issue of universality versus targeting. It is reasonable to target welfare benefits when, but only when, this does not generate perverse incentive structures and impose heavy informational and administrative costs on welfare institutions. These conditions are rarely met except in the area of benefits for the disabled and long-term sick, where incomes and capital holdings are fairly easily assessed, and incentive considerations are insignificant. Elsewhere, there are massive incentive and epistemic objections to targeting, and good arguments for universal provision. Targeting policies in welfare face grave epistemic problems in assessing needs that are often variable, and whose measurement is disputable. In respect of the favoured neo-liberal measure of the negative income tax, how would it cope with the fluctuating incomes of seasonal and part-time workers? What would be the unit of assessment: individual or household? If household, how could that be defined? In addition to massive epistemic difficulties, the negative income tax, with its usual marginal tax rate of around 70 per cent, would generate huge disincentives and a deep poverty trap. It is extraordinary that this absurd measure (with its inevitable consequence of a further large socialisation of income) has gained the support of so many neo-liberals.

Because of the epistemic and incentive difficulties of targeting, there is a strong case for universal provision where, as in the unreformed National Health Service (with all its imperfections), costs can be maintained at comparatively reasonable levels and a decent basic level of treatment provided in most areas of need. It is a signal advantage of universal provision that, unlike targeting schemes, it does not skew incentives perversely so as to create poverty traps, make unreasonable demands on the knowledge possessed by providers, or generate vast administrative apparatuses. It is therefore preferable to targeting in such areas as the NHS and, as has already been suggested here, perhaps also the basic state pension. This is not to say that means-testing is never appropriate, since policy areas have been noted where it may well be; only that in many policy areas the costs of selectivity far outweigh the benefits.

Consider next the issue of discretion versus entitlement in welfare benefits. Neo-liberals have shown a fondness for discretion in welfare policy that is exceedingly strange, given their concern for the limitation of power over the lives of individuals.

The model of discretionary allocation by governmental authority (as practised in Switzerland, for example) should be objectionable to liberals for several reasons. It concentrates power over the lives of individuals, often vulnerable or defenceless individuals, to a wholly objectionable extent. Because the authority exercised is discretionary, it cannot conform to any ideal of the rule of law, which in other areas liberals affect to cherish. In practice, welfare benefits will be allocated at the discretion of welfare professionals whose decisions will often (if experience is any guide) be animated by questionable orthodoxies and ephemeral fads. And, because in practice the discretionary authority is bound to be subject to budgetary constraints, the integrity of that authority as the guardian of the recipients' interests and needs will inevitably be compromised. This is a major defect of the Griffiths Report on community care, which proposes replacement of the present system's voucher arrangement by bureaucratic assessment of individual needs, and of current reforms of the NHS which reinforce discretionary allocation of medical resources while at the same time compromising the clinical freedom of doctors. Finally, liberals who oppose entrenched welfare entitlements may care to recall that they were also rejected by socialists, such as the Webbs, apparently because they believed that they accorded to individuals freedom of choice that was excessive and unwarranted.

None of this is to say that discretionary allocation of welfare benefits may not sometimes be desirable, or else inevitable – as, perhaps, in the case of the Social Fund in Britain. Over a large area of benefits, however, there is a strong case for their entrenchment as entitlements, given the uncertainty and arbitrariness that go with discretionary allocation. In many cases, voucher schemes should be expanded or instituted, being themselves (as has already been observed) entrenched welfare entitlements. Critics of welfare entitlements may, therefore, reasonably be asked why they support species of them (such as voucher schemes) and yet resist the extension of similar schemes into other areas of welfare policy.

A genuinely liberal approach to welfare policy will, accordingly, favour an enabling welfare state, featuring universality and entitlement in many areas of provision. It will, however, be a pluralist institution, containing policies and practices of targeting and discretionary allocation, where these seem the only appropriate measures. It will not attempt the impossible (and, in my view, undesirable) task of imposing any pattern of distribution on society, a task ruled out by the same epistemic and incentive arguments that defeat central planning. It will rely, so far as is feasible, on the institutions and informal life of civil society, where local knowledge can be best deployed. In its own operations, the enabling welfare state will see to it that benefits such as workfare confer obligations, where they can reasonably be imposed; that they be means-tested, where (as in the context of chronic illness) incentive considerations are insignificant; and it will seek to devolve welfare functions to the lowest level of government, thus observing the principle of subsidiarity while acknowledging the necessity of central governmental funding. Where feasible and cost-effective it will separate governmental funding from governmental provision, using vouchers and other devices to give state support to market provision of welfare services. It will not, however, endorse the doctrinaire supposition that privatisation and marketisation are the answers to all problems in welfare policy.

The enabling welfare state here advocated differs from others in that its ethical foundation is not in ideas of justice or distribution, still less in ideas of fundamental rights, but rather in the values of autonomy and enablement that ground market institutions. The individuals who are enabled to act autonomously by market institutions and by the institutions of an enabling welfare state will enjoy worthwhile autonomy only if there are forms of common life, rich in choiceworthy options, available to them. It is these forms of community that the social market economy aims to nurture and protect.

THE SOCIAL MARKET ECONOMY: AN OUTLINE

According to the perspective which animates this chapter, there is an essential indeterminacy about which goods are to be produced in markets. There is no general, universal principle that can tell us which goods are best provided by markets, by voluntary associations, by the institutions of an enabling welfare state, by collective political decision-making or by the application of a rule or the invocation of an entitlement. Time, place and circumstance have always a major contribution to make to our deliberations on these matters. In any particular historical context, however, there are considerations or maxims which assist us in our detailed, circumstantial reasonings as to which goods are best supplied by markets and which by other institutions. Elsewhere,[79] I have stated a few of these maxims, including the central one that, aside from the core state activities of national defence and law and order, the vast majority of economic goods are in a modern state such as Britain most appropriately supplied in free markets (supplemented, where necessary, by voucher and other schemes for the provision of purchasing power to those otherwise without income or resources). This maxim is further supported by the upshot of the argument earlier in this chapter, which is that no modern state can in the end avoid the bulk of economic activities being conducted within the institutions of a free market economy. This is so, both for practical (epistemic and incentive) reasons and for ethical reasons having to do with the promotion of individual autonomy. Another way of stating this result is to say that it is only through the institutions of a liberal civil society – in which contractual freedom, personal liberty and private property are protected under a rule of law – that a modern civilisation can reproduce itself. I have passed over here the important area of those individual liberties that are exercised in economic and commercial life, not because they are unimportant, but because others have shown their indispensable role in a liberal civil society, and I have elsewhere myself argued to that effect.[80] It is maintained here that market institutions are an aspect of individual freedom, conceived as autonomy, that is indivisible from other dimensions of autonomy, such as those protected by freedoms of conscience, expression and so on. This is a result of the argument that will be taken as given in the subsequent discussion, and which underpins the later discussion of the outlines of a social market economy in Britain and other, similar countries.

My topic here is that of the limits of market institutions – the question of the areas in which there is market failure, or in which market provision is inappropriate for other reasons, or requires supplementation. It may be worth repeating here that the shape of market institutions is not something that can be known a priori, or which can be derived from any theory, say, of rights. On the view developed here – a view which I owe to the Freiburg School of social market theorists – market institutions are social constructions, artefacts which we may not have designed, and which are for us historical inheritances, but which we may properly alter and reform so that they better contribute to human well-being. There is not, in other words, an ideal market, a condition of pure *laissez-faire*, to which real markets approximate; there are only the varied institutions that make up markets in all of their diversity. Like every other human institution, the market is imperfect (and imperfectible); and there is no single, unique set of market institutions that is everywhere and always appropriate. The spirit in which we approach market institutions ought, perhaps, to be that of Popper's piecemeal social engineer,[81] who seeks to improve institutions bit by bit, without the dubious assistance of any model of perfection. If we approach markets in this spirit, we will find that they often need to be supplemented or informed by government action if they are to achieve their ends and make their contribution to human well-being.

The most obvious area in which the limits of market institutions are revealed is that of public goods, which, because they are not partitionable or excludable, must be supplied to all or none. I shall not address here goods such as clean air, say. Many other writers have said all that can be usefully said on the subject, including the wise observation that the dangers of market failure must always be weighed against the hazards of government failure. I shall instead focus upon another kind of public good; those inherently public goods (in Raz's term)[82] that are associated with a common culture in which autonomous individuals have a rich array of options and amenities to choose from. In part, to be sure, this latter species of public good overlaps with the former. A clean city or natural environment may be a public good in both senses. I am here concerned, however, with the sense in which a city, say, that is not only clean but also safe, pleasing to the senses and contains a good variety of cultural amenities, forms the public space in which individuals may make autonomous choices among valuable options. The insight that is being exploited here (which I owe to Raz's work) is that autonomy, if it is to be meaningful and valuable, requires not only capacities for choice on the part of the individual but also a span of worthwhile options in his or her cultural environment. In the absence of this, autonomy wanes, and the lives of individuals become the poorer, however many choices they make. Autonomy is not worth much, if it is exercised in a Hobbesian state of nature.

The area of policy identified by this concern is primarily that of environmental policy, both in respect of the natural and the humanly constructed environment. In both cases, a rich environment which is conducive to valuable autonomy can be promoted by market institutions, by road pricing in cities as an antidote to traffic congestion, and by an appropriate tax regime for polluters and the creation or refinement of property rights in natural spaces. It is silly, none the less, to suppose that market institutions alone can protect the integrity of the environment. No market solution exists, so far as we know, for the greenhouse effect. Further, providing or renewing a decent urban environment requires both private and public investment in infrastructure. A liberal state committed to assuring the public space in which autonomous individuals make their choices cannot be indifferent to the physical and social environment. In that regard, the model from which we have most to learn is that of Austria, Germany and Scandinavia, in which the social market economy provides the resources whereby a graceful and elegant urban environment is maintained. It is to the countries of continental Europe, again, rather than to the United States, whose history and geography may make other policies more appropriate, that we should look for a model for transport policy in which otherwise excessive reliance on the private automobile is diminished and public transport systems encouraged, where necessary by subsidy.

It is in regard to the cultural environment in which autonomous choices must be made that a liberal state has its most controversial responsibilities. A cultural environment in which family breakdown is commonplace, in which the arts and the sciences are neglected and in which the level of public taste is vulgar, is an impoverished one in which few options will be choice worthy. For the most part, of course, we must rely on the autonomous intermediary institutions of civil society to prevent this impoverishment, and there is much that can be done by way of tax deductibility in these areas whereby the vitality of civil society can be maintained and enhanced. This is not to say that Britain, or any other modern state, can sensibly do without an arts policy which encourages and supports cultural activities (such as opera) which could not otherwise be sustained. The libertarian objection that such subsidy is regressive in its incidence on the population is a silly one, since the goal of such support is not distributional. Its justification is what is termed in recent philosophy 'perfectionist':[83] it aims to support forms of activity that are intrinsically valuable, whosoever consumes or enjoys them. Nor is the argument that public support for the arts depends on an arbitrary judgement about the value of the activity one which has any force. It has force, if at all, only if we adopt a blank value-scepticism in which we view judgements of the value of pigeon-fancying or pornography against the plays of Shakespeare or the novels of Dostoevsky, say, as entirely subjective, reflecting or expressing only the personal preference of the judge. Such a perspective, containing only preferences, may seem a natural one for economists, but it is not one which a sensible policy-maker has any good reason to accept.

Given the argument that a society without a flourishing artistic life and a higher culture in which art objects have a status other than commodities is an impoverished society, in practical policy terms the implication may be, in the area of the deregulation of television, for example, the proposal for an Arts Council of the Air, as advanced by distinguished classical liberals such as Brittan and Peacock.[84] An analogous argument can be made for science policy, whose aim should be to encourage and support pure research, and to prevent science being reduced to an entirely utilitarian activity conducted in a context of chronic resource-scarcity. In both areas, the underlying argument is that the activity, art or science, is itself an intrinsic good, whose value is not reducible to the satisfaction of personal preferences. Moreover, it is an intrinsic good which opens up for the autonomous chooser options in the common culture without which, like it, he or she would be the poorer, and which thereby enhance his or her autonomy. In respect of the cultural environment, there is a strong case to be made that institutions such as the BBC should not be undermined in a circumstance in which alternative institutions, at least as efficacious in maintaining cultural standards, have yet to prove themselves.

Autonomous choosers cannot flourish in an environment of anomic individuals, lacking in the capacities necessary for responsibility and for intrinsically valuable relationships such as those of romantic love and friendship. An autonomous chooser surrounded by wantons[85] – by persons without ethical standards, long-term projects or deep attachments – will lead an empty life, however resourceful he or she may otherwise be. A liberal state therefore has the vital responsibility of tending and sheltering the social matrix of responsible choosers, the family. It cannot shirk the formulation of a family policy. In this, though it ought to eschew the spurious liberal ideal of neutrality with regard to all forms of family life, it is bound to respect the legitimate variety of forms of family life in society today. In other words, though policy should aim to discourage forms of family life, such as that of single-parenthood, where it is demonstrably injurious to children, it cannot engage in projects of social engineering aiming to revive a vanished form of traditional family life. Appropriate policies in this area might include tax deductibility or subsidies for child care at work, an increase of child benefits for the under-fives and compelling absent parents to provide for their offspring at the levels determined by the courts.[86] Whatever the detailed mix of measures, a liberal government cannot responsibly avoid developing a policy on the family.

This is only one instance of a more general point, that a liberal regime concerned to promote the autonomy of its subjects cannot avoid concerning itself with the social forms in which autonomy is exercised. The worth, perhaps the very existence, of autonomous choices depends on the existence of these social forms. As Raz has again put it:

> individuals inevitably derive the goals by which they constitute their lives from the stock of social forms available to them, and the feasible variations on it.... By being teachers, production workers, drivers, public servants, loyal friends and family people, loyal to their communities, nature-lovers and so on they will

be pursuing their own goals, enhancing their own well-being, and also serving their communities, and generally living in a morally worthy way.[87]

In general, valuable autonomy presupposes a stock of roles, statuses, institutions and social forms, a structure of intermediary institutions embodied in a common culture, from which individuals derive worthwhile options. A liberal government has a positive responsibility to tend and nurture these intermediary institutions, and ought never to make policy on the model of the atomistic individual related to others only by a variety of contractual agreements.

What are the responsibilities of government in respect of the market economy itself? By far the most important is that of the provision of a stable currency, an objective on which all recent British governments have defaulted. It is naïve in the extreme to suppose that this can be achieved while monetary policy remains politicised. A market solution, such as the Hayekian[88] proposal for competing currencies, may well be defensible but is not at present in the realm of the politically possible and might not provide an antidote to inflation until that had reached unacceptable levels. In all likelihood, the institutional framework best suited to monetary stability may not be that of the market, still less that of the political sphere in which democratic governments will inevitably debase the currency in the attempt to bring into an advantageous alignment the electoral and the economic cycles. The most promising framework may be that of a regime of rules, whether as embodied in an independent central bank (as in New Zealand) or in a regime of fixed exchange rates, as advocated by the earlier Hayek. The paramount dangers to stable money in our times are those of democratic political competition and of monetary nationalism. For this reason the custody of a sound currency is, in contemporary circumstances, not something that can safely be left to national governments or to the devices of markets that governments will unavoidably attempt to manipulate. Instead, the provision of a sound currency can only be solved by a regime of rules that constrains or prevents monetary debasement by government. In the British case, ERM membership, with all of its costs and imperfections, at least proved a significant constraint on currency debasement by government. However, ERM membership, because of its distortive effects on the British economy and the difficulty – perhaps, for epistemic reasons, the impossibility – of determining the 'right' rate of the pound within it, was a poor substitute for sound domestic monetary policy. In the British case, the best prospects for stable money may lie in the establishment of a truly independent bank, modelled on the New Zealand example, in which its policies are guided by rules, rather than on the American model of the Federal Reserve Bank, whose discretionary authority allows it to pursue (as at present) devaluationist and perhaps inflationary policies. If in Britain there were a central bank that was genuinely independent of government in its policies, ERM membership would have been at best unnecessary or, more likely, undesirable.

Aside from depoliticising monetary policy, one of the most important tasks of a liberal state is a negative one – that of refraining from developing an industrial strategy. Such a policy of picking winners, and supporting them by tariff or subsidy, is one of the inheritances of corporatism in Britain and has a dismal record of failure. In this connection, there is much to learn from Germany and Japan, in which (contrary to popular opinion) the effect of government superintendence of the economy has been to promote intense internal competition. The epistemic argument against socialism, though it is certainly not a conclusive argument against all forms of government intervention in the economy, is certainly a powerful one against an industrial policy that aims to guide the economy as a whole. In this respect, nothing could be more pernicious than the idiom of UK plc, with its insidious echoes of a bankrupt corporatism.

This is not to endorse *laissez-faire* (itself probably a historical illusion), nor to say that there should be a 'hands-off' policy of government in all areas of the economy. A regional policy of tax reductions, enterprise zones and so forth is plainly arguable. A labour policy, preferably on Swedish lines, has already been mentioned as an element in the enabling welfare state which aims to return to autonomy and productivity those who have fallen out of (or never been in) the market economy. Without returning to the corporatist illusion of incomes policies, it is not clear that a wage policy cannot be formulated by government which assists wage bargaining in the market environment. And it is hard to see how any modern state can eschew the formulation of an energy policy, itself an integral part of policy toward the environment.

It has not been the aim here to discuss exhaustively all of those governmental activities which seek to supplement market provision of goods and services. I have not discussed tax policy, save in passing, nor have I said much about education policy or social policy, since, crucially important as they are, they are beyond my brief here. The philosophical thesis of this chapter is that completeness or determinacy in regard to a specification of the proper spheres of government, market and voluntary association is in any case an impossibility, a figment spawned by the hubris of theory. The aim here has been the humbler one of arguing that this ineradicable indeterminacy need not inhibit reasoned circumstantial discourse and debate about the roles of market, voluntary association and government in a modern state such as Britain. The functions that I have ascribed to government, and the range of policies that I have argued come under its responsibility, are far larger than anything acceptable to a libertarian or a classical liberal perspective, yet considerably smaller than those required by a socialist or an egalitarian social-democratic perspective. It has been one of the postulates of my argument that no modern state will in fact retreat to the sphere of minimum government, any more than any modern state will succeed in generating an egalitarian community. Brute historical facts, such as mass democracy and cultural pluralism, together with the imperatives of the market economy itself, render these visions utopian fantasies (or, as I would view them myself, dystopian nightmares). But I have also tried to exhibit the ethical and philosophical reasons why these ideals have no claim on morality or on our reason.

On the positive side, my argument has been that market competition is not a natural feature of human behaviour but an institutional artefact, a process occurring within or generated by a definite (though variable across time and space) matrix of laws and policies. It was, in fact, one of the central insights of the German social market model which animates much of my argument that the free market requires more than non-intervention by government to preserve competition; it requires a competition policy, as recognised in the Dusseldorf Principles enunciated by the Christian Democrats in 1949, which stipulated 'competition guaranteed by control of monopoly'. The recognition that governmental intervention may be a necessary precondition of market competition is one of the essential features of the social market economy model.

What, in outline, are the other constitutive features of the social market economy? It may be worth pausing here, if only briefly, to rebut the standard objections, made by classical or fundamentalist liberals, to the very expression. Often, it is maintained that the expression is tautologous, since markets are themselves social institutions, presupposing and generating a host of social relationships, not all of which are economic in the narrow sense. Alternatively, though incompatibly, it is often held that the expression is oxymoronic, in that markets exist not to serve any social or collective end but simply to satisfy the disparate purposes of individuals. Or, lastly, it is commonly alleged that the expression has no clear meaning at all.

These common objections are mentioned, not because they have any force, but in order to explain the central tenets of the social market economy, as it is theorised in the Freiburg School and as it might be realised in the specific context of contemporary Britain. One of the key ideas has already been stated in the argument thus far: that the market is not a natural social phenomenon, but instead a creature of law and government. A second idea is that the market is not free-standing or self-justifying but part of a larger nexus of institutions, sharing with them a justification in terms of the contribution it makes to human well-being. A third idea is that the market lacks ethical and political legitimacy unless it is supplemented or complemented by other institutions that temper its excesses and correct its failures. Market institutions will lack legitimacy if market exchanges occur in filthy or unsafe environments, if there is not a rich infrastructure of public amenities that undergirds them, or if there exists an underclass that is denied access to them. The theory of the social market economy, at its core, is that market institutions are always embedded in other social and political institutions, which both shape them and legitimate them. The central ideas of the *Soziale Markwirtschaft* have been characterised by Hutchinson as Smithian in mode:

> This 'Smithian' mode, starting from a realistic view of man and his psychology, and recognizing the all-pervasiveness of ignorance in human affairs, gives as important a place in its objectives to freedom and the rule of law as it does to the attainment of some ideal, optimal economic efficiency. The ideals behind the launching of the Social-Market Economy, coming down, as they did, in part from the Historical School, followed this 'Smithian' mode. For example, Walter Eucken laid great emphasis on the 'interdependence between the economic order and all other forms of order (i.e. legal, social and political)'.... Eucken condemned the policy of *laissez-faire* as incompatible with the maintenance of a

legal order based on the idea of a *Rechtstaat*, because such a policy conceded too much power to monopolies and partial monopolies.[89]

It had been Eucken, of course, who, in his seminal 1948 article, 'On the Theory of the Centrally Administered Economy: an Analysis of the German Experiment', had shown not only the inevitable inefficiency but also the incompatibility with individual freedom and the rule of law of central planning in the German case. It was these ideas which animated the bold experiment in deregulation, inaugurated by Erhard against the wishes of the Allied Occupying Powers, which began the German economic miracle. It is these ideas of *Ordoliberalismus* and the Freiburg School that most merit study in Britain at present. They do so, in the first place, because the German case is the only one, so far, in which the role of government in the economy and in society has been radically, and seemingly irreversibly, reduced. As Hutchinson observes:

> so persistent, and seemingly ineluctable, has been the extension of the role of government in so many economically advanced, democratic countries, that it is difficult to cite any case from such countries where a significant rolling back of the interventionist tide has been achieved, *except after major wars*. Even there, the role of government in the economy has usually only been reduced as compared with the all-pervasive central regulation of wartime, and not nearly pushed back to the previous peacetime level.
>
> To these generalisations the Social Market Economy of the German Federal Republic has provided the outstanding exception among leading Western democratic countries.[90]

Published in 1981, Hutchinson's statement needs no revision a decade later, when the delusive revolutions of Thatcher and Reagan have left government larger than ever before in peacetime in their respective countries. There is a second reason why these ideas, which have been carried on by such thinkers as Gottfried Lutz and have influenced others such as Alfred Müller-Armack, should be studied in Britain. This is that the social-market theorists of a free economic order, or *Ordnung*, recognised (as the neo-liberal architects of the failed Thatcher and Reagan revolutions evidently did not) that free-market institutions, if they were to be enduring and legitimate, had to be embedded in broader, social and political institutions, which shaped and constrained them. As Hutchinson puts it:

> The other (Smithian or social-market) kind of case for the competitive market economy is (by contrast with the neoclassical, Ricardian case) formulated in much broader terms, comprehending the political and social order, and especially the legal foundations and framework of the economic order.[91]

And Hutchinson remarked of Eucken that 'the launching of the Social-Market Economy was and had to be an explicitly "constructivist" act'. As Eucken put it: 'The economic system has to be consciously shaped.'[92] Market institutions, therefore, although they always comprehend an inheritance of evolved conventions and practices, are always open to reform or redesign, and such modifications are and should be part of a deliberate policy which recognises and takes into account the embeddedness of market institutions in other, legal, social and political institutions.

Such institutions will have no unique structure, but will vary in their shape and content from time to time and place to place. It is not here being proposed that the German model, in its theory or its practice, should (or could) be simply transplanted to Britain. The proposal is that market institutions in Britain, and perhaps other similar modern states, require for their legitimacy a variety of governmental policies and institutions, including the institution of an enabling welfare state. This is to say that the structure, content and legitimacy of market institutions is guaranteed by the legal and social intervention of an active government. (It is not claimed that an enabling welfare state, as such, was ever a part of the German social market economy; only that, in Britain today, it best complements market institutions, and so captures well the spirit of the social market economy.)[93] Freeing up the market and reducing the invasive state require accordingly a positive, not merely a negative, agenda of governmental policy. This is affirmed against the background of a prior affirmation that government should enter only where private provision and voluntary association are demonstrably inadequate. In other words, as has already been noted, the principle of subsidiarity, that government ought not to usurp functions which can be well discharged by intermediary institutions, ought to be observed throughout policy.

It may nevertheless be reasonably asked how large will be the kind of state mandated by my theorising. In part, the answer is that the legitimate concern ought to be with what the state properly does, not with its overall magnitude. After all, a state could have only a few functions, most of them undesirable, and yet pre-empt most of society's resources in order to discharge them. Again, there will presumably be few who would opt for a state that pre-empted a quarter of society's resources but wasted most of them, over a state that controlled slightly more but spent them judiciously in the service of agreed and desirable objectives. It cannot, therefore, sensibly be the sheer size of a state, independently of any other criterion, that determines its legitimacy.

Nor is the demand at all sensible that the state, which is justified by the theory that I have advanced, be determinate in its size. Such a demand is radically flawed at both philosophical and empirical levels. It expresses the superstition, cherished by classical or fundamentalist liberals, that there is a talismanic formula, an infallible theory or an unfailing legal or constitutional device which can determine, presumably forever, the proper scope and functions of the state. In its most primitive form, this is the theory of the minimum state, with all its incoherencies. Its inadequacies are patent. Do the minimum functions of government include the provision of a sound currency, or not? If those functions are restricted to national defence and law and order, how is their size to be determined, and how are they to be financed? If minimal government is to encompass voucher schemes or negative income tax schemes, how is their size to be decided and their costs defrayed? These are questions to which classical liberal theory gives no determinate answers, if only because there are none to be given. The indeterminacy that they fail to overcome is not a defect of any theory, including that developed in this chapter; as I have already observed, it is merely a truth about the world.

The objection that the state emerging from the theory that is defended here is indeterminate in its size or cost is similarly absurd at the level of practice. It is true that the public choice process, which is theorised in the economic theories of bureaucracy and democracy, could have the perverse effect of inflating an enabling welfare state, say, beyond the functions envisaged here. This danger is inherent in every other governmental institution and policy. It would occur in the minimum state, as will be recognised by anyone with any knowledge of the realities of military procurement in the United States (and elsewhere). It would occur on a stupendous level if the disastrous neo-liberal panacea of the negative income tax were instituted: like any other guaranteed income scheme, it would at once be bid up by the vote motive to the level of tolerance of consequent taxation, or beyond. It would manifestly be the case in respect of such other neo-liberal measures as voucher schemes: since their size and cost would undoubtedly be inflated by the pressures of political competition, they have (in that respect) no advantage whatever over other forms of governmental provision. The same is true of tax credits, for which there would in practice be an undignified political auction. Note, in passing, that public choice theory predicts expansionist tendencies in governmental services, even in the absence of the democratic vote motive, in virtue of bureaucratic rent-seeking. Partly for this reason, the knee-jerk classical liberal response to the objections here advanced, that such measures be governed by constitutional rules or analogous devices, is (perhaps incorrigibly) naïve. The example of balanced budget rules, which have everywhere been circumvented and honoured in the breach, illustrates the futility of such devices. The truth is that, aside from the constant vigilance of a citizenry steeped in a culture of liberty, there is no remedy for the expansionist tendencies inherent in all forms of government activity. This is as true for the so-called minimum state, and for the favoured measures of neo-liberalism, as it is for any other. Is this simple point in fact so subtle as to elude the understanding of latter-day classical liberals? It is, after all, only an instance of the imperfectibility of all human institutions – itself an exceedingly ancient truth.

At the same time, the concern that an invasive state will stifle the autonomy of civil society is a compelling one that must be addressed. The argument of this chapter is that reductions in government expenditure ought to be qualitative, not quantitative, across-the-board cuts. A state which sheltered a liberal civil society, in which the freedoms of the market economy were tempered by the institution of an enabling welfare state and supplemented by a variety of other institutions and measures, need not be a large state. It would likely be much smaller than most existing democratic states.

The size and invasiveness of the state can be reduced significantly, in ways compatible with the measures advocated here, principally because much current government expenditure consists in a wasteful system of cross-subsidies to the middle classes. In Britain, for example, state expenditure on the so-called under-class is probably only about one-sixth of total expenditure on welfare as a whole.

The situation is likely to be little different in the United States. It is therefore a travesty to represent the existing British or American welfare state either as a system of organised altruism for the benefit of the poor and needy, as socialists sometimes do, or a vast system of unjust transfers from the majority, as many classical liberals and conservatives sometimes do. In harsh reality, the income transfers of the welfare state, especially when taken in conjunction with the tax regime, are in substantial part transfers from the rich and the poor minorities to the middle-class majority. (In Britain, there may be good reason to retain universal provision in some areas, such as the NHS, where there are perverse transfers, but where the costs of targeting are excessive. This may not be so in other countries, such as New Zealand, where the health care delivery system which is to be reformed has long contained charges.) With the exception of a few of its programmes, the British welfare state is a middle-class racket without ethical justification or standing, and which (because of its vast transaction costs and its wastefulness) does not in the end benefit even the middle classes.

The size and cost of a welfare state which instituted a system of welfare rights could well be far less than that of the current welfare state, if (like present crypto-voucher schemes in community care) welfare benefits were targeted, if many welfare benefits conferred obligations on their recipients, and if the tax system offered better incentives for self-provision. A system of proportional taxation, in which redistributions were made transparently from the affluent majority to the needy minorities, might make clearer to all the advantages of a welfare state which was streamlined to serve the genuinely needy. It is a cardinal point of the present argument that, whereas much welfare spending in Britain is wasteful and ineffective, an enabling welfare state ought to aim for a far more complete satisfaction of the basic needs of the unfortunate than is presently achieved.

In the British case, if there is any substance in neo-liberal, supply-side arguments about tax revenue rising as marginal rates are lowered, better provision could possibly be made for the beneficiaries of an enabling welfare state at the lower income tax rate of, say, 20 per cent, levied proportionally.

It is hard, but perhaps not altogether impossible, to see how these harsh realities could be reformed, given the facts of political competition in mass democracy. They could be so reformed, only if the middle classes were persuaded that a smaller state, in which under a lower tax regime they were free to provide most services privately for themselves, was more in their interests than the current ruleless and wasteful *mélange* of arrangements. That is a demanding political task for any party. Excessive cynicism about democratic political life in Britain should not be allowed to convince people of the impossibility of such a reform. There is a real danger that the Public Choice model of the economics of politics (which has illuminated much, especially in the work of James Buchanan, that is vitally important for the understanding of the processes of political competition) could blind people to the shared norms which pervade political life – in Britain at any rate – and which constrain policies founded solely on a calculation of their economic costs and benefits to voters. The fiasco of the so-called community charge or poll tax, which offended the sense of fairness even of many who were gainers from it, has a lesson to teach (for those who have the wit to learn from it) about the limitations of a purely economic analysis of political life, and the dangers of policies based on such a model. More positively, the manifest limitations of the Public Choice model, in its application to British political life, suggest that the moral appeal of the sort of society resulting from the reforms suggested may have a political resonance, even for those who might initially lose from such reforms, which should not be dogmatically discounted. This is the challenge that must be addressed by any serious liberal reform of current arrangements.

Unless it is confronted, there is no real prospect of reforming present arrangements so that the genuinely needy, who are at present very ill-served, receive the resources which are due to them, and which should be a matter of entitlement for them. Nor is the reintegration of the underclass in society likely to occur. Instead, there will remain a wasteful and invasive Leviathan, whose resources are squandered on middle-class subsidies generated by collusive interest groups and by the operation of the vote motive, and which leaves those truly vulnerable to their own devices.[94] An ambitious goal, but one achievable over the long term by administrations which were committed to limited government with a positive responsibility for the satisfaction of basic needs and the conservation of the common culture, would be the reduction of state expenditure to around a quarter of national product, as advocated by Hayek.[95] Such a goal, though it would amount to a transformation of government little short of revolutionary, will not satisfy fundamentalist advocates of *laissez-faire*. However, it is probably a goal that no British government will for the foreseeable future even approach, given the inheritance of earlier interventionist policies (including an increase of the portion of national product appropriated by government to around 38 per cent) and the political memory of ill-conceived measures which reduced government expenditure without due regard to their human costs and the impact of such cuts on established expectations. Since, over more than a decade, a policy aimed at reducing the role of government in society has resulted in an increase of state expenditure as a proportion of national product, and state activity is in absolute terms probably higher than ever before, the argument here is that a genuine and lasting reduction in the size, cost and invasiveness of the state is to be achieved only by a revision and revaluation of the agenda of government in which its positive responsibilities are clearly and explicitly specified.

CONCLUSION

The argument of this chapter is that, once market socialism has been struck off the policy agenda, the spectrum of reasoned debate that remains extends, at least in Britain and in other similar modern states, from unconstrained libertarian capitalism at one end to egalitarian social democracy at the other. Yet more radically, I have argued that neither extreme of that spectrum can be given a compelling ethical or philosophical rationale. Both libertarianism and egalitarianism lack credibility as fundamental political moralities, and for that reason should also be removed from the intellectual and political agenda. The real space for reasoned debate is much narrower than the spectrum so conceived, even though both ends of it accept the necessity in a modern economy of free market institutions and of the institution of private property in the means of production on which effective market pricing depends. The real space for public discourse is not between the two extremes, but in the area of detailed debate about the scope and content of public goods, the depth and limits of the common culture, the relative costs of government failure and market failure, and the content and levels of provision of basic needs. This is the agenda of policy that should inform public discourse henceforth, and upon which political consensus in Britain and similar countries should in future be established.

A liberal civil society cannot hope to be stable if political life is polarised between ideological extremes. If the argument of this chapter is sound, the ideologies of libertarian capitalism and egalitarian social democracy lack any persuasive defence in ethical or philosophical terms. Abandoning these doctrinaire positions does not mean adopting a middle ground of muddled pragmatism: it means occupying the only real space for disciplined reasoning. For conservatives in Britain, such a move entails abandoning the simplistic formulae and utopian panaceas of the libertarian New Right and recognising the dependency of the market economy on a common culture which contains institutions that protect those whom the unconstrained market would neglect. Such a recognition need not prove difficult for conservatives who have not forgotten the communitarian concerns of traditional Toryism and who know something of the achievements and policies of Christian Democratic governments in Europe. For British social democrats, the move toward a new consensus means shedding the disabling illusions of egalitarianism in order to consider the detailed failings of the market and of the current welfare state. The example given by the European social-democratic parties, especially in Germany and Austria, should make this move more easily negotiable. It would be a hopeful augury for liberal civil society in Britain if, by the abandonment of fundamentalist positions in the major parties, a new consensus were to emerge that facilitated civilised public, political discourse about the agenda and limits of governmental intervention in society and the economy. It is such a space of convergence or consensus, with all of its variations and disagreements, that I have tried to stake out under the general category of the social market economy, and whose content I have sketched through the particular example of the enabling welfare state.

In its critical application to neo-liberal thought and policy, the argument has been that an individualist order is not free-standing, but depends on forms of common life for its worth and its very existence. Equally, autonomy is valueless if it is exercised in a community that is denuded of the inherently public goods which create worthwhile options and which thereby make good choices possible. One of the basic needs of human beings is membership in a community. Such membership will be stable if, and only if, the community is seen to be meeting basic human needs through the institutions of the market, and, where these fail, through other institutions, such as the enabling welfare state.

The morality of the market is one that prizes and rewards integrity and responsibility. It is one that has as its ultimate ethical justification the role of the vital interest in autonomy in individual human well-being. The morality of the market is the only morality consistent with the reproduction of a liberal civilisation. Defenders of this morality must acknowledge that a principled commitment to its values carries with it, logically, morally and politically, a commitment to measures that protect the well-being and autonomy of the vulnerable and the defenceless. A market economy without this commitment lacks both ethical and political legitimacy. It is the argument of this chapter that a humane social market economy is the only sort of free economy likely to survive in the years to come, and the only sort that deserves to survive.

4   An agenda for Green conservatism

INTRODUCTION

> Man's conquest of nature, if the dreams of some scientific planners are realized, means the rule of a few hundreds of men over billions upon billions of men. There neither is nor can be any simple increase of power on man's side. Each power won *by* man is a power *over* man as well. Each advance leaves him weaker as well as stronger. In every victory, besides being the general who triumphs, he is also the prisoner who follows in the triumphal car.
>
> (C.S. Lewis)[1]

It is fair to say that, on the whole, conservative thought has been hostile to environmental concerns over the past decade or so in Britain, Europe and the United States. Especially in America, environmental concerns have been represented as anti-capitalist propaganda under another flag. In most Western countries, conservatives have accused environmentalists of misuse of science, of propagating an apocalyptic mentality, and of being enemies of the central institutions of modern civil society. Nor are these accusations always wide of the mark. Indeed, in considerable measure they show conservatives endorsing the self-image of the Greens as inheritors of the radical protest movements of earlier times, and as making common cause with contemporary radical movements, such as feminism and anti-colonialism. In other words, both the Greens themselves and their conservative critics have been happy to share the assumption that socialism and environmental concern go together.

The aim of this present argument is to contest that consensus. Far from having a natural home on the Left, concern for the integrity of the common environment, human as well as ecological, is most in harmony with the outlook of traditional conservatism of the British and European varieties. Many of the central conceptions of traditional conservatism have a natural congruence with Green concerns: the Burkean idea of the social contract, not as an agreement among anonymous, ephemeral individuals, but as a compact between the generations of the living, the dead and those yet unborn; Tory scepticism about progress, and awareness of its ironies and illusions; conservative resistance to untried novelty and large-scale social experiments; and, perhaps most especially, the traditional conservative tenet that individual flourishing can occur only in the context of forms of common life.

All of these and other conservative ideas have clear affinities with Green thought, when it is not merely another scourge of the inherited institutions of civil society. The inherent tendency of Green thought is thus not radical but the opposite: it is conservative. At the same time, the absorption of Green concerns into conservative thinking will necessitate some radical changes within conservative philosophy and policy; particularly within those strands of conservative thought that have, during the past decade or so, come to be animated by neo-liberal doctrines whose origins are, in fact, not conservative at all, but rather in the classical liberal rationalist and libertarian ideologies which were spawned in the wake of the Enlightenment.

In one of its thrusts, the argument advanced here is a further critique, building on earlier criticisms I have developed elsewhere,[2] of the neo-liberal doctrines of the New Right, within the particular context of environmental policy. This New Right ideology is, in effect, the most recent eruption of secular liberal utopianism, a species of rationalism in politics[3] which affirms that the dilemmas of political life can be resolved, once and for all, by the application of a system of first principles for the regulation of governmental activity. This rationalist dogma is here rejected, as novel problems arise for government from people's unanticipated interactions with the natural environment. But the conception of human nature, and of human well-being, that underlies this species of liberal rationalism is also rejected. On the view developed here, though human beings need a sphere of independent action, and so of liberty, if they are to flourish, their deepest need is a home, a network of common practices and inherited traditions that confers on them the blessing of a settled identity. Indeed, without the undergirding support of a framework of common culture, the freedom of the individual so cherished by liberalism is of little value, and will not long survive. Human beings are above all fragile creatures, for whom the meaning of life is a local matter that is easily dissipated: their freedom is worthwhile and meaningful to them only against a background of common cultural forms. Such forms cannot be created anew for each generation. We are not like the butterfly, whose generations are unknown to each other; we are a familial and historical species, for whom the past must have authority (that of memory) if we are to have identity, and whose lives are in part self-created narratives, woven from the received text of the common life. Where change is incessant or pluralism too insistent, where the links between the generations are broken or the shared raiment of the common culture is in tatters, human beings will not flourish. They will wither, or else fall into anomic violence. In so far as neo-liberalism has been an ideology of radical change, whose debts are to liberal individualism rather than to traditional conservatism, it has tended to reinforce the disintegrative processes of modernist societies. This chapter may be understood as an attempt to restore a balance within conservative philosophy which has in recent years shown signs of being lost.

It is also an attempt to correct some of the radical excesses of Green theory. On the whole, Green theory is inspired by an anti-capitalist mentality that neglects the environmental benefits of market institutions and suppresses the ecological costs of central planning. In the real world, environmental degradation has been at its most catastrophic where, as under the institutions of the former Soviet system, planners are unconstrained in their activities by clearly defined property rights or by the scarcities embodied in a properly functioning price mechanism. (The situation appears to be little different, or worse, in the People's Republic of China.) For reasons that are perfectly general, and which will be explored in greater detail later in the argument, environmental despoliation on a vast scale is an inexorable result of industrial development in the absence of the core institutions of a market economy, private property and the price mechanism. This is a vital truth as yet little understood by Green theorists, even though it is all too plain in the post-communist countries.

Green theorists also harbour an animus, very often, to the distinctive technological and social forms of modern life, which is quixotic and counter-productive. It is eminently sensible for Green theorists to seek for forms of technology and of productive association whicht are less environmentally invasive, and so more sustainable over the long term, than many of those that characterise the highly industrialised societies of our age; but it is absurd to suppose that we can return to the technologies or the productive associations of pre-industrial societies, and it is unreasonable to stigmatise some of the least invasive modern technologies, such as nuclear power, as especially environmentally hazardous. It is reasonable to be concerned about the growth of vast mega-cities, such as Shanghai and Mexico City, in which vast aggregations of human beings are concentrated, without the amenities or the public spaces that distinguished the historic European cities. This is not a reason for hostility to cities – one of humankind's most civilised institutional inventions – or for rural nostalgia, but rather a ground for a project of restoration of the city in something akin to its classical historic forms. There is much that is amiss in modernity, and much to reject in modernism; but we can hope only to temper the modern age and its ills, not to abolish them, as some of the Green theorists suppose.

As against the neo-liberal strand within recent conservatism, on the other hand, my argument is that market institutions, although they are indispensably necessary, are insufficient as guarantors of the integrity of the environment, human as well as natural. They must be supplemented by governmental activity when, as with the restoration or preservation of the historic European city, private investment cannot by itself sustain the public environment of the common life. The environmental case against doctrinal neo-liberalism is yet stronger than this. The unfettered workings of market institutions may damage the natural and human environments, even if it is true (as I argue later) that in most cases they act to protect them. Though there is in many Western countries a good case for freer selective immigration, a policy of *laissez-faire* in immigration, by undoing settled communities, mixing inassimilable cultures and thereby triggering dormant racisms, would serve only to undermine the political stability on which successful market institutions depend for their existence; yet such a policy continues to be advocated by fundamentalist liberals who cannot, or will not, perceive that labour is a factor of production which is categorically distinct from others, inasmuch as it is wholly constituted by human beings, whose relations with each other are not at all like those of different sorts of assets in a global portfolio. Equally, despite the economic rationality of global free trade, the real evils of trade war, and the fact that multilateral free trade pacts remain often beneficial, global free trade as envisaged, say, in recent GATT discussions, can often have disastrous effects on local and regional communities, wiping out entire ways of life while supplying no sustainable alternatives. Mechanical application of the simplistic panaceas of neo-liberalism spells ruin for communities in many parts of the world and, parenthetically, it is a recipe for disaster throughout the post-communist world.

Neo-liberal ideas have been attractive to conservatives in many Western countries, and in parts of the post-communist world, partly in virtue of the real excesses of twentieth century statism, to which they provide a healthy corrective. They are nevertheless a distraction from the central concerns of traditional conservatism, and they inhibit conservatives in addressing the problems that arise for them in an age in which economic growth on conventional lines has begun to come up against genuine environmental constraints. Conservative policy in the post-war world has been governed by the strategy of securing legitimacy for market institutions by so aligning the electoral and the economic cycles as to yield uninterrupted economic growth. This is a strategy which, in neglecting the deeper sources of allegiance, is risky when the economy turns sour. It offers nothing in an age – not so far off, and perhaps imminent in some Western countries – when economic growth on the old model is not sustainable, and has in any case come to a shuddering halt.

The prospect of open-ended growth in the quantity of goods, services and people is in any case hardly a conservative vision. Though the eradication of involuntary poverty remains a noble cause, the project of promoting maximal economic growth is, perhaps, the most vulgar ideal ever put before suffering humankind. The myth of open-ended progress is not an ennobling myth, and it should form no part of conservative philosophy. The task of conservative policy is not to spread the malady of infinite aspiration, to which our species is in any case all too prone, but to keep in good repair those institutions and practices whereby human beings come to be reconciled with their circumstances, and so can live and die in dignified and meaningful fashion, despite the imperfections of their condition. Chief among all of the objects of conservative policy, for this reason, is the replenishment of the common life; the shared environment in which, as members of communities and practitioners of a common culture, people can find enjoyment and consolation.

As against the values and policies of neo-liberalism, which tend to deplete further and even to destroy the resources of this common life, a Green conservatism animated by the concerns of traditional Toryism would seek, wherever this is feasible, to repair and renew the common life. It would acknowledge the vital role of the core institutions of civil society, private property and contractual liberty under the rule of law, in any civilised modern state, and, more particularly, in any polity which seeks to protect the common environment, human and natural. It would recognise that unlimited government has been the greatest destroyer of the common environment in our age, and would accordingly support measures for the limitation of government, often by the devolution or hiving-off of its activities. It would affirm that governmental monopoly, or near-monopoly, in a variety of vital services – perhaps even in the supply of money – has proved an evil against which the extension of market institutions may be the best remedy. It would nevertheless resist making a fetish of market institutions: it would be ready to extend them where their absence is a cause of environmental degradation (as when environmental depletion occurs through the occurrence of tragedies of the commons); but it would also be ready to curb them, when their workings are demonstrably harmful to the common life, and when the costs of such curbs are not prohibitive. It would recognise that the introduction into such services as education and health care of market institutions might often be an appropriate measure, helping to correct their tendencies to bureaucratisation, and to make them more responsive to the needs of individuals.

At the same time, it would not follow the neo-liberals in supposing that marketisation is the sovereign remedy for the failures of modern education and health care, which derive, in large part at least, from their ever more pronounced character as industries, conceived as adjuncts to governmental economic policies, rather than as forms of practice each having its own *telos*. The most profound failings of modern education and of health care require remedies more radical than any that neo-liberals have proposed, and they demand the adoption toward current educational and medical practice of an attitude that is far removed from uncritical reverence or unreflective conservatism. There is nothing at all unreasonable about a contemporary conservative adopting such radical attitudes to contemporary institutions, since these are in substantial part the results of very recent, and often very ill-considered, innovations. In respect of education and health, in particular, my argument will be that the conservative goal of restoring to them a distinctive *telos* and a traditional ethos will demand rather radical reforms in current practice, going well beyond the extension into them of market processes which, though it may enhance individual choice and the quality of service, does not by itself make of contemporary educational and medical institutions guardians of conservative values. Achieving this latter goal may require the radical remedies of disestablishing the school and curtailing the professional monopoly of doctors; just as conserving and restoring the historic European city may demand drastic controls on the private passenger car, or recovering personal responsibility for health may demand conferring on patients the responsibility of choosing when it is best that life be ended. These are only a few instances of an ancient paradox, with which the modern world abounds in examples, that conservatives cannot help becoming radicals, when current practice embodies the hubristic and careless projects of recent generations, or has been distorted by technological innovations whose consequences for human well-being we have not weighed. This is a paradox that a Green conservatism will often confront. It will confront it at a most fundamental level, inasmuch as Green thought – especially that variety of Green thought that is associated with the theory of deep ecology and with the Gaia hypothesis – embodies a challenge to the ruling world-view of the age, which is a sort of scientific fundamentalism allied with liberal humanism. This is a world-view which is thoroughly alien to conservative philosophy in virtue of the nihilism that it breeds in relations with nature and with fellow humans but which conservatives are nevertheless hesitant to resist, since it is associated with the prestige of science as the animating force of modernity. This scientistic world-view must be brought into question among conservatives, as it has already been among Greens, and it is part of the agenda of Green conservatism that it be so questioned. Green conservatism will, first and last, repudiate the hubristic rationalist ideology that suffuses neo-liberal thought and policy, which has captured and subjugated recent conservatism, but which is merely the most recent excrescence of modernist humanism – a creed that both genuine conservatives and Greens have every reason to reject.

THEORY

Ecological functions of market institutions

the rational herdsman concludes that the only sensible course for him to pursue is to add another animal to his herd. And another; and another.... But this is the conclusion reached by each and every rational herdsman sharing a commons. Therein is the tragedy. Each man is locked into a system that compels him to increase his herd without limit – in a world that is limited. Ruin is the destination toward which all men rush, each pursuing his own best interest in a society that believes in the freedom of the commons. Freedom in the commons brings ruin to all.

(Garret Hardin)[4]

The central ecological function of market institutions is in the avoidance of the tragedy of the commons.[5] This occurs when, in the absence of private or several property rights in a valuable natural resource, separate economic actors – individuals, families, corporations or even sovereign states – are constrained to deplete the resource by over-use, given their realisation that, if they do not do so, others will. Tragedies of the commons occur because, in the absence of the institutions of private property, no one has an incentive to adopt a long-term view of the utilisation of resources. Tragedies of the commons also have features akin to those of Prisoner's Dilemmas,[6] in that each has an overriding incentive to do what is not in his or her own interest – in this case, to run down the resource to extinction. Examples of such tragedies are manifold in environmental literature, unfortunately, but two may suffice to illuminate the central point about them. If a forest, say, belongs to no one, then no one will have an interest in planting the next generation of trees, or, for that matter, in developing logging techniques that leave saplings standing. Since no one stands to benefit from such foresight, no one will exercise it. Hence the reckless deforestation, for agricultural and other purposes, including timber harvesting, that has occurred in parts of Latin America and South-East Asia. Or consider natural resources in fish. In so far as shoals of fish are in the commons – unowned assets in a state of nature – they will be harvested to extinction, since the only operative incentives on fisherfolk will be to catch the fish and reap a fast profit on them, before their competitors do. True, where fisherfolk live in isolated communities without competitors for their resources, they may develop traditions which limit the overexploitation of fish; but these will always go by the board when competitive fishing communities, or enterprises, come on to the scene. The moral of this example is a perfectly general one. Competition for natural resources, living or otherwise, in the absence of private property rights in them, spells inexorable ruin for such resources. The commons will always be doomed, and its resources fated to disappear, when there is a diversity of competing demands upon them. The lesson – rightly drawn by free market economists – is that the extension of private property institutions to cover resources, such as shoals of fish, hitherto in the commons, is a potent corrective to the over-exploitation of the natural environment.

Market institutions have another crucial ecological virtue: that of reflecting through the price mechanism shifting patterns of resource-scarcities. In the broadest terms, market pricing overcomes, at least partially, the otherwise insuperable epistemic dilemma facing all economic agents: that of utilising information which is dispersed throughout society and which, in virtue of its often fleeting and circumstantial nature, and the fact that it is sometimes embodied in dispositions and traditions whose content is not fully articulable, cannot be collected or gathered together by any planning agency.[7] By allowing this, often tacit and embodied, knowledge to be expressed in price information available to all, market institutions mitigate the ignorance in which we must all act in our capacity as economic agents. They in this way allow for a measure of rationality in the allocation of resources, and of efficiency in their uses, that is unavoidably denied to central planners and their agents. The point may be put differently. Critics of central planning often focus on the perverse incentives that socialist institutions create for planners, bureaucrats, managers and workers. They point to the political factors that skew the allocation of capital into unproductive enterprises, the reinforcement of risk-aversion (and consequent low levels of technological innovation) that planning institutions yield via their inability to attach costs to unexploited opportunities, the disastrous state of labour morale in the absence of rewards for real productivity, and so on. All of these observations are pertinent, but they miss the mark in failing to note that resource-allocation would be immensely wasteful and chaotic under socialist institutions even if they did not have this perverse impact on incentives, simply in virtue of the fact that planners, managers and workers would still lack the information regarding resource-scarcities that only market pricing can make available to them. Even perfect servants of the plan could not help but generate economic chaos. In so doing, they would also, no less inexorably, produce environmental catastrophe.

Socialist planning and environmental destruction: the case of the USSR

The Soviet record after over seventy years of central planning is instructive for anyone who supposes that socialist institutions have any advantage over market institutions in ecological terms. Let us consider a few figures. According to Andrei Yablokov, the Russian government's adviser on the environment, life expectancy in Russia has, because of pollution, declined from 70.4 years in 1964 to 69.3 in

1990. In some especially badly polluted cities, it has fallen to 44 years.[8] Yablokov asserts that about 20% of the population of the former Soviet Union lives in ecological disaster areas, while 30–40% live in areas of 'ecological stress'.[9] An official report in 1988 admitted that in 103 industrial cities, with a total population of about 40 million, air pollution levels are more than 10 times the official limit; in 16 cities they are 50 times the limit.[10] The mortality rate of native peoples in the former Soviet Union is even lower than that of the average citizen. According to Stefan Hedlund,[11] the death rate among these peoples is two to three times higher than among Russians, and one group of native people – the Evenks – have a life expectancy of only 32 years. The human cost of environmental degradation in the former Soviet Union cannot be measured by such figures: it is incalculable. It is one of the blackest ironies of our age that, until very recently, the anti-capitalist mentality of Western Greens induced them to look to socialist institutions as solutions for the incomparably less serious environmental depredations of the Western European nations.

The destruction of nature in the former Soviet Union has consequences that go far beyond the régime that brought it to pass. It will affect the whole world for centuries to come. The dangers of the Soviet nuclear industry, though enormous, are perhaps only the best known of the threats that the Soviet ecological catastrophe pose for the environmental integrity of large parts of the planet.

> Radioactive lakes, created over the years by waste from the Soviet nuclear weapons programme, are at risk from earth tremors which may send the polluted waters into the Caspian sea ... and cause an environmental disaster comparable to, or even greater than, the Chernobyl accident.... Lakes around the Urals city of Chelyabinsk, the centre of the Soviet nuclear industry, are oozing with plutonium.[12]

Built by slave labour immediately after the Second World War, Chelyabinsk – the name of the city as well as the province in which the long-secret nuclear complex, officially called Mayak, is sited – has been the scene of three nuclear disasters, each comparable with, or worse than, the Chernobyl meltdown of April 1986.[13] Further, the first of these nuclear disasters was not, like Chernobyl, an accident, but instead a result of conscious, deliberate policy: 'From 1940, when the Mayak complex produced its first nuclear weapon, to 1956, Mayak officials poured nuclear waste directly into the nearby Techa River.'[14] The effect of 'the unrestrained nature of Soviet "economic development"' has been that 'Both morbidity and mortality rates (in Chelyabinsk) rocketed during the Eighties. Growth in diseases of the blood circulation system ... grew some 31% during the last decade, while bronchial asthma increased by 43%, congenital anomalies by 23% and gastro-intestinal tract illness by 35%.' These were figures acknowledged even in an official report commissioned by Gorbachev.[15] It is clear that it is not alarmist to describe the Chernobyl incident as one of a number that have occurred in the Soviet Union; and one of a much larger number that are still likely to occur. The situation in China is still largely unknown, but is very likely to be comparable or, if ominous reports from Tibet (where part of the Chinese nuclear arsenal is sited and tested) are at all well-founded, even worse.[16]

The nuclear hazards of Soviet institutions are the most dramatic, but not necessarily the most serious, evidences of what has recently been termed 'ecocide in the USSR'.[17] 'Normal' policies of economic development may yet take a greater toll on the global environment. As Hedlund has observed,

> In Soviet Central Asia, irrigation and overfertilisation to support a senseless cotton mono-culture has led to the virtual disappearance of the Aral Sea, once the world's fourth largest inland water.... Desertification is comparable to the Sahel, and health indicators compare to those of Bangladesh ... Giant herds of sheep, grazing in numbers 20 times greater than the land can sustain, have caused a disaster in the Kalmuck region between Stavropol ... and the Caspian ... the result has been the creation of a sand desert.... This desert is spreading by 10% annually and is forecast to reach the southern Ukraine within five years....
> Europe is threatened both by its first sand desert and by massive waves of ecological refugees.[18]

The inheritance of Soviet institutions is environmental destruction on an almost apocalyptic scale. And the environmental destruction has not ceased with the collapse of the Soviet Union. According to a recent report by the Lithuanian Department of the Environment, fifty years of Soviet military occupation have incurred environmental degradation that will cost at least 150 billion dollars to repair; indeed, Soviet troops are continuing to degrade the environment (by, for example, dumping benzene into water near the Soviet airfield in central Lithuania at levels ten times those judged safe for human consumption).[19] The collapse of the Soviet state has revealed an environmental wasteland, which the remnants of the Soviet system are further despoiling.

The causes of this catastrophe are not to be found in the wickedness of Soviet bureaucrats, in the backwardness of Soviet peoples, or in errors in the implementation of economic planning, but in the nature of the system itself. Soviet institutions explain the Soviet ecological apocalypse, because they contained no mechanisms for accountability of the planners or their servants, no institutions for the transmission of negative popular feedback on the adverse effects and hazards of the plans, and for that matter no provision for monitoring those adverse effects. The fundamental explanation for the Soviet destruction of the environment, however, is that it occurred in a Hobbesian state of nature – a lawless condition without property rights in which human life was (and indeed is) indeed 'nasty, brutish and short'. Apart from the complete absence of institutions of democratic accountability, the lack of a law of property meant (and means) that no one can in general know, even with the best will, who might have responsibility for which aspect of the environment; and, of course, every incentive of the system tends to suppress such knowledge, even where it exists.

The lesson of the Soviet example is the same as that of the broader theory of the role of market institutions in protecting the environment. The destruction of the environment proceeds most swiftly, and often most irreversibly, in a state of nature lacking in law and property rights. The institutions of a civil society, in which these lacks are remedied and a market economy built up, though long derided by Western Greens, are a vitally important necessary condition not only of human well-being but also of the conservation of the natural environment. This is a truth well understood by the Green movements of the post-communist world, but yet to be absorbed (or accepted) by Western Greens, with a few noteworthy exceptions.

Ecological limitations of market institutions

The ecological case for market institutions is undoubtedly a very strong one. If private property provides incentives for conservation of scarce resources, the price mechanism supplies a measure of the relative scarcity of different resources. Further, the price mechanism will encourage the search for alternative resources when existing resources of a certain sort grow too expensive, just as it will spur technological innovation in respect of the extraction and use of known resources. In these ways, market institutions embody the least irrational of available mechanisms for the allocation of resources, and, by comparison with socialist planning institutions, they are highly environmentally friendly.

Market institutions have, nevertheless, very serious ecological limitations. As they are described and defended by their most ideological advocates, market institutions are a sort of perpetual motion machine, an engine of unlimited growth, which only the ill-conceived interventions of government stalls. This conception is defective for several reasons. There are, in the first glance, forms of environmental market failure that it fails to capture. Consider the phenomenon of global warming. (From the point of view of my argument here, it does not matter whether this phenomenon exists, whether the evidence shows it to be a real danger, or whether there is no conclusive evidence in support of such propositions. It could be merely a hypothetical danger and still do the work I want it to do in my argument.) Global warming reveals the limits of market institutions, from an environmental perspective, in that it is a threshold phenomenon, coming about via billions of separate acts, each of which individually is innocuous or even imperceptible. Market pricing of each of these acts will not prevent the totality of them generating the phenomenon. In this, and in similar cases of a pure public bad, only prohibitive governmental intervention can prevent or alleviate the problem. The class of environmental market failures may be a larger one than the example of global warming suggests, if (as is surely plausible) there are areas where the extension of property rights is inviable or merely too costly to be reasonably envisaged. This may be true of endangered species that are migratory over vast distances and across several legal jurisdictions: only an intergovernmentally agreed and enforced ban, or a quota system similarly set up, can protect them from extinction. In other words, even where a pure public bad is not at issue, the public good of protection of endangered species will be underprovided whenever market institutions cannot sensibly be extended to create property rights in the species in question, and where market institutions are not supplemented by governmental institutions and policies.

It will often not be enough to supplement market institutions for the sake of environmental protection. Their workings will have to be constrained. Global markets, left to themselves, will often decimate local trades and modes of production and will destroy the ways of life that they support. (Conventional programmes of 'aid' to 'developing countries' often have the same effect.) Global markets in food, along with dumping from developed countries with artificial and unnecessary agricultural surpluses, have destroyed agrarian ways of life in many poor countries, promoting migration into unsustainably gigantist cities, with all of their familiar costs and hazards. Ending economic aid that is self-defeating or counter-productive, and curtailing agricultural protectionism in the developed countries, as advocated by free-marketeers, is *not* an adequate response to the dilemma of protecting otherwise sustainable agrarian communities in poor countries, even if such measures are part of the solution. Such countries may need protection (in the form of tariffs and subsidies) for their peasant farmers – whatever GATT, the IMF, or the World Bank may dictate. In this, and other contexts, market institutions must be restricted in their workings, and not merely supplemented.

We find another limitation of market institutions in their insensitivity to inherently public goods.[20] These are goods which do not necessarily satisfy the technical requirements of an economic public good, such as indivisibility and non-excludability, but which are ingredients in a worthwhile form of common life. Consider public parks in the context of a modern city – an example to which I shall return towards the end of this chapter, when I consider the implications for conservatives of a Green agenda for urban policy. There are, of course, no insuperable technical obstacles to turning urban parks into private consumption goods. Fences can be set up, electronic ID cards printed for subscribing members, private security patrols hired, litter collected by profit-making agencies, and so on. Public parks are not, in the conventional economic sense, public goods. However, they are inherently public goods in the sense that I intend, inasmuch as public parks that are safe, well-tended, pleasing to the senses and easily accessible to urban dwellers are elements in the common form of life of the historic European city. The point is generalisable. Public spaces for recreation and for lingering, whether streets, squares or parks, are necessary ingredients in the common life of cities, as conceived in the European tradition, and elsewhere. Where such public places atrophy or disappear, become too dangerous or too unsightly to be occupied, and so vanish into a state of nature, the common life of the city has been compromised or lost. This is a nemesis, long reached in many American urban settlements and not far off in some British and European cities, which market institutions can do little to prevent. It is only one example, though perhaps a peculiarly compelling one, of the indifference of market institutions to inherently public goods.

If their workings are not to compromise the integrity of the environment, human as well as natural, market institutions must be both supplemented and constrained. They need such constraint and supplementation, in any case, if they and their various environmental benefits are to survive. Market insitutions, except in their most rudimentary forms, are not natural phenomena, the spontaneous results of human action, but artefacts of law and creatures of government. They are as frail and as vulnerable to the onslaughts of war, revolution and dictatorship as any other civilised institution. This is an especially important point, in so far as market institutions may throw up problems which they cannot themselves solve, and which sometimes threaten their very stability. We do not need to look far for examples of this hazard. Left to themselves, no doubt, market institutions would throw up a cornucopia of narcotic designer drugs, even larger than that which has grown up underground and beyond the reach of law; in this, and in other areas of policy, a strategy of legal prohibition, though not without its own costs, has in many countries (though not, apparently, in the United States) contained the problem within a manageable compass. Again, unhampered market institutions may generate forms of entertainment, such as violent or horrific video films, whose general availability is manifestly harmful to the common life. Here, as elsewhere, market institutions must be curbed, or at least restrained in their workings, if a civilised and peaceful form of common life is to be preserved and transmitted across the generations.

On a larger scale, if market institutions generate demands which they cannot themselves satisfy, they will be swept away by revolution or popular dictatorship – as may happen in countries, such as some in Latin America, where the spread of market-generated prosperity has not been accompanied by a demographic transition and where overpopulation has supervened. Free-marketeers who repose their faith in market institutions forget that they are artefacts of human actions which human action can undo. In this they forget a crucial Hobbesian truth: that the integrity of market institutions, and ultimately their very survival, depend on the efficiency of coercive authority, in the absence of which market institutions collapse or else suffer capture by exploitative predators. Market institutions depend, in other words, on a Hobbesian peace for their very existence. The office of government, in this connection, is the superintendence of market institutions, with the aim of ensuring that their workings are not self-defeating or such as to endanger themselves. This is a rudimentary tenet of conservative philosophy of which many contemporary conservatives, whose vision has been occluded by the empty vistas of neo-liberal dogma, appear ignorant.

Ecological theory and conservative philosophy

change is a threat to identity, and every change is an emblem of extinction. But a man's identity (or that of a community) is nothing more than an unbroken rehearsal of contingencies, each at the mercy of circumstances and each significant in proportion to its familiarity. It is not a fortress into which we may retire, and the only means we have of defending it (that is, ourselves) against the hostile forces of change is in the open field of experience; by throwing our weight upon the foot which for the time being is more firmly placed, by cleaving to whatever familiarities are not immediately threatened and thus assimilating what is new without becoming unrecognizable to ourselves. The Masai, when they were moved from their old country to the present Masai reserve in Kenya, took with them the names of their hills and plains and rivers and gave them to the hills and plains and rivers of the new country. And it is by some such subterfuge of conservatism that every man or people compelled to suffer a notable change avoids the shame of extinction.

(Michael Oakeshott)[21]

One of my central theses is that Green thought and conservative philosophy converge at several crucial points, the very points at which they most diverge from fundamentalist liberalism. There are at least three deep affinities between Green thought and conservative philosophy that are important to my argument. There is first the fact that both conservatism and Green theory see the life of humans in a multi-generational perspective that distinguishes them from liberalism and socialism alike. Liberal individualism, with its disabling fiction of society as a contract among strangers, is a one-generational philosophy, which has forgotten, or never known, the truth invoked by David Hume against Thomas Hobbes: that, in our species, wherein sexual and parental love are intertwined, the generations overlap, so that we are *au fond* social and historical creatures, whose identities are always in part constituted by memories (such as those which are deposited in the languages that we speak) which cross the generations.[22] The forms of common life in which we find our identities are the environments in which we live and have our being: they are our human ecology.[23] Again, contrary to the antinomian impulse that animates Marxian and other socialist liberationist movements, the traditions that we inherit from our forebears are not fetters on our identities, shackles which repress our self-expression, but the necessary conditions of having selves to express. We may sometimes legitimately seek to amend our historical inheritance, when it no longer meets human needs, but never to emancipate ourselves from it: that project, the project of making the world over anew, is the gnostic delusion that beset Paine, Robespierre and Lenin. For conservative philosophy, therefore, as for ecological theory, the life of our species is never to be understood from the standpoint of a single generation of its members; each generation is what it is in virtue of its inheritance from earlier generations and what it contributes to its successors. In so far as one-generation philosophies prosper, the links between the past and the future are weakened, the natural and human patrimony is squandered, and the present is laid waste. The modernist idea that each of us is here only once, so we had better make the most of it, is a popular embodiment of the one-generational world-view, which finds expression in much liberal and socialist thought.

A second, connected idea, shared by conservative philosophy and Green theory, is the primacy of the common life. Both conservative and Green thinkers repudiate the shibboleth of liberal individualism, the sovereign subject, the autonomous agent whose choices are the origin of all that has value. They reject this conception, to begin with, because it is a fiction. Human individuals are not natural data, such as pebbles or apples, but are artefacts of social life, cultural and historical achievements: they are, in short, exfoliations of the common life itself.[24] Without common forms of life, there are no individuals: to think otherwise is to be misled by the vulgarised Kantian idea of the person which, shorn of the metaphysics that is its matrix in Kant and that gives it all the (slight) meaning it has, dominates recent liberal thought.[25] But liberal individualism also embodies a mistaken conception of the human good. For conservatives, as for Green thinkers, it is clear that choice-making has in itself little or no value: what has value are the choices that are made, and the options that are available – in short, what is chosen, provided it is good. As I have already argued elsewhere,[26] individual well-being presupposes an array of choiceworthy options which can only be supplied by worthwhile forms of common life. It is from the options provided by such forms of life that choices, however autonomous, derive all of their value. The ultimate locus of value in the human world is not, therefore, in individual choices but in forms of life. This should lead us to qualify, even to abandon, the ideal of the autonomous chooser (which I have myself elsewhere endorsed)[27] in favour of the recognition that the good life for human beings – as for many kindred animal species – necessarily presupposes embeddedness in communities. It is an implication of this point that Green theorists who extend to other animal species the legalist categories of individual rights are moving in precisely the wrong direction: what is required is the recognition that, among human beings, it is not individual rights but often forms of life that need most protection, if only because it is upon them that individual well-being ulti-mately depends.

A third idea shared by conservative and Green thinkers is the danger of novelty; in particular, the sorts of innovation that go with large-scale social (and techno-logical) experimentation. It is not that conservatives (or sensible Green thinkers) seek to arrest change: that would be to confuse stability, which is achieved through changes that are responsive to the cycle of life and to the shifting environment, with fixity. It is rather that both Greens and conservatives consider risk-aversion the path of prudence when new technologies, or new social practices, have conse-quences that are large and unpredictable, and, most especially, when they are unquantifiable but potentially catastrophic risks associated with innovation. It is an irony that conservatives, whose official philosophy emphasises reliance on the tried and tested, should often embrace technological innovation, as if it were a good in itself. To be sure, there is little likelihood that the flood of technological innovation can in our time be stemmed; but that is no reason to welcome it or to refrain from curbing it, where this is feasible and there are clear dangers attached to it. It is at least questionable, for example, whether experimental advances in genetic engineering will on balance add to the sum of human well-being; whether their prohibition in any one country, or group of countries, can successfully halt their development, however, is another matter. It is more than questionable whether current high-tech policies in farming are defensible from a conservative perspective that is prudently risk-averse, since current farming technology, like other branches of industrial food technology, encompasses a myriad of interventions in natural processes, each of which has consequences that are unknown and whose effects, when taken together, are incalculable and unknowable.

A sound conservative maxim in all areas of policy, but especially of policy having large environmental implications, is that we should be very cautious of innovations, technological or otherwise, that have serious downside risks – even if the evidence suggestive of these risks is inconclusive, if the risks are small, or if their magnitudes cannot be known. A tiny chance of catastrophe may be a risk that can prudently be assumed, if all that is at stake is a human life or a few human lives. It is hard to see how any genuinely conservative philosophy can warrant risk-taking of this sort when the catastrophe that is being hazarded is environmental and millennial in its consequences. This is a truth which is acknowledged – and acknowledged as an element in a sane conservatism – by at least some Green thinkers.[28]

The conservative and Green aversion to risky change does not, of course, entail any policy of immobilism. It may indeed entail radical alternatives in current policy, if such policy encompasses substantial and unwarranted risks. Such alternatives will not, however, be animated by any conception of open-ended progress. It is a cardinal element in my argument for the consilience of conservative philosophy with Green thought that both reject the modernist myth of progress, and for very similar reasons. It is rejected by Green thought because it incorporates the idea of infinite growth – an idea alien to every tenet of ecology.[29] The characteristic that best distinguishes flourishing ecosystems is never growth, but rather stability (a conservative virtue in its own right). This is a truth which is acknowledged in the discipline of ecology in all of its varieties, but which is expressed most beautifully in James Lovelock's idea of Gaia:[30] the idea of life on the Earth as constituting a single organism, one which regulates the species and environments of which life on Earth is composed so as to maintain its stability as a whole. This is an idea, resisted by scientific fundamentalists on the ground that it restores teleology to nature, which should commend itself both to Green thinkers who seek to escape from anthropocentric conceptions of the place of the human species in the biosphere, and to conservatives who have not lost the sense of nature (preserved in the Judaeo–Christian tradition) as an order or *cosmos*. Both Green and conservative thinkers should welcome the idea of Gaia, not least as a counterweight to the dominant humanist heresies of modernism. Modernist political faiths which advocate the unlimited growth of population, production and knowledge – political religions such as Marxism and liberalism – are effectively in rebellion against every truth we have established about order in the natural world. Only a sort of secular, humanistic fideism – not any rational assessment of the human lot – could support the otherwise groundless conviction that our species is exempt from the natural constraints that govern every other species of which we have knowledge. The idea of progress is rightly anathema to the most reflective Green thinkers, one of whom has stigmatised it as expressive of 'the anti-way', the way downwards, to entropic disorder and final extinction.[31]

Conservatives have, or should have, their own good reasons for rejecting the idea of progress. Several come at once to mind. The idea of progress is particularly pernicious when it acts to suppress awareness of mystery and tragedy in human life. The broken lives of those who have been ruined by injustice or by sheer misfortune are not mended by the fact – if it were a fact – that future generations will live ever less under these evils. Meliorism, as embodied in the idea of progress, corrupts our perception of human life, in which the fate of each individual is – for him or her – an ultimate fact, which no improvement in the life of the species can alter or redeem. Again, the idea of progress presupposes a measure of improvement in human affairs which, except in limiting cases, we lack.[32] This is not to deny that we can meaningfully judge there to have been improvements in specific spheres of human life: no one who has read Thomas de Quincey's *Confessions of an English Opium-eater* can doubt that anaesthetic dentistry has made a not inconsiderable contribution to human well-being. But improvements in one sphere are accompanied by new evils in others: who is bold enough to affirm that the technological advances of modern medicine have, on balance, promoted human well-being? The facts of iatrogenic illness, of meaningless longevity and of the medicalisation of the human environment, well documented by Illich,[33] are telling evidences to the contrary. The deeper truth, however, is that, when assessing goods and evils across very different spheres of human life, we are trying to weigh incommensurables – longevity against the absence of pain, security against adventure, and so on. Although there are generically human evils – of torture, of constant danger of violent death, of human lives cut off in their prime – which are obstacles to any sort of human flourishing, even these universal evils cannot be weighed in the scales against each other. Like the goods of a flourishing human life, they are incommensurables. The conception of human history as a project of universal improvement, in so far as it is at all meaningful, is questionable, given that the eradication of one evil typically spawns others, and many goods are dependent for their existence on evils. At root, however, the idea of history as progressive amelioration is not so much debatable as incoherent; as Herder perceived when, acknowledging the incommensurability of the goods that are distinctive of different forms of cultural life, he rejected even the qualified meliorism of the Kantian philosophy of history.[34]

If the idea of history as the progress of the species is without meaning, it cannot afford a meaning to human life. And here we have the root of the conservative objection to the notion of progress: that it serves as a surrogate for spiritual meaning for those whose lives would otherwise be manifestly devoid of sense. The idea of progress is detrimental to the life of the spirit, because it encourages us to view our lives, not under the aspect of eternity, but as moments in a universal process of betterment. We do not, therefore, accept our lives for what they are, but instead consider them always for what they might someday become. In this way the idea of progress reinforces the restless discontent that is one of the diseases of modernity, a disease symptomatically expressed in Hayek's nihilistic and characteristically candid statement that 'Progress is movement for movement's sake'.[35] No view of human life could be further from either Green thought or genuine conservative philosophy.

The modern conception of progress is only one symptom of the hubristic humanism that is the real religion of our age. As against that debased faith, both conservative and Green thought have as their ideal peace and stability. They seek a form of society that is sufficiently at ease with itself that its legitimacy does not depend on the illusory promise of unending growth. Neither Greens nor conservatives, if they are wise, are in any doubt as to the magnitude of the obstacles in the way of such a society. There can be no doubt that the project of a social order that does not rest on the prospect of indefinite future betterment creates problems for policy that have as yet been barely addressed by conventional thought, including the mainstream of conservative philosophy. Securing the legitimacy of political and economic institutions in a stationary-state society, which is without open-ended growth in population or production, is a hard and central problem for policy, which ought to concern Green thinkers as deeply as it should conservatives.

POLICY

The stationary state

It is perhaps only in transmissible arts that human progress can be maintained or recognised. But in developing themselves and developing human nature these arts shift their ground; and in proportion as the ground is shifted, and human nature itself is transformed, the criterion of progress ceases to be moral to become only physical, a question of increased complexity or bulk or power. We all feel at this time the moral ambiguity of mechanical progress. It seems to multiply opportunity, but it destroys the possibility of simple, rural or independent life. It lavishes information, but it abolishes mastery except in trivial or mechanical efficiency. We learn many languages, but degrade our own. Our philosophy is highly critical and thinks itself enlightened, but it is a Babel of mutually unintelligible artificial tongues.

(George Santayana)[36]

If the project of unbounded progress is to be rejected as a sensible social and political ideal, both in virtue of the ecological limits that it will soon meet and because of its spiritual emptiness, is there an alternative conception of the good society to which conservatives and Greens can alike repair? One may be found, I submit, in J.S. Mill, in his conception of a stationary-state economy, which he describes canonically as follows:

in contemplating any progressive movement, not in its nature unlimited, the mind is not satisfied with merely tracing the laws of its movement; it cannot but ask the further question, to what goal?...

It must always have been seen, more or less distinctly, by political economists, that the increase in wealth is not boundless: that at the end of what they term the progressive state lies the stationary state, that all progress in wealth is but a postponement of this, and that each step in advance is an approach to it ... if we have not reached it long ago, it is because the goal itself flies before us [as a result of technical progress].

I cannot ... regard the stationary state of capital and wealth with the unaffected aversion so generally manifested towards it by political economists of the old school. I am inclined to believe that it would be, on the whole, a very considerable improvement on our present condition. I confess I am not charmed with the ideal of life held out by those who think that the normal state of human beings is that of struggling to get on; that the trampling, crushing, elbowing, and treading on each other's heels which form the existing type of social life, are the most desirable lot of human kind, or anything but the disagreeable symptoms of one of the phases of industrial progress. The northern and middle states of America are a specimen of this stage of civilization in very favourable circumstances; ... and all that these advantages seem to have yet done for them (notwithstanding some incipient signs of a better tendency) is that the life of the whole of one sex is devoted to dollar-hunting, and of the other to breeding dollar-hunters....

Those who do not accept the present very early stage of human improvement as its ultimate type may be excused for being comparatively indifferent to the kind of economical progress which excites the congratulations of ordinary politicians; the mere increase of production and accumulation.... I know not why it should be a matter of congratulation that persons who are already richer than anyone needs to be, should have doubled their means of consuming things which give little or no pleasure except as representative of wealth.... It is only in the backward countries of the world that increased production is still an important object: in those most advanced, what is economically needed is a better distribution, of which one indispensable means is a stricter restraint on population.

There is room in the world, no doubt, and even in old countries, for a great increase in population, supposing the arts of life to go on improving, and capital to increase. But even if innocuous, I confess I see very little reason for desiring it. The density of population necessary to enable mankind to obtain, in the greatest degree, all the advantages both of cooperation and of social intercourse, has, in all the most populous countries, been attained. A population may be too crowded, though all be amply supplied with food and raiment. It is not good for a man to be kept perforce at all times in the presence of his species.... Nor is there much satisfaction in contemplating the world with nothing left to the spontaneous activity of nature; with every rood of land brought into cultivation, which is capable of growing food for human beings; every flowery waste or natural pasture plowed up, all quadrupeds, or birds which are not domesticated for man's use exterminated as his rivals for food, every hedgerow or superfluous tree rooted out, and scarcely a place left where a wild shrub or flower could grow without being eradicated as a weed in the name of improved agriculture. If the earth must lose that great portion of its pleasantness which it owes to things that the unlimited increase of wealth and population would extirpate from it, for the mere purpose of enabling it to support a larger, but not a happier or a better population, I sincerely hope, for the sake of posterity, that they will be content to be stationary, long before necessity compels them to it.

It is scarcely necessary to remark that a stationary condition of capital and population implies no stationary state of human improvement. There would be as much scope as ever for all kinds of mental culture, and moral and social progress; as much room for improving the Art of Living and much more likelihood of its being improved, when minds cease to be engrossed by the art of getting on. Even the industrial arts might be as earnestly and as successfully cultivated, with this sole difference, that instead of serving no purpose but the increase of wealth, industrial improvements would produce their legitimate effect, that of abridging labour.[37]

A universal stationary state may well be a utopia; but it is a better measuring-rod for attainable improvement in the human lot than the wholly unrealisable fantasy of infinite growth. It captures the core of what is often described as sustainable development, and, because it respects the varieties of finitude by which we are surrounded, it should commend itself not only to Green theorists, but also to conservatives. It has a vital element, however, which many conservatives and Greens find offensive, although it is eminently sensible, namely the neo-Malthusian commitment to the control of human population. Such a commitment, I shall argue, is indispensable to any policy seeking to avert regional and global ecological degradation; and the idea that market institutions and their matrices, civil societies, can flourish, or even hope to survive, in a world of rapidly but unevenly increasing populations is, in truth, sheer fantasy. It is to this global perspective on population, and to related topics of sustainable development, that I turn first in my consideration of policy. I proceed then to consider what might be an agenda of policy for Green conservatives as applied to the common environment at the national level in Britain, focusing on six related policy areas: energy and agriculture, urban and transport policy, and education and health. In all, I shall argue, conservative values dictate radical departures from current practice – changes that can also be seen as congenial to Green concerns.

The global perspective: population

If there were only 500 million people on earth, almost nothing that we are now doing to the environment would perturb Gaia.

(James Lovelock)[38]

In the days before Pasteur man's population was maintained approximately constant from generation to generation by a cybernetic system in which the principal feedback element at the upper limit was disease. The crowd-diseases – smallpox, cholera, typhoid, plague, etc. – are, by the ecologist, labelled 'density-dependent factors', whose effectiveness in reducing population is a power function of the density of the population. No growth of population could get out of hand as long as the crowd-diseases were unconquered.... With the development of bacteriological medicine, all this has been changed. Now, the feedback control is man himself. The reality of this truth is temporarily obscured by the increasing size of the feast, through technological advances, but this is only a passing phase which must soon come to an end.... Having eliminated all other enemies, man is his own worst enemy. Having disposed of all his predators, man preys on himself.

(Garrett Hardin)[39]

The single greatest threat to global ecological stability other than large-scale nuclear war comes from human population growth. According to United Nations estimates, there are around 5.5 billion people in the world today. Within thirty years, this number will have increased to 8.5 billion, and by the middle of the next century it will – barring demographic collapses of one sort or another – have topped 10 billion. These latter extrapolative figures take account of the demographic transition: the point in economic and social development at which families (in many, but not by any means all, poorer countries) begin to shrink in size. Even given that the rate of increase of world population fell from 2.04 per cent per annum in 1970 to around 1.8 per cent at present, it is worth noting that an annual growth rate of the latter figure will double the number of parents every 39 years. Nor does the story end there. Even given the very large and doubtful supposition that a demographic transition occurs everywhere and at a similar rate, the world's total population will swell for a long time. The age-structure alone of many populations, such as that of Bangladesh, in which perhaps a majority are under fifteen, guarantees this further increase. The prospect is of a doubling of the world's human population in under sixty years. Is there anyone who can reasonably suppose that the world's ecological balance can cope with this unprecedented demographic growth? Or that it will occur unattended by vast economic and political (and military) convulsions?

It may be salutary to review briefly the principal reasons why population pressures are likely, unless sensible policies are adopted, to render the coming century one of wars and migrations even greater and yet more terrible than those of the twentieth century. To begin with, the growth of populations is very uneven as between different countries, and different parts of the world. In the former Soviet Union, for example, the population of Russians is in steep decline, whereas the Muslim population is, in general, increasing rapidly. The huge differences in size of different populations further increase the absolute magnitudes resulting from these different rates of growth. The population of mainland China, perhaps around twelve hundred million at present, is roughly ten times that of neighbouring Japan, whose population is static or declining. The population of Indonesia is such (well over a hundred million) that it would find no difficulty in fielding a land army larger than the entire population of New Zealand. Such examples could easily be multiplied. It requires a faith in the resilience of human institutions that borders on the absurd to imagine that discrepancies of these magnitudes will not occasion migrations and wars of the classical Malthusian varieties.

Nor is the celebrated demographic transition occurring evenly in all parts of the world. The theory itself, though it has a measure of leverage on historical and contemporary evidence, is a piece of economic imperialism. Like other applications of the model of *homo economics*, it neglects the crucial variable of culture. The theory tells us that families will shrink in size when parents, themselves growing richer and so able to provide for their old age, or sheltered from destitution by welfare programmes, cease to regard their children as investment goods and come to view them as consumer goods. Family size will then fall. This desiccated model leaves out the influence on fertility of very diverse moral and religious traditions. The demographic transition is likely to be most pronounced where – as in Taiwan and Japan – mores are such that birth control is unproblematic and abortion not a moral issue; and this is borne out by evidence from these countries. Where the local religion puts a premium on large family size, and anathematises contraception and abortion, as with some varieties both of Roman Catholicism and of Islam, we may expect the demographic transition to be slow and slight, or else indefinitely delayed – as appears to be the case in parts of Latin America and North Africa. Such differences in the rate of demographic transition will magnify existing disparities in population size. They will generate waves of illegal immigration – of the sort already occurring from the Maghreb in Africa to Southern and Western Europe – that are likely to have highly destabilising effects on both the recipient societies and the societies subject to such haemorrhagings of population. It is not difficult to foresee major military conflicts occurring as a result of actual or prospective population movements of this sort.

Resistance to population policy among conservatives is deep and widespread, and it is paralleled by Maoist attitudes among radical Greens, who see calls for population control as veiled policies of genocide on poor peoples. Such resistance is folly of the worst sort, from the standpoint both of conservative philosophy and of Green thought (not to mention common sense). For Greens, it must surely be clear that a vast uncontrolled expansion of human population will endanger and disrupt the biological community of which our species is only a part: it is a recipe for instability, or, if not, for the sort of stability that, if the Gaian hypothesis is at all well-founded, comes about via catastrophic reduction in human numbers.[40] And such a reduction is most likely, in the absence of a well-conceived policy of population control, to occur in the poorest countries.

For conservatives, the sheer inordinacy, the defiance of natural finitude that is involved in open-ended population growth, and the hazards that it poses to civilised economic and political institutions, should be sufficient to caution them against that species of technological optimism about our capacity to cope with ever growing human populations that is found in such nineteenth-century thinkers as Herbert Spencer and Karl Marx. Such technological hubris – advocated, or presupposed, in our own time by thinkers such as Julian Simons and, in some of his later writings, by F.A. Hayek – is objectionable, in the first place, because of its overestimation of human inventiveness and its underestimation of the fragility of any natural or Gaian order that has a place in it for humans. It is to be resisted, secondly, because, even if human technology had the virtuosity attributed to it by these forms of positivism and scientism, human institutions would break down long before technology could develop to such levels of virtuosity, or be applied in practice. Or, to put it another way: the growth of technology itself depends on human institutions that are always unstable and often desperately fragile; it is disrupted, or retarded, when human institutions break down. For this reason, the growth of technology cannot be guaranteed, and a technical fix for the problems of humankind, even supposing it to be possible, will always be beyond its reach.

If such philosophical considerations prove insufficiently compelling, perhaps the threat to liberty posed by human population growth will be persuasive. Overpopulation is itself an encroachment on individual liberty, as more and more of our activities are constrained by the density of human settlements.[41] The sudden and dramatic increase in human numbers has been identified by at least one twentieth-century conservative thinker[42] as but an aspect of the ascendancy of mass humanity which is the chief threat to individuality in our age. It is scarcely a conservative point of view to value the quantity of human beings in the world over the quality of their lives; to prefer a crowded world choked with noise and filth to a world of space and amenity that is peopled on a smaller scale; or to deny the human need for solitude and wilderness. All of these conservative considerations mandate a policy for population when, as now in most parts of the world, medical progress has removed natural constraints on overpopulation. The forms of population policy will naturally vary from time to time and place to place; and, for a conservative, it is important that they should conform, so far as they can do so feasibly, with local customs and beliefs. There will nevertheless be occasions when, unless local beliefs and values – about the sanctity of human life, say, or the evils of contraception – are radically reformed, the deeper conservative values of the stability and integrity of the common environment will be compromised, perhaps irreversibly. This is only one example of a truth to which my argument will recur: that, in our age of cataclysmic change, conservative values can sometimes be renewed only by radical revisions in current thought and practice.

Economic development

Man's continuous tapping of natural resources is not an activity that makes no history. On the contrary, it is the most important long-run element of mankind's fate. It is because of the irreversibility of the entropic degradation of matter – energy – that, for instance, the peoples from the Asian steppes, whose economy was based on sheep-raising, began their Great Migration over the entire European continent at the beginning of the first millennium. The same element – the pressure on natural resources – had, no doubt, a role in other migrations, including that from Europe to the New World.... Nothing could be further from the truth than the notion that the economic process is an isolated, circular affair – as Marxist and standard analysis represent it. The economic process is solidly anchored to a material base which is subject to definite constraints. It is because of these constraints that the economic process has a unidirectional irrevocable evolution.

(Nicholas Georgescu-Roegen)[43]

The economic activities of modern man are interfering ever more dramatically with the most fundamental Gaian cycles – water, carbon, sulphur, phosphorus – thus disrupting the critical order of the biosphere and reducing its capacity to support life. This is unfortunately inevitable if economic development remains modern man's overriding goal. For it is a one-way process, in which the

Biosphere is systematically transformed into the technosphere and technospheric waste – a process that cannot continue indefinitely.

(Edward Goldsmith)[44]

The ideal of a stationary-state society implies stable levels of human population throughout the world; in most parts of the world, stability at levels lower than at present. In some Western countries, the ageing of current populations may support more liberal selective immigration policies; but the population of the world as a whole, and of most of the countries in it, is by any sensible standard far too high. Alleviation of the human lot lies not in a further growth in human numbers, but in stability at much reduced levels. To this end, attitudes and policies in regard to fertility and procreation will need to alter radically. If they do not, human numbers will be curtailed by other, more traditionally Malthusian means.

It is no less important to stress that economic development cannot proceed much longer on the traditional lines of indefinitely expanding output. Such policies carry with them an indefinite expansion of the toxic side-effects of hyper-industrialisation, in pollution, ozone depletion, the disappearance of wilderness, and so on. Certainly, the proposition that the 'developing' world can ever hope to have the levels of production of the most industrialised nations is thoroughly absurd – but only slightly more so than the idea that the so-called First World can expect to return to the trajectory of uninterrupted economic growth that it enjoyed in the sixties and eighties. Both propositions underestimate the fragility of the world's ecological balance, and the impact on its stability of ever higher levels of industrial activity. Most absurd of all is the notion that a population around twice that of the world at present could ever expect to generate the industrial production that the world's richest nations presently exhibit.

The industrialisation of the world on the model of its richest nations is a dystopian fantasy. It probably exaggerates even the capacity of the First World to renew itself on the conventional path of economic growth. The past few years have seen the abortion of the Reaganite and Thatcherite 'dashes for growth', and the stubborn resistance of the world's most advanced economies to a resumption of expansion on the old lines. In the United States, the artificial lowering of short-term interest rates to levels unknown for nearly thirty years, and probably in real terms negative, has so far failed to rekindle economic activity. In Europe and Japan, neither monetarist nor Keynesian strategies of the old sorts appear efficacious in restarting the engine of growth, and asset values are in ominous decline. The prospect for the First World – fraught with terrible implications for the rest of the world – may be a Great Depression, akin to that of the 1930s (or worse) in that it is accompanied by trade wars, financial meltdowns and geopolitical convulsions. This is not a prospect to be welcomed by any sensible conservative or Green, or by any sane observer; but it is one that should at least pose a question mark over the feasibility, if not the desirability, of a resumption of economic growth along the lines – almost certainly unrepeatable – of the 1960s and 1980s.

Even if the real prospect for the First World is one of continued stagnation rather than of cataclysmic depression, it bodes ill for the future of the transitional post-communist countries. It is in any case highly contestable whether – as the conventional wisdom would have us believe – that future lies in a replication of the central institutions of Western democratic capitalism. As I have argued in detail elsewhere,[45] such a transplantation of Western institutions to the post-communist countries is, in general, neither desirable nor possible. Except in a few areas, where development can piggy-back on the innovations of the military–industrial complex, it is fantastic to suppose that the future for Russia, say – whose environment is already virtually ruined by Faustian projects of industrialisation – lies in further industrial growth: it is much more likely to be in the renewal of agriculture, if that can still be achieved. In any case, except perhaps in the Czech lands of Bohemia and Moravia, in Hungary, in Slovenia, in Estonia and possibly Lithuania, and in the Silesian parts of Poland, where Germany, Austria and Finland have historic interests and the capacity for investment, there is likely to be insufficient Western inputs of capital to finance the reconstruction of the post-communist economies on any Western model. Most of the post-communist peoples will therefore be compelled, by force of sheer economic stringency, to consider other paths to development.

The model of First World affluence and industrial productivity is, perhaps, especially pernicious in its applications to the world's poorest countries, in most of which it will be forever unrealisable. It may well be feasible, at least for a while, for small countries, such as Taiwan and Singapore, to follow in the tracks of Japan and to catch up with, and overtake in affluence and productivity, formerly First World countries, such as New Zealand; it is very doubtful whether a country of the size, geography, resources and population of mainland China can do likewise. (It is worth recalling that average levels of wages in mainland China are perhaps about a hundredth of those in Japan.) In this connection, whatever the other aspects of the present Chinese government, one cannot withhold admiration from their recent policies which initiated economic reform first in agriculture, where it reaped the boon of a surviving peasant tradition that the Bolsheviks, and Stalinist collectivisation, destroyed in Russia. In countries such as China, the renewal of agriculture, along with population control and the search for light, intermediate technologies having the least destructive impact on the natural environment, should be corner-stones of policy, rather than the futile project of emulating Western industrial societies which are already in evident decline, and which may be headed for a fall.

Policies of emulation of First World economic development are pernicious, also, because of their adverse effects on local ways of life. In some instances, at least, there are ways of life that have long achieved an ecological balance with their environmental niche, in which poverty is unknown or even unthought-of, and in which all the evidences of human flourishing are present. Modernisation of a culture such as that of Ladakh, say, has thus far been an almost unmitigated disaster,[46] encompassing the ruination of ancient traditions that had served the Ladakhis well for many centuries. This is not to say that modernisation can realistically be halted, since the introduction of Western medical technologies, with their explosive consequences for population growth, is already probably irreversible. In the case of Ladakh, as of that of analogous Bhutan (where the situation is complicated by ethnic strife between Nepali immigrants and native Bhutanese which threatens to resemble the conflicts that have decimated Sri Lanka), the precipitate introduction of Western medicine alone spells ruin for the people and their culture, unless countervailing modernising measures – such as the introduction of birth control – are also soon adopted. Even assuming that the demographic crises of countries such as these can somehow be averted, they face the daunting task of negotiating a highly selective assimilation of Western technologies at a time when all of the international organisations, such as the World Bank and the United Nations, favour development on the First World model. If there are any safe bets in this field, one may be found in the prediction that such policies, which aim for unsustainable economic development at the cost of the irreversible destruction of traditional cultures, will end in tragedy. This is a wager that the post-colonial history of Africa, no less than the history of Western cultural imperialism that preceded it there, already amply supports. The result of such policies in Africa has so far been only the deracination of local peoples from their traditional tribal cultures and their impoverishment by a global market that drives out their local products. It is hard to see by what rationale this scenario should be replicated in other parts of the world.

Western models of economic development for poor countries should be objectionable both to conservatives and to Green thinkers. Where Western development has taken root, as in Japan, it has been able to do so precisely because (and in so far as) indigenous traditions have not been displaced: a fact which should reinforce the conservative precept that development policy should always conform with local traditions, and never amount to an attempt at a wholesale transplantation of an alien culture. For Greens, the very notion of universalising Western affluence should be suspect, given its costs to the natural environment, and its unsustainability over the long term. Even conservatives who judge the imperatives of economic growth in an industrial society to be irresistible need not sanctify the fiction that such growth has furthered the cause of human happiness. Is any conservative ready to affirm that the city-dweller complete with ghetto-blaster is happier than the destitute Eskimo (prior to the fatal contact with Western culture), or the pious and cheerful Tibetan? Human experience suggests otherwise. We are led to the absurd view of economic growth as an inherently desirable phenomenon, partly by the fetish of calculability that has overtaken the social studies, and partly because we have few decent measures for the costs of economic growth.[47] This will prove a dangerous folly for policy-makers to persist in.

Western advice that poor countries abandon the First World model of development is often, and not always without reason, viewed as hypocritical. It is not unreasonably asked: what alterations are the First World peoples (so called) willing to make in their form of life for the sake of the integrity of the environment? If modernisation on a First World model is to be resisted, how are the First World countries to reform themselves? More to my present purpose, how are conservatives to respond to the challenge posed by the fact that Western affluence cannot be made universal or enduring? What, in particular, are the implications for policy of a Green conservatism for an industrial society such as that of Britain? Let us consider what such an agenda of policy ought to be if it had as its object, not the resumption of economic growth on conventional lines, but instead the conservation and renovation of the common environment.

The national perspective: an agenda for Green conservatism in Britain

Two caveats are in order before we explore the implications of a convergence of Green and conservative perspectives at a national level in Britain. It is far from clear that the nation-state is the appropriate unit for environmental policy, since some policy issues transcend it, while others are most manageable at regional and local levels. Nor is it at all self-evident that the nation-state is an institution that accords well either with conservative or with Green values (in so far as they are ultimately distinguishable). The nation-state is a very recent institution, a construction of the nineteenth-century classical liberal political élites, who were animated by Romantic thought rather than by conservative philosophy. Further, it has in the twentieth century, under institutions of mass democracy, been the arena for rival political élites whose one point of convergence in thought and policy has been a Promethean attitude to nature and a commitment to indefinite economic growth. These latter are hardly Green values. It is not clear that there is anything deep in either conservative or Green thought that commits them to the sanctity of the nation-state as we know it at present.

The nation-state is also, in some important respects, an inappropriate vehicle for environmental concern. Many environmental problems are global: they have effects that spill across territorial jurisdictions. This is true not only of phenomena such as ozone depletion and global warming but also of acid rain pollution, and of many other injurious impacts on the natural environment. There is also a difficulty for Green theorists, which few, if any of them, have as yet confronted: the difficulty created by the ecological terrorism and environmental destruction that is wrought by bandit states. Here is meant not only deliberate acts of ecological vandalism of the sort that were committed in Kuwait by the present ruler of Iraq, which are increasingly likely in the future, but also the phenomenon of environmental holo-causts, having global or regional spillover effects, which are wreaked by lawless states. The former Soviet Union and present mainland China probably fall into this latter category. These phenomena lead by a clear train of reasoning to another set of vast hazards to the natural and human environments, which is typically ne-glected or very inadequately treated in Green thought: the hazards generated by the ever more rapid development, proliferation and deployment of military tech-nologies of mass destruction. This is an issue to which I will return at the end of this chapter. Here I wish only to note that the proliferation of such technologies is not halted, or even significantly retarded, by unilateral acts of national renuncia-tion; and it is of very little profit to anyone to have installed exhaust controls on cars, or to have curtailed the peaceful development of nuclear energy, if we are thereafter subject to the lethality of biological, chemical, conventional and nuclear weapons technologies. The proliferation of such technologies throughout an increasingly anarchic world that contains a growing number of terrorist states casts a lengthening shadow over the future of our species, and over all of the others that it presently dominates, which should inform all serious projects of environmental conservation. In this area, above all, as in many others, unilateral action by nation-states is bound to be typically ineffectual: what is needed is effective concerted action by national governments.

The contemporary nation-state has been, and continues to be, an agency of centralisation; as such, it is an institution that should be endorsed by conservatives and Greens only with considerable reserve and suspicion. Much environmental destruction has occurred because national governments have acted with indifference or ignorance upon local ecologies, natural and human. Again, there are many activities of existing nation-states that need not, and often should not, be performed by national governments, and that sometimes can be done most effectively without any action by government beyond the provision of a legal framework for private initiative. One of the most radical suggestions of neo-liberal thought has been that even the monopoly on the supply of moneys by national governments may be unnecessary and indeed undesirable from the standpoint of price stability.[48] This is a thought that should be congenial to Greens, since it opens up the possibility of local communities having their own local money, issued by local banks that are independent of central governments. Again, much welfare policy has been filtered through national government, when it is often best made and implemented at lower levels, closer to local communities, and often by intermediary and voluntary institutions. Though (as I shall argue) the contemporary nation-state is now the only political institution to retain legitimacy and, for that reason, cannot responsibly be dismantled, there can be no doubt that its responsibilities are currently massively over-extended.

In general, policies toward local environmental issues are best made at local level, if only because, in the human world, all policies turn on the stability and vitality of local communities. Here a further caveat needs issuing. Returning environmental initiative to regions and localities need not, and typically (at least in Britain) should not, mean a multiplication of tiers of local and regional government. In Britain, local government has often been in the forefront of environmental vandalism – wrecking working-class communities by hubristic projects of urban renewal, demolishing serviceable buildings and despoiling countryside. What is needed is rather the strengthening of local and regional non-governmental institutions, the enabling of local communities – a task that may often require the intervention of national government to break the power of local bureaucracies and entrenched interests.

We see here a paradox from which neither conservative nor Green thought can escape: whereas there is nothing sacred in the nation-state that we are bound to revere, still less (after the fashion of modernist humanism) to worship, it remains none the less the only effective agency of environmental action. It acts by making and policing intergovernmental agreements and by conferring Hobbesian protection on local communities and regional ecologies that would otherwise surely be objects of predation by criminal states. And it uses its coercive powers to curb forces, such as uncontrolled migration, and to limit organisations, such as the transnational corporation, which might otherwise endanger local communities and environments. (I do not mean here to stigmatise the transnational corporations, which can sometimes take a larger view than national governments; merely to affirm that the activities of transnational corporations need to be subject to a monitoring that only national governments often can supply.) The nation-state can discharge this task, not only in virtue of its coercive powers, but because of that upon which they rest, namely, the fact that nation-states are in our time the only political institutions that retain authority in a world that has otherwise lost it. It is a lesson which wise conservative philosophy has to teach Green theory that only by working with and in institutions, such as the nation-state, which possess authority and legitimacy, can environmental problems be stably resolved.

The political economy of the stationary state: the limits of market capitalism

There is nothing in front but a flat wilderness of standardisation either by Bolshevism or Big Business. But it is strange that some of us should have seen sanity, if only in a vision, while the rest go forward chained eternally to enlargement without liberty and progress without hope.

(G.K. Chesterton)[49]

The capitalist state is unstable, and indeed more properly a transitory phase lying between two permanent and stable states of society.

(Hilaire Belloc)[50]

One of the central facts of our time is the historical vindication of market institutions. Central planning has not achieved economic security at the price of individual liberty; it has assured general poverty and sustained tyranny. By the conventional standard of its contribution to economic growth, central planning has been a comprehensive failure except in the strategic–military sector. As we have already seen, the inability of central planning institutions to deliver prosperity has not prevented them from devastating the environment. On the contrary, central planning has accomplished a near-ecocide[51] in the former Soviet Union without even a temporary compensating growth in prosperity, and with most of its gigantic industrial projects being ventures in absurdist pyramid-building which lack the aesthetic appeal and spiritual significance of their Egyptian prototypes.

The historical vindication of market institutions has been, popularly and wrongly, perceived as expressive of the triumph of Western capitalism. It is true enough that such absurd variants on a 'third way' as market socialism are utopian (or dystopian)[52] fantasies; but this is not to say that Western capitalism has triumphed, that it will or should be adopted throughout the post-communist world, that it is a single set of institutions without distinctive varieties, or even that some of its varieties – those found in the Anglo-American world, especially – may not now be in steep decline. The simple fact is that market institutions come in an immense diversity of forms, of which Western capitalism is only one and is not necessarily the most stable.

From a standpoint that is acceptable to authentic conservatives and Greens alike, Western capitalism, at least as it is found in a country such as Britain, has two large and connected disadvantages, which disable it in ecological terms. The first is that Western capitalism – like socialist central planning but unlike medieval feudalism, say – is predicated upon indefinite economic growth. For Western capitalism, the stationary state represents the nemesis of secular stagnation, dreaded by mainstream economists from Ricardo to Hansen: any faltering in growth, any disruption of rising living standards is perceived – as indeed it is correct so to do – as a defect in the prevailing economic system. For Green theorists, accordingly, Western capitalism is predicated upon an ecological impossibility, and it is for that reason doomed to instability and ephemerality. The second disadvantage flows from the first. This is that the political legitimacy of Western capitalist market institutions depends upon incessant economic growth; it is endangered whenever growth falters. This is a feature of Western institutions that should be profoundly distasteful to all true conservatives, for whom the legitimacy of institutions, and the authority of government, has (or should have) ethical and spiritual foundations, whereby they can weather even protracted periods of economic hardship. The dependency of Western capitalism on uninterrupted economic growth for its political legitimacy has allowed it to evade addressing its chief defects, which account for its systemic tendency to instability: the insecurity that it generates for ordinary people by its prodigious technological virtuosity and inherently innovative character; and the maldistribution of capital whereby this insecurity is compounded. There are, indeed, varieties of market institutions in which this endemic insecurity is addressed, such as that of Japan, in which at least a substantial proportion of the working population enjoys lifetime job security in a company. (It is the stability which such practices confer on Japanese market institutions that addresses one reason among many others why Japan is very wise to resist emulating Western, and especially Anglo-American, models for business enterprise, which bear all the marks of bankruptcy.) In most capitalist countries, however, the insecurities of the economic system are at best mitigated by a range of welfare institutions, which foster a culture of dependency and do nothing to spread the advantages and responsibilities of ownership.

Such welfare institutions, when they are not confined to their proper function of assisting those incapable of productive employment to lead lives that are nevertheless dignified, abound with moral hazards and self-defeating effects. It is, in fact, hard (but essential) to envisage reforms of our inherited capitalist institutions which would obviate the necessity for a welfare state that has, on the whole, done little to emancipate its supposed beneficiaries from poverty and dependency, but has instead institutionalised these conditions. I have suggested elsewhere[53] reforms of current welfare institutions and policies which might go some distance towards achieving their original intent and rendering less significant their counter-productive side-effects. Here I want to argue that only a radical extension of the benefits of ownership will sufficiently mitigate market-generated insecurity for market institutions on a roughly capitalist model to be stable in the context of a stationary-state economy. In Britain, policies for the dispersion of wealth have been destructively perverse in the extreme. On inheritance, they have encouraged not wider ownership, but the transfer of wealth to the state.[54] In tax policy, the absurd fetish of home-ownership has been subsidised, while savings, dividends and capital gains have been subject to double taxation. Schemes for wider dispersion of wealth have taken the form of encouraging investment in highly volatile equities arising from privatisations. The combination of progressive income taxation with virulent inflation has rendered the accumulation of capital from earnings an impossibility for virtually everyone. The result has been the Servile State described by Belloc, which is little different from the new serfdom (one wholly lacking the redeeming features of its medieval predecessor) diagnosed by Hayek.[55]

Tax and welfare policies must urgently be reformed, so as to promote re-skilling and to enhance the opportunities for the private accumulation of capital – itself a necessary condition of the Green virtue of social stability and the conservative values of harmony and independence. In addition, consideration should be given to a negative capital tax[56] whereby each citizen would receive at maturity a patrimony of capital that would confer on him or her the possibility of independence and of self-provision against most forms of market-generated insecurity. In Britain, such a patrimony could be denominated in government bonds, perhaps index-linked against inflation and tax-exempt, which were redeemable on stated terms for purposes of investment, saving, provision for retirement, and so on. The aim would be to guarantee a minimum of capital as a patrimony for each and all. (To be sure, such a scheme could not guarantee that the patrimony would not be wasted or malinvested, and so it could not obviate the need for all welfare institutions; but we are dealing here, as always, with exercises in imperfection, not utopias.) Such a distributivist measure in no way mandates egalitarian levelling (since it could easily be financed from proportional income taxation) and it needs for its justification none of the dubious notions of social justice rightly criticised by neo-liberals. In truth, it probably embodies one of the few viable means of reducing the systemic instabilities of market capitalism while substantially dismantling the elephantine apparatus of the welfare state.[57] It is vastly preferable to hare-brained neo-liberal schemes for a negative income tax, which I have criticised elsewhere.[58] And it might conceivably engender that fund of legitimacy that would enable market institutions to renew themselves stably across the generations in a stationary-state economy, in which only individual effort or the lottery of the market, but not an engine of forced economic growth, can alter individual positions in society.

New institutions and policies of other sorts will doubtless be necessary if market institutions are to adapt themselves to the constraints of a stationary-state economy. Daly has suggested, as an alternative to pollution taxes which attempt to cost the externalities of industrial production, depletion quotas on natural resources, which would be set by government but would be auctioned off as marketable assets. He commends this radical policy proposal on the grounds that 'It does not expropriate land and capital, but does further restrict their use at an across-the-board level. It provides the necessary macroeconomic control with the minimum sacrifice of microeconomic freedom. It minimises centralised, quantitative planning and maximises reliance on decentralised, market decision-making.'[59] Similar proposals have been made for the control of population.[60] It does not matter, for the purposes of my argument, whether these proposals are acceptable as appropriate responses to current environmental concerns. They have the merits (not always possessed by policies advocated by Greens) of seeking to turn to advantage the workings of market institutions, rather than to repress them; and in that respect, they accord maximal feasible respect to individual liberty. They accept that the task of Green policy is that of reforming civil society and its market institutions, not abolishing them. In this such policy proposals are exemplary. Even if the proposed measures were to prove defective, they will be less delusive than attempts to kick-start economic growth on the old models; and they will have some prospect of generating the legitimacy for market institutions that they have in recent times borrowed spuriously from an unsustainable expansion in material living standards.

ISSUES ON THE NATIONAL POLICY AGENDA

It is no part of the object of this chapter to address every issue in national political debate in Britain in order to identify a convergence of conservative and Green perspectives on it. Instead I shall, from the shifting and inevitably indeterminate subject-matter of public discourse in Britain, address six broad policy areas – energy and agriculture, urban and transport policy, and health and education – to see how a Green conservative agenda might be applied. In every case, we will find a substantial convergence of perspectives, along with significant revisions in both standard conservative and conventional Green thinking.

Energy and agriculture

The natural energy of the Universe, the power that lights the stars in the sky, is nuclear. Chemical energy, wind and water wheels: such sources of energy are, from the viewpoint of a manager of the Universe, almost as rare as a coal-burning star. If this is so, and if God's universe is nuclear-powered, why then are so many of us prepared to march in protest against its use to provide us with electricity?

The very concept of pollution is anthropocentric and it may even be irrelevant in the Gaian context.

(James Lovelock)[61]

A feature of Green thought has been its opposition to novel technologies for the production of energy; most particularly, its opposition to nuclear power. At first glance this may appear to be one of the many points of convergence between Green thought and conservative philosophy which it is the purpose of this chapter to exhibit. After all, conservative philosophy insists that it is collectively imprudent to incur even tiny risks, if they are risks of catastrophe and are avoidable; and we have had more than one instance thus far (as the opponents of nuclear power never cease to remind us) of serious accidents in nuclear power plants. Are not the Greens therefore in conformity with conservative philosophy in opposing nuclear power, in virtue of its novelty and its potentially vast hazards to the environment?

Almost all of the commonly accepted arguments against nuclear power are substantially spurious; elements of a pseudo-Green conventional wisdom, part Luddite, which is suspicious of new technologies, however benign they may be, and attached to old technology, no matter how demonstrably environmentally pernicious. It is true, of course, that there are in the world unsafe (because now obsolete) nuclear power stations, especially in the post-Soviet world, and, very probably, in China: the risk of further Chernobyls amounts, for that reason, to a likelihood. These dangers are good arguments against unsafe reactors, and therefore for the closure of such reactors; they are not arguments against nuclear power. The fact is that, by comparison with older energy-producing technologies, nuclear power is environmentally benign, and not especially hazardous. As Lovelock has observed:

> It is true that calculations have been made of the cancer deaths across Europe that might come from Chernobyl, but if we were consistent, we might wonder also about the cancer deaths from breathing the smoke fogs of London coal and look on a piece of coal with the same fear now reserved for uranium. How different is the fear of death from nuclear accidents from the commonplace and boring death toll of the roads, of cigarette smoking, or of mining – which taken together are equivalent to thousands of Chernobyls a day?[62]

The public perception of nuclear power as peculiarly risky is an illusion, partly created by the failure to compare its hazards with those forms of power with which we are familiar. (Compare the frequency and devastating impact on the natural environment of oil spills – of which only the worst are reported – with the publicity given to nuclear accidents; or the havoc wrought on nature by the antediluvian, pre-nuclear industrial technologies of the former Soviet bloc – virtually screened out from Western perceptions – with the global publicity accorded to the Chernobyl meltdown.) Indeed, if time travel were possible, a visitor from an earlier period of industrial society – say, the nineteenth century in Britain – would most likely be astonished by the cleanliness and integrity of our environment, which early industrialism ravaged. There is a lesson here for Green thought, which is that, whereas the reckless adoption of novel technologies without due consideration of their consequences is imprudence or folly, new technologies are not always maleficent. Sometimes, as is arguably the case with nuclear power, they are a major improvement on the cumbrous, costly and ecologically invasive technologies of the past (such as coal-mining). In any event, nuclear power is with us; it behooves us to make the best of it. As Lovelock has put it:

> If we cannot disinvent nuclear power, I hope that it stays as it is. The power sources are vast and slow to be built, and the low cost of the power itself is offset by the size of the capital investment required ... I have never regarded nuclear radiation or nuclear power as anything other than a normal and inevitable part of the environment.[63]

This is not an argument for the indiscriminate adoption of nuclear power, or for everything that has been done by the nuclear industry or said on its behalf. It is, rather, an argument for a rational energy policy, formulated at national level, in which nuclear power, along with other forms of energy-production, would have an important role. That there is need for a national energy policy is questioned, I take it, only by free-market doctrinaires, whose positions are grounded in a metaphysical faith in market institutions rather than empirical reasonings about their operations and limitations. As in a good many other respects, we can take a cue here from Japan, which responded to the oil-shock of the seventies by a host of governmentally sponsored energy-saving initiatives, including further development of its nuclear power programme. We will also be sensible if we treat the progressive curtailment of the role of the private passenger car as being, among other things, an element in a reasonable national energy policy.

After the size of the world's human population, the greatest threat to the integrity of our common environment is to be found not in the peaceful uses of nuclear energy, but most probably in current farming practices. Once again, the Green conventional wisdom, with its nostalgia for a lost rural arcadia and its contempt for the contrivances of city living, neglects or misperceives the real threats to our common life, and that of the planet. The impact on global ecological stability of even the world's most bloated cities is a trifle by comparison with that of the agricultural technologies that have been adapted to feed a swollen human population. As Lovelock again puts it:

> we are moving towards eight billion people with more than ten billion sheep and cattle, and six billion poultry. We use much of the productive soil to grow a very limited range of crop plants, and process far too much of this food inefficiently through cattle. Moreover, our capacity to modify the environment is greatly increased by the use of fertilizers, ecocidal chemicals, and earth-moving and tree-cutting machinery.... Bad farming is probably the greatest threat to Gaia's health.[64]

Or, as Edward Goldsmith has observed:

> The rapid degradation of the world's remaining agricultural lands is invariably attributed by governments and international agencies to traditional agricultural techniques. Thus US Aid attributes the rapid deterioration of 'the soil resource base' in arid lands to mismanagement, based on the use of 'traditional technology and agricultural practices' – though these technologies have been used sustainably for thousands of years.... Malnutrition and farming are also attributed to archaic agricultural practices, and, in particular, to low inputs of fertiliser. A report based on a 20-year study jointly undertaken by the Food and Agricultural Organisation (FAO) and other organisations insists that the amount of food produced in the world is a direct function of fertiliser use, without mentioning the diminishing returns on excessive applications of fertiliser experienced whenever farmers have adopted modern agricultural methods.[65]

What does this mean for farming policy in a country such as Britain? Writing over twenty years ago, Robert Waller observed that

> The whole framework of prices, grants, subsidies and incentives within which he [the farmer] will be working will ... favour intensification. It developed basically within the 1947 Agricultural Act. This well-intentioned Act was designed to shield the farmer against the forces of the free market by fixing prices and subsidies that would assure him a reasonable livelihood. In practice it has had the opposite effect.[66]

Commenting on the ecological effects of intensive farming practices, Waller notes that:

> Each one of the different technologies used to increase intensification is subject to a fundamental law of diminishing returns. Slowly the countless disadvantages resulting from each new input of machinery, fertilizer, pesticides, etc., will begin to outweigh their initial advantages. This process must render each further increment of growth achieved by these means progressively less profitable, until such time as negative returns set in.[67]

Intensive farming practices of this sort have been further reinforced by the provisions of the European Community's Common Agricultural Policy, which subsidises overproduction. The question arises as to what policy framework for agriculture in Britain can be commended on grounds common to both Green and conservative perspectives, and by what standards current practices are to be assessed.

It is plain that the iniquitous Common Agricultural Policy must be phased out. At the same time, it is no less evident that subjecting farming, in Britain or in similar countries, to the exigencies of global markets is a recipe for environmental short-termism. (It is possible that the market reform of agriculture in New Zealand constitutes an exception to this generalisation; but I cannot pursue the point here.) Wherever there remain small and medium sized farms which are embedded in local communities to whose viability they make a decisive contribution, they deserve support and shelter from the global market if they cannot otherwise survive. The policy of subsidising highly intensive, 'efficient' farming is precisely the opposite of that which is appropriate, when less 'efficient' farms, which have perhaps renewed themselves over several generations in contexts of markets that were not globalised, are at risk. The general function of tariffs and subsidies in relation to agriculture should be to act as an incentive to move away from high-intensive 'efficiency', rather than the contrary. (Agricultural subsidies may have, also, a strategic military justification, as in the Swiss and Japanese examples. This provides a further reason against the adoption of unrestrained free markets in farming.) In Britain, it is at least arguable that current CAP subsidies should be redirected to the support of organic farming methods which have a low impact on the soil and its related ecosystems, including a less intensive and more humane regime of life for breeding and caring for farm animals. It is not only arguable but also manifestly sensible, from any point of view which can be shared by genuine conservatives and Greens, that the destruction of small farms in the present economic depression should be arrested by reforms of current subsidy arrangements which take proper account both of the impact of farming practices on the natural environment and of the contribution of farming to the maintenance of rural community life.

It is no part of my brief here to try to specify the details of a sensible policy for agriculture in Britain. The goal of the argument is the simpler one of urging the repudiation of any agricultural policy which applies to farming norms of industrial productivity that neglect the non-renewability of many of the natural resources that enter into farming, which promote the further industrialisation of farming, and which do not recognise the contribution that farming makes to the renewal of rural communities as one of its larger social benefits. It is this general framework of thought that must be applied to the details of policy as they pertain to the different varieties of farming which currently exist in Britain.

Urban and transport policy

A village or small town must ... be arranged so as to confer on it a feeling of wholeness and oneness. In south-west France, the two neighbouring towns of Marmande and Villeneuve-sur-Lo are said to exert very different influences on their inhabitants. The former is stretched out along a main road, the latter, an ancient *bastille*, is built round a central square. Of the two, it is the latter which is known for its spirited community.

   Cities ... should also be designed on similar principles if they are to satisfy social needs. The central square is a very important feature, offering a place where the citizens can gather to run their affairs. The Greeks could not conceive a city without its *agora*. Significantly, in the industrial cities of the West, as economic concerns take over from social ones, it is the shopping precinct with its multi-storied car park that is the focal point.

(Edward Goldsmith)[68]

The typical American male devotes more than 1,600 hours to his car.... He spends four of his sixteen waking hours on the road or gathering his resources for it. And this figure does not take into account the time consumed by other activities dictated by transport: time spent in hospitals, traffic courts and garages.... The model American puts in 1,600 hours to get 7,500 miles: less than five miles per hour. In countries deprived of a transportation industry, people manage to do the same, walking wherever they want to go, and they allocate only three to eight per cent of their society's time budget to traffic instead of 29 per cent. What distinguishes the traffic in rich countries from the traffic in poor countries is not more mileage per hour of life-time for the majority, but more hours of compulsory consumption of high doses of energy, packaged and unequally distributed by the transportation industry.

(Ivan Illich)[69]

One feature of the Green conservative agenda that is central to my case has been intimated already, at several stages of the argument: namely, the rejection of a Green nostalgist hostility to the city, and of the corresponding arcadian conception of country life. To be sure, our discussion of agricultural policy has stressed the vital need to preserve rural communities, and to resist their destruction by crass development programmes and by the unfettered global market; and it will not be suggested that the good life can only be lived in cities. Green nostalgism for a lost (and, no doubt, substantially delusive) rural idyll is dangerous, nevertheless, in that it tends to obscure the real threats that now exist to one of humankind's most civilised institutional inventions, the city. It is the overdevelopment of the city, its deformation as a megalopolis, and its increasing insensitivity to the needs of those who labour and dwell in it that should be at the heart of an agenda of policy which is held in common by Greens and conservatives alike. In truth, the death of the city – an accomplished fact in parts of the United States – should be seen as a disaster in human ecology. The real and present danger is that it is occurring, in many modern countries, slowly and all but imperceptibly, but with ultimate effects on human social order which are all too visible in the limiting case of Detroit.

Urban policy and transport policy are, of course, closely interlinked – so closely that it may be worth looking at some of the absurdities of current transport policies (and the lack of them) before proceeding, with London as our exemplar, to try to say something on the larger issues of urban conservation and reconstruction. Since transport policy is a large and complex subject, my aim here, as elsewhere in this chapter, is not to prescribe in detail; such a task would be not only beyond my competence but also profitless, given the very different policy dilemmas in different countries, and even within Britain. Instead, my aim is to sketch a rough outline of thought for policy which is animated by values of conservation and concern for the common life. The inevitable point of departure for critical reflection in the arena of transport policy, in Britain and in many Western countries, is its fatal domination by the private motor car and its requirements. The private motor car will always have a place in transport, and the argument I shall develop against it does not aim to eliminate that role; instead, my goal is to question the dominant place of the car in modern transport, and to do so by showing that its dominance is prejudicial to the common environment.

It may be worth glancing at a few global facts about cars and their effect on the environment before we look at their national and local impact. In under forty years (1950–88) the number of cars on the road across the world has multiplied by nearly ten times, from 53 million to 500 million. Cars account for about one half of all air pollution, with three hundred pounds of 'greenhouse gas', carbon dioxide, being eventually released into the atmosphere for every fifteen gallons filled up. Worldwide, car accidents kill around a quarter of a million people, and seriously injure three million. The number of passenger cars rose by five times between the fifties and the late eighties. In Britain, each mile of a British motorway demands 25 acres of land, and each year up to 4,000 acres of rural land are paved over to be used as roads. Further, cars are extremely inefficient as a mode of transportation, both in terms of the number of people they carry, and because cars efficiently convert only 2–3 per cent of the potential energy in the oil refined for their use. The case against the private passenger car as a mode of transportation, stated solely in terms of its effects on the physical environment, is overwhelming.[70]

It is not the physical costs of over-reliance on the car but its impact on the life of urban (and other) communities that I want to focus on here. The impact of the car on cities is to destroy them as human settlements in which generations of people live and work together. It is well to recall that cities have not, traditionally, been concrete wastelands to which people repair only to work, and then flee; they have not been segregated by occupation or age, or carved up into residential and business areas; and they have, in consequence, been communities, not traffic intersections for transients whose lives are elsewhere and which at night have the funereal character of a deserted stage-set. Yet, at any rate in Britain today, this is what cities are fast becoming. As has recently been observed, 'London is becoming more mono-functional, increasingly divided into ghettos of poverty and affluence disrupted by traffic noise and pollution.'[71] And the reason for this degeneration is, in substantial part, to be found in the tyranny of the car: 'Leaving aside the costs of lost productivity caused by congestion, and the toll of deaths, injury and ill health, road traffic does more than anything else to undermine city neighbourhoods. Streets meant for shopping and meeting, green areas designed as places of recreation and relaxation become, respectively, trunk roads and roundabouts.'[72] The restoration of cities as public places for the enaction of the common life demands, first and foremost, policies for the drastic curtailment within cities of the motor car; a policy objective that is in any case justified by the deleterious effect on the health of city dwellers of car-related pollution.

No doubt an extension of market institutions into traffic control will be helpful to this end. Road-pricing, which has been technically feasible for some time but remains politically disfavoured, is a good example of the imaginative use in urban contexts of the price mechanism in the service of environmental concerns. It is hard to see how market solutions, by themselves, can be of much further use. An increase in petrol taxation might be defensible, though it is a blunt instrument of policy. Emission taxes on larger, less efficient cars are more worthy of serious consideration. Most importantly, however, is the recognition by policy-makers that only a massive expansion of public transport in Britain will diminish the role of the private car, with all of its environmental costs. One feature of such an expansion would undoubtedly be the enhancement of facilities for walkers and cyclists: in Britain, 37 per cent of passenger journeys and 32 per cent of travel time occur via walking or cycling, but these basic freedoms of mobility are very poorly planned for. The expansion of bus, railway and (in London and similar cities) underground services is a vital part of a policy aiming to curb the appetite (and the need) for the private car. Here we need to note that public transport may be privately owned and operated, and may (as with the growth of jitney services since coach deregulation in Britain) benefit from measures of economic liberalisation. In transport, as elsewhere, there may well be a case for public funding of privately operated services, and so for privatisation, where this does not create a private monopoly but rather promotes market competition. What cannot be shirked is the necessity in many areas of transport policy – rural buses being an obvious example – of governmental subsidy for environmental purposes. (In this connection, current proposals for the privatisation of British Rail are, at best, an exercise in irrelevance.) In transport, as in urban policy, few things are more pernicious than the market model of private persons making their several decisions. Such a model is bound to result in the running down of infrastructure – except for elements of it which benefit powerful interest groups, such as the motor industry – and the further erosion of communities and of cities as human settlements that contain communities.

The renewal and development of infrastructure in cities, at least in those built on the classic European model, requires decision-making by strategic planning authorities of a sort that can only be unthinkable to doctrinaire advocates of *laissez-faire*. This is not to say that intervention in the life of cities by governments has always been, or is ever likely to be, invariably beneficial: in Britain it involved the destruction of working-class communities by municipal housing programmes, and in the United States the further marginalisation of black communities by urban renewal policies.[73] The risks of further policy mistakes of this sort are unavoidable but against these we must set the certainty that uncontrolled private development will evacuate cities of their common life, and produce a common environment that is anomic, chaotic and aesthetically repellent. Both conservatives and Greens must acknowledge that only strategic planning authorities, of the sorts that are active in all of the other major European cities, can preserve British cities as places of aesthetic integrity and human amenity, as human settlements in which the inherently public goods of common life are protected.

Concern for the aesthetic integrity of cities confers on planning authorities another important responsibility: that of preserving the city as a place of pleasing buildings, in harmonious styles, and of composing a beautiful landscape and living-place. In part, the task of such authorities will reasonably be conservative and restrictive, that of denying planning permission to developments which would disrupt local architectural styles or would diminish the city as a setting for common life. An excellent example is that of the municipal authorities in Salzburg, who granted permission for a McDonald's outlet in that city only on condition that its architecture conform to the traditional style of the city. Such authorities will also reasonably concern themselves with restoration: with removing the uninhabited ruins of architectural modernism and replacing them with buildings which are worth living in and looking at. That this is not a utopian vision is shown by the real examples that we have in such European cities as Siena and Barcelona. Throughout much of Europe, but as yet very intermittently in Britain where planning institutions remain weak, cities have been renewed and conserved by imaginative and resourceful planning. Such planning will be rejected by *laissez-faire* dogmatists, who cannot grasp that the city is a form of life in itself, and not an individualist congeries of strangers; but the conservative pedigree of such planning policies for cities is impeccable, reaching back in Europe for centuries.

Such policies are radical in effect, but conservative in inspiration. Limiting the private passenger car – which one American conservative has called 'the mechanical Jacobin'[74] – is a potent corrective against the further weakening of the ties of street and local communities. Restoring cities as public places which are safe and pleasing, and in which we may take pride, gives an occasion for civic virtue, in the absence of which we are a society of transients. Even where, as will often be the case, national governmental funding is necessary for urban regeneration, it is best disbursed at local level, where it will be most responsive to the feedback of local people. Wherever market institutions can be introduced which facilitate this feedback, there is a strong case for their adoption. On this basis, it may well be worth considering charging for local services, when these are not elements in inherently public goods and so aspects of the common life, and where the price is genuinely responsive to consumers. However, for conservatives who are not mesmerised by the delusive harmonies of neo-liberalism and for Greens, the task of protecting and renewing the city cannot be envisaged, let alone achieved, without strategic planning by local authorities of infrastructural development, which reproduces the common environment within which cities can renew themselves as living human settlements whose members span the generations.

Education and health

> When cities are built around vehicles, they devalue human feet; when schools pre-empt learning, they devalue the autodidact; when hospitals draft all those who are in critical condition, they impose on society a new form of dying.
>
> (Ivan Ilich)[75]

It is obvious that the current condition of educational institutions in Britain, and still more in the United States, offers little of comfort to conservatives. Schools regularly fail to achieve their most basic goals of inculcating literacy and numeracy in children; they are staffed by teachers whose competence and performance are not monitored, and who often cleave to out-moded progressive teaching methods that have long proved demonstrably ineffective; and, in the inner cities, they are plagued by mass truancy. Higher education is a bastion of an antinomian counter-culture whose relationship to the rest of society is one of well-cultivated hostility. It is plain that educational institutions are transmitting neither the skills nor the values whereby a stable society renews itself.

The response to this predicament by neo-liberals has been to advocate the privatisation of schools and other educational institutions, or at least the introduction into them of market institutions. I have elsewhere criticised the commonest variation on this neo-liberal response, the proposal of a voucher scheme for schools, on a variety of grounds.[76] It should be said that actual conservative policy on education in Britain has not followed the voucher route, but has instead focused on releasing state schools from the control of local educational authorities by giving them the freedom to 'opt-out' and become centrally funded, but self-governing institutions, constrained only by the provisions of the national curriculum. This is a framework for policy in schooling that neo-liberals predictably attack, despite the fact that bringing state schools under the national funding umbrella emancipates them from far more invasive local authorities, and to that extent insulates them from political influence. The resultant situation can hardly be worse than that which preceded it, and may well in some respects be significantly better.

Voucher schemes do not in any case go to the root of the problems of modern schooling in a country such as Britain, which arise from the transformation of education into an arm of industry, and from the institutional monopoly which schools themselves have over learning. Schooling as we know it in Britain today is not much more than a century old. Literacy and numeracy were spreading quickly and widely among ordinary people in the nineteenth century well before compulsory schooling was instituted,[77] and the contribution of schools to their further promotion – like that of medical care to the prevention of disease – is easily exaggerated. The decline that has occurred in educational standards in Britain since the 1960s, say, has further limited the role of schools in transmitting essential skills and values. It has done so, pretty well across the board of the different varieties of schools, with some private schools doing less well than some state schools when measured by traditional standards. Doubtless the reckless experimentation with teaching methods and curricula in the state schools in the sixties, the headlong rush into comprehensivation and the near-abolition of selective state schools during that period, all contributed to the erosion of educational standards. It is noteworthy, however, that it is the adoption of progressive methods of teaching which seems the decisive variable here, and that this was spread across both state and private schools. Privatisation of itself would accordingly be no remedy for this decline, which has deeper institutional and cultural roots. From this point of view, neo-liberal voucher schemes are merely an irrelevance.

The chief defect of voucher schemes, from the standpoint of a conservative (or a Green) who is concerned with the renewal of community, is that they fail to address the institutional monopoly of learning by schools. Such a monopoly was tolerable, when teaching in schools was governed by a tacit curriculum of inherited skills, values and cultural understandings that expressed the traditions of local communities; it becomes insupportable when schools are estranged from the communities that they are supposed to serve, and reproduce themselves (rather than their communities) in alienated unemployables. Though Britain contains many good schools, in the maintained as well as in the private sector, in which something akin to a traditional education is still offered, it is increasingly plain that schools as institutions have, on the whole, become insensitive to the skills and traditions that they exist to transmit, and often indifferent to the communities that they serve. Voucher schemes have the merit of extending to the poor a range of choice which is currently enjoyed by the affluent, and of ending the inequity whereby families of modest means, who nevertheless scrape up the means to finance private education for their children, end up paying twice. It is unclear that voucher schemes, as currently advocated by neo-liberals, would do much, if anything, to remedy the failings that belong generically to the majority of contemporary schools, state-supported and private.

One solution to this dilemma may be in a system of educational credits for all, which is not tied to attendance at schools but instead to measured achievement in literacy and numeracy, the two most basic skills which present schooling inculcates least successfully. The basic content of such a scheme has been set out by Illich, programmatically:

> Right now educational credit good at any skill center could be provided in limited amounts for people of all ages, and not just to the poor. I envisage such credit in the form of an educational passport or an 'edu-credit card' provided to each citizen at birth. In order to favour the poor, who would probably not use their yearly grants early in life, a provision could be made that interest accrue to later users of cumulated 'entitlements'. Such credits would permit most people to acquire the skills most in demand, at their convenience, better, faster, cheaper and with fewer undesirable side effects than in school.[78]

There is little doubt that enabling pupils, or their families, to choose among a range of venues and methods of learning, which were not restricted to the institution of the school, would result in a blossoming in many fields of teaching of traditional teaching methods. As Illich notes:

> The strongly motivated student who is faced with the task of acquiring a new and complex skill may benefit greatly from the discipline now associated with the old-fashioned schoolmaster who taught reading, Hebrew, catechism or multiplication by rote. School has now made this kind of drill teaching rare and disreputable, yet there are many skills which a motivated student with normal aptitudes can master in a matter of a few months if taught in the traditional way. This is as true of codes as of their encipherment; of second and third languages as of reading and writing; and equally of special languages such as algebra, computer programming, chemical analysis, or of manual skills like typing, watchmaking, plumbing, wiring, TV repair; or, for that matter, dancing, drawing and diving.... At present schools pre-empt most educational funds. Drill instruction which costs less than comparable schooling is now a privilege of those rich enough to bypass the schools, and those whom either the army or big business sends through in-service training.[79]

The central idea of such a proposal is akin to that of the voucher, in that it confers purchasing power on individuals for the acquisition (in a context of market competition for their provision) of a specified range of services; but it differs radically from the voucher scheme, as it figures in recent neo-liberal policy proposals, in not requiring that the services be provided in a specific institutional setting (the school) and therefore in not presupposing attendance in schools. In this way it goes much further than any neo-liberal measure could: it not only severs public financing of a good from its market provision but also severs its provision from the narrow context of any specific institution – in this case, the declining institution of the school. It thereby cuts a Gordian knot in neo-liberal policy: that surrounding compulsory schooling and the definition of schools themselves. In this proposal, education credit could be used in any institutional context (including that of schools) which could show a record of achievement in transmitting specific skills. The obligation on families would not be to assure school attendance by their children, but to enable them (with the use of the educational credits) to acquire specified basic skills. These latter could be subject to assessment by state examinations (as proposed over a century ago by J.S. Mill)[80] and the institutions, or 'skill centres', which taught them would also be subject to governmental accreditation, based on objective performance criteria for the transmission of the skills; both of these would be legitimate uses of governmental activity. (Of course, the obligations of families in bringing up their children to specified levels of literacy and numeracy would need to be qualified with respect to disability and retardation; but this is, I think, a matter of detail in the overall proposal, which does not affect its major thrust.) At the same time, the compulsory element in schooling would have been removed, and the privileging of schools with governmental finance (an objectionable feature of all current voucher schemes) would have been ended: school would have been disestablished. One predictable result of exposing schools in this way to competition by non-school institutions would be a drastic and rapid improvement in the quality of schooling itself.

The educational credit proposal, like the voucher schemes it is designed to supplant, need not come in only one form; it could have many variations and be introduced in a series of incremental steps. For the vast majority where incomes are adequate, it could take the form of a tax credit for each child, to be spent at any accredited school, state or private, and at any accredited, non-school 'skill centre'. For those whose incomes are too low for tax credits to be feasible, an educational credit card (akin to the voucher) would be needed, usable on the same liberal terms as tax credits. Providing that a poverty trap was not thereby created, there is no reason why, in the interests of opening up opportunities for the worst-off, such a credit card for learning purposes need not be worth significantly more than the tax credits of more affluent families. Equally, as Illich indicates, there is no reason why such a learning credit card should be restricted to children: it could, and should, be available as a means of re-skilling (or skilling for the first time) those who discover, later in life, that schools have failed them, or whose existing skills have been rendered obsolete by economic or social change. In this proposal, learning is conceived as a life-long engagement whose limits are not those of the institution of the school, but only of the lives of learners. The basic skills specified for children would, by necessity, be different from (and far more uniform than) those needed by most people later in life, and monitoring and accreditation procedures would differ accordingly. The device of an educational credit would link learning at all levels, nevertheless, while freeing it from the disabling confines of an institution from which traditional understandings of learning and teaching have often vanished.

From a conservative perspective, a radical proposal on the lines sketched has the advantage of promising to revivify traditions of learning in all of their variety. From a Green perspective that is shared by conservatives, it should be welcomed as rendering more permeable the barriers between learning and working, between work and leisure, that disfigure modernist societies. The prospect opened up by such a proposal is that of learning occurring in the context of a common life which harbours flourishing schools, but in which the school is no longer a hermetic institution, whose funding and legal status separate it from the vernacular transactions of its supporting communities. Of course, the disestablishment of school does not mean that there will be no schools, any more than the disestablishment of churches means that there are to be no more churches; nor, in the proposal here advanced (as distinct, perhaps, from that of Illich) does it mean that people may not use their educational credits to acquire an education in schools. The proposal is designed to foster greater institutional pluralism in learning and, as a likely result of such diversity, to restore or save otherwise disappearing (but none the less highly effective) traditions in education. It may be that the disestablishment of school is now, in some countries such as Britain and the United States, the only measure that can rescue traditional understandings of teaching and learning. Arguably, and ironically, it may be the only way to save schools from what is otherwise their manifest fate – that of becoming adjuncts to an industrial economy, for which, no less ironically, they produce workers lacking in most of the skills and moral capacities that are demanded by work in the conditions of late industrial society. It is in order to deliver schools from this fate of becoming a hybrid institution, part prison, part playground, part outdoor poor relief, that the radical measure of disestablishment is contemplated.

It is not envisaged that a radical measure of this sort could or should be introduced rapidly in Britain, or similar countries. Incremental and gradualist measures are clearly appropriate. A reduction (rather than outright abolition) of the compulsory school leaving age, together with the provision of educational credit for those who choose this option, is one such incremental measure. No doubt there are many others which might be conceived. A weighty consideration in framing all such gradualist measures is that they enhance the capacity for exit – currently zero, aside from that afforded by truancy – of the poorest members of our society, who are worst served by schools. Accordingly, if vouchers are to figure as an element in a phased policy of school disestablishment, they should begin by being conferred upon the poorest families, who have most need for them. No measure could do more to prevent the further growth in Britain of an estranged underclass, unemployable across several generations, which – as the American experience graphically illustrates – constitutes one of the greatest impediments to a harmonious common life in our cities. And, in any case, no measure can be justified, in this or other areas of policy, which does not enhance the well-being of those positioned in the underclass as the direct result of their being trapped in ghettos created by the misconceived interventionist policies of an earlier generation.

Sensible reflection on a conservative policy for health care begins with the recognition that ideally acceptable institutions for the promotion of health and the care of the sick exist nowhere in the world. Countries, such as those of the post-communist bloc, which have attempted a full-scale, comprehensive socialisation of medical care have produced a morass of corruption in which medical resources are scarce and very inequitably distributed. They embody a model for health that no sane conservative (or Green) would wish to emulate. However, the American market-driven system of medical care is hardly a model that any sane conservative would adopt either. With costs climbing inexorably towards a sixth of US gross domestic product, plagued by litigation and defensive medicine, strait-jacketed by the worst drug-testing bureaucracy in the world, and leaving nearly forty million of its citizens without medical coverage of any systematic sort, the American system of medical care performs extremely poorly by comparison with the systems of countries such as Britain and Greece which, unlike the USA, spend only a fraction of their GDP on medical care. In fact, the British National Health Service performs remarkably well, both in terms of cost-containment and in terms of its adequacy as perceived by its users in many areas of care. Indeed, current reform measures, aiming at the creation within the NHS of markets through the transformation of hospitals into independent trusts, may well prove costly remedies for tolerable ills in the old system, which a genuine conservative policy should probably have left alone. (This is not to say that current reform measures can or should be reversed; any future administration has no option but to try to make them work.) Certainly, no policy for the National Health Service could be worse conceived than one of privatisation or marketisation on the American model, given its record.

Reform of the National Health Service in Britain, like reform of other systems of health care in other countries, begins by accepting a few truisms which are denied by many in the current Pelagian climate of opinion but which are central to both conservative and Green outlooks on human life. There must first be acceptance of the limits of medical care. We are all going to die, and it cannot be the proper office of medical care to thwart the course of nature; rather, to assist and smooth its way. Many, if not most, episodic ailments are self-limiting: either the healing resources of the body cope with them or else death supervenes. Medical care can help in moments of crisis and can assist in adapting to chronic illness; it cannot wipe out sickness or conjure away our mortality. When it attempts to do so, iatrogenic illness becomes a worse affliction than those that befall us in the natural course of things. Much modern medicine is pathological in its denial of death and reflects the broader culture of which it is a part in refusing to recognise that we may thrive in dying, even as our souls may perish in senseless longevity. Virtually all of modern medical care resists this implication, but it is an inexorable result of existing medical technology, which can keep us 'alive' almost indefinitely, that death must henceforth be for us – except in the context of catastrophic accident – a chosen option, if we are to be spared the death-in-life that follows from many forms of illness, disability and senility. This is a crucial point to which I shall return.

Medicine can do little about the frailties of our condition, and nothing about our mortality; these remain subject to fortune and genetic fate. It must be accepted, also, that medical care has contributed comparatively little to the improvement of health that has undoubtedly occurred in recent times. This, as Illich and others have amply shown,[81] arises far more from improvements in sanitation and other aspects of the environment, in diet and in lifestyle, than from any sort of medical intervention. The task of medicine, which is understood in Britain by wise general practitioners, is often, if not typically, to help patients to cope with ailments which arise from their lives as a whole and which medical intervention cannot hope to cure. For the most part, our ailments arise from the way in which we live (or the genes that we have acquired in the genetic lottery); we cannot hope for a medical cure for them, we can hope only, at best, for their alleviation. This is a truth which is obscured by popular discourse of 'the war against cancer' – as if death were an enemy that could be vanquished rather than, at last, a friend to be welcomed – and which is denied in macabre high-tech medicine involving organ transplantation. The major phases in the human life-cycle are not necessarily occasions for medical intervention. For millennia, people have been born, have suffered pain and illness, and have died, without these occurrences being understood as treatable disorders. There remain many who wish their children to be born at home, their illnesses and old age to be lived through at home, and who want to die at home. The medicalisation of human life, which has occurred in all modern societies, increasingly denies us these options. As Illich has put it, describing one end of the spectrum of this medicalisation of the human life-cycle: 'Only the very rich and the very independent can choose to avoid that medicalisation of the end to which the poor must submit and which becomes increasingly intense and universal as the society they live in becomes richer.'[82] The question remains, what is to be done to reverse this trend to ever greater medicalisation of human life? And how might such an objective be achieved, while preserving (or extending) access to basic, decent medical care, where this is a manifest human need? Illich has stated, in the most general terms, what needs to be done:

> In several nations, the public is now ready for a review of its health-care system. Although there is a serious danger that the forthcoming debate will reinforce the present frustrating medicalisation of life, the debate could still become fruitful if attention were focused on medical nemesis, if the recovery of personal responsibility for health care were made the central issue, and if limitations on professional monopolies were made the major goal of legislation.[83]

Let us see how this programmatic statement might be applied in the context of a country such as Britain.

It must be acknowledged, first of all, that many medical procedures, which are currently restricted to members of the medical profession, can be performed safely and intelligently by trained laypeople. The tendency to further professionalisation of medical care must be resisted and reversed, professional monopolies curbed or broken, and competency in a variety of medical tasks allowed to para-medical personnel. Even the licensure of physicians itself – the corner-stone of the privilege of the medical guild in the United States, but important in Britain also – must come under critical questioning, as should the ever-increasing designation of medicines as prescription-only medications. It would, of course, be absurd to propose, in the fashion of radical libertarian critics of contemporary institutions such as Szasz, that all legal limitations on medical practice and on pharmaceutical freedom be abolished forthwith; that is a measure that no conservative or Green thinker could sensibly support. There is nevertheless every reason for professional monopolies to be curtailed and pharmaceutical freedoms enhanced, in order to achieve the recovery of personal responsibility for health and the reversal of the dehumanising medicalisation of life. The contemporary world contains a variety of regimes for the medical profession: pharmaceutical freedom is significantly greater in Continental Europe and in Latin America than in English-speaking countries (of which the United States is, by far, the most restrictive); the freedoms and competencies of nurses, midwives, pharmacists, opticians and others in the medical professions vary widely across jurisdictions; and different countries are at different stages on the road to the medicalisation of life that the omnicompetent authority of the medical guild carries with it. There is no reason why a policy of restoring personal responsibility for health should not borrow eclectically from these differing regimes for the medical profession, with a view to relaxing and, perhaps, eventually curtailing the professional monopoly of doctors.

In this connection, the recovery of personal responsibility for health would be assisted by reforms in the funding of health services. In Britain, where the National Health Service will remain the corner-stone of health care, there is a good case for a hypothecated health tax, with an exit option for those who prefer private arrangements solely. Such an exit option should be framed to permit those who exercise it to use the resources so released not only on conventional medical care but also on alternative therapies which are, at present, only rarely available within the NHS. Two further fundamental points must here be recognised: first, the relative performance and the epistemological credentials of conventional medicine, as compared with many alternative therapies, are far less impressive than mainstream opinion allows; second, the choice among therapies, conventional or alternative, should so far as is practicable be that of the patient him/herself. An enabling condition of such freedom among therapeutic regimes, however, is a revision of the neo-liberal health voucher, analogous to that proposed earlier for the education voucher, such that it covers alternative traditions of medicine and not only that of conventional, scientist Western medicine. To be sure, there will always be a shifting borderline between what is counted as medical care and what is regarded as a genuine alternative tradition of medical theory and practice. In part, this arises from our irremediable ignorance – obscured by much mainstream medical authority – of what is best for our health. As Illich observes,

> Nobody knows how much health care will be worth to him in terms of money and pain. In addition, nobody knows if the most advantageous form of health care is obtained from medical producers, from a travel agent, or by renouncing work on the night shift. The family that forgoes a car to move to a Manhattan apartment can foresee how the substitution of rent for gas will affect their available time; but the person who, upon the diagnosis of cancer, chooses an operation over a binge in the Bahamas does not know what effect his choice will have on his remaining time of grace. The economics of health is a curious discipline, somewhat reminiscent of the theology of indulgences that flourished before Luther. You can count what the friars collect, you can look at the temples they build, you can take part in the liturgies they indulge in, but you can only guess what the traffic in remission from purgatory does to the soul after death. Models developed to account for the willingness of taxpayers to foot rising medical bills constitute similar scholastic guesswork about the new world-spanning church of medicine.[84]

Our ignorance as to what are the best remedies for our ailments justifies the most liberal form of voucher, or health credit scheme, for those who wish to opt out of the NHS. (It also supports moves towards greater diversity in medical traditions within the NHS, as I shall argue later.) Of course, this amended voucher proposal could not escape all of the difficulties of standard neo-liberal proposals: difficulties created by disability, uninsurability, and so on. It would therefore be a serious error to regard it – as neo-liberals regard their own pet measures – as a panacea for all of the dilemmas of health care. In promoting choice and pluralism in health care, however, it would also do its bit for the recovery of personal responsibility for health that should be the aim of conservatives and Greens alike. Recognising that both the perception of health and the definition of illness are personal judgements rooted in cultural traditions, it would devolve health care decisions to the level of specific individuals in definite communities. The aim would be to promote individual choice of medical services in the context of a pluralistic diversity of medical institutions and traditions, with professional monopoly being progressively relaxed, so that an ever greater variety of practitioners – herbalists, homeopaths, acupuncturists, holistic and traditional doctors, and so forth – could, through the unfettered choice of individuals in their communities, receive support from an extended health credit system. (As noted above, such credits would need to be fine-tuned, so as to be significantly greater for those – the disabled, the chronic sick, and so on – with greater medical needs. The problems that are raised by such fine-tuning do not seem to me to be insoluble or to affect the proposal decisively.) The proposal which is advanced would have the inestimable advantage, not possessed by standard neo-liberal measures, of promoting competition not only between the NHS and private practice but also between orthodox and alternative medical practices and traditions.

All systems of health care, including one containing an extended medical credit scheme of the sort sketched above, are systems for the rationing of medical resources. Not all medical needs are insatiable (contrary to neo-liberal dogma); but enough of them have the property of insatiability to make rationing – by price, formula or clinical discretion – unavoidable. Often such rationing involves decisions of life or death, or decisions which dictate the future quality of life of patients irreversibly. Any reform of medical care aiming to promote responsibility and enhance dignity must encompass measures enabling patients to reject medical care, and to prevent their unwilling survival. No scheme of reform of health care is adequate which does not contain measures for enabling and empowering patients as agents in these decisions. This entails the legal empowerment of patients, or of those whom they have assigned as their guardians, to request euthanasia, under conditions specified by the patient. Conservatives who resist arguments for euthanasia have not noticed that a natural death is, perhaps, rarer now than at any time in human history. It is threatened, for those in the highly industrialised societies, not (as hitherto in our history) by war or civil violence but instead by the medicalisation of human life: 'The technical and the non-technical consequences of institutional medicine coalesce and generate a new kind of suffering: anaesthetised, impotent and solitary survival in a world turned into a hospital ward.'[85] Only the legal availability of euthanasia, physician-assisted where necessary, as provided for in a version of the Living Will mandating termination of life under specified conditions, can end the absurdity and moral horror in which we currently warehouse for survival those who would, often enough, vastly prefer to exercise the ultimate form of exit option. Where natural death is an uncovenanted blessing which is denied to virtually all of us, resistance to the death-by-choice of voluntary euthanasia is not wisdom, conservative or otherwise, but rather a fetishisation of physical survival, which is condemned by all of the world's religions and offensive to human dignity. If patients are not in this most crucial of all decisions empowered as agents, then we transfer authority from responsible persons to the servants of medical institutions, themselves increasingly conceived as industries for the maintenance of human machines. We are then not far from the transforming of the patient into an object, and of medicine itself from a humane profession into a branch of biological engineering, whose ultimate output is soulless survival.

Reform of contemporary medical institutions and practice – in Britain, and in similar countries – cannot avoid taking the road of deprofessionalisation, of curbing and limiting professional monopoly over health care. An extended health voucher or health credit scheme of the sort proposed, though not without its difficulties, could assist in promoting this objective in the context of legal reforms to break down professional monopoly. No doubt there will always be a place for governmental involvement in health care, even in countries where health care is entirely privately provided, if only to guarantee that children's health be protected and public health safeguarded. In respect of adults, however, considerations of personal responsibility for health, and of our ignorance as to what is best for our health (shared by the medical profession in many cases), argue for the greatest feasible individual freedom. The extended health voucher, as discussed so far, together with provision for the ultimate exit option of euthanasia (in many circumstances, though not all, itself merely a refusal of further treatment) would go a very considerable distance toward this goal. A health credit which was usable in a diversity of medical traditions would meet Paul Feyerabend's desideratum that 'health and sickness are to be determined by the traditions to which the healthy or sick person belongs and within this tradition again by the particular ideal of life a person has formed for himself'.[86] Of course, there will always be a question, which can never be decided a priori, as to what is to count as a *bona fide* tradition of medical treatment and what as a medical service. It may be, for this reason, that individual freedom can only be safeguarded (the interests of children and the problems of public health aside) if the extended health credit, which is advanced here as part of an exit option from the National Health Service in Britain but which is applicable in other, similar countries, be returnable entirely to the individual as free purchasing power. This appears to be the logic of returning health care to personal responsibility.

It is not my argument that deprofessionalisation and the enhancement of personal freedom in medical care be applied solely in the context of an exit option from the NHS. On the contrary, the aim – as with an educational credit for non-school institutions, one of whose aims is the revitalisation of schooling – is to encourage these developments within the NHS also. This reflects my belief that, though a hypotheticated health tax with an exit option that is in the end redeemable as free purchasing power is defensible on grounds of personal freedom, the crucial considerations in the reform of health care are not whether its funding or organisation is public or private, but instead the degree of professional monopoly within it, the diversity of medical traditions available to the patient, and his or her opportunities for controlling the care offered to him or her. These are the decisive considerations that should govern health care reform in countries such as Britain, not narrow concerns about funding. The mix of funding and organisational arrangements for health care will, inevitably and desirably, vary considerably from country to country, and from time to time. Even in the case of Britain, there is no a priori way of determining the institutional mix that will be most appropriate for medical care in the future, except to say that the NHS will remain the point of departure for sensible reform, even if (as proposed here) there be instituted an exit option from it. No doubt the best institutional framework for health care in Britain is one that allows for the maximum of diversity in a setting that allows for, and has incentives for, further unplanned developments; but there is a variety of forms that this institutional framework might take, and I have not tried to settle here the issues between them. It is no part of the argument here to try to settle which of these arrangements is to be adopted, since none will be universally desirable and the relevant reasonings are always circumstantial, not applications of first principles. The general thesis remains: that conservative values of respect for individuals and for the communities in which they live their lives mandate a reform of health care which is aimed at limiting professional monopoly within it and promoting the recovery of personal responsibility for health. This – together with the recognition that frailty and mortality are parts of our condition, not treatable disorders in it – should be a framework of thought that is eminently acceptable to Greens.

CONCLUSION

> The project of science, as I understand it, is to solve the mystery, to wake us from our dream, to destroy the myth; and were this project fully achieved, not only should we find ourselves awake in a profound darkness, but a dreadful insomnia would settle upon mankind, not less intolerable for being only a nightmare.
>
> (Michael Oakeshott)[87]

> We know now that a completely planned heaven is either impossible or unbearable. We know that it is not true that design can come only out of planning. Out of luxuriant waste, unmoved by selection, come designs more beautiful and in greater variety than man could plan.
>
> (Garrett Hardin)[88]

My argument has been that there are many natural affinities between conservative philosophy and Green thought, from which both may profit. Conservatives must learn from Green thought that the promise of open-ended global growth, held out by today's neo-liberal descendants of Herbert Spencer, is delusive; instead they must turn their attention to the sources of legitimacy by which social institutions could be sustained in a stationary-state economy. In repudiating the fashionable heresies of neo-liberalism, conservatives are merely returning to an older and sounder Tory tradition, which perceived the illusoriness of the sovereign, autonomous chooser of liberal theory, and so insisted on the primacy of the common life. The importance of Green thought for conservatives today is that it recalls them to their historic task of giving shelter to communities and reproducing them across the generations – in a context of finite resources which dictates stability, not growth, as the pre-eminent conservative value.

An encounter between conservative and Green thought compels important revisions in some standard conservative positions. It is unreasonable for conservatives to disregard the dangers inherent in the present growth of human population, and perverse for them to resist measures for its control. Conservatives must learn to be open to radical criticism of current institutions of market capitalism and of the health and education professions, in so far as they are predicated on spurious promises of indefinite growth or open-ended progress, and so depart both from Green thought and from genuine conservative philosophy. Conservatives need to explore, with Greens and others, as yet unthought-of dilemmas of life in societies which are no longer buoyed up by the prospect of incessant economic growth or by modernist pseudo-religions of endless world-improvement.

On the other hand, Greens need from conservatives a vital tincture of realism without which their thought, and so their policy proposals, become merely utopian. It is supremely pointless for Greens to insist that the alternatives before our species are only a total transformation of our condition or oblivion. If that is so, we may confidently predict oblivion as our fate. In this, we would only be applying an aspect of the Gaia hypothesis, well stated by Lovelock:

> Gaia, as I see her, is no doting mother, tolerant of misdemeanours, nor is she some fragile and delicate damsel in danger from brutal mankind. She is stern and tough, always keeping the world warm and comfortable for those who obey the rules, but ruthless in her destruction of those who transgress. Her unconscious goal is a planet fit for life. If humans stand in the way of this, we shall be eliminated with as little pity as would be shown by the micro-brain of an intercontinental ballistic missile in full flight to its target.[89]

The prospect of a Gaian decimation of the world's human population has indeed been welcomed by the most radical supporters of the *wild-politik*, such as John Aspinall:

> Some of us are now drawn to believe that a demo-catastrophe will be an eco-bonanza. In other words, a population readjustment on a planetary scale from 4,000 million to something in the nature of 200 million would be the only possible solution for the survival of our species and of the eco-system or systems that nurtured us.

But Aspinall goes on immediately to ask what might the price be in terms of the well-being of other species, of such a catastrophic curtailment of human hubris:

> The next great death might last a millennium, but during it, and indeed before it, who knows how many genera of plant and bird and beast would be swept away?... What will be left? What will survive the holocaust? The surviving world must be a diminished world; at its worst, a world in apocalyptic, irreversible decline; at its best, one savagely mutilated, even dismembered.[90]

Only Panglossians – Marxist, neo-liberal, humanist or Pelagian – will gainsay Aspinall's apocalyptic vision. If there is any consolation, it comes from the Gaian hypothesis itself, which suggests that a reduction in bio-diversity might be the route to stability for the remaining life-forms on earth.

Lest these prospects seem overly apocalyptic, it is well to remind ourselves of one of the facts of our age that is rarely addressed by Greens, save in a spirit of pacifist wishfulfillment: that is, the apparently inexorable proliferation of ever cheaper technologies of mass destruction. It is worth recalling that the international order in which, for the while, we live, is a Hobbesian state of nature, an anarchy containing well over a hundred sovereign states. Of these states, many are desperately unstable, riven by internal ethnic and other conflicts; some, like Bangladesh or Indonesia, confront insuperable Malthusian problems; others, such as some African, Middle Eastern and Balkan states, are ruled by criminals or fanatics. To all of these states there is an uncontrollable leakage of weaponries of spiralling lethality – a leakage that has been massively increased in speed, magnitude and danger by the collapse of order in the former Soviet Union. It beggars belief to suppose that these weapons will not be used in the coming decades, with incalculable cost to human and other life. In former Yugoslavia, ethnic war of the sort that is likely to dominate the coming century has already ruined a fragile and precious part of the human environment, the city of Dubrovnik, and is degrading much of what is left of the natural environment. It is difficult not to foresee military convulsions, far vaster in scale than those in former Yugoslavia and using far more destructive technologies, wreaking irreparable harm on the environment in the years to come. If, for our species, the coming century looks like being one of wars, massacres and forced migrations, of which the holocausts of our own century are but precursors, for the other species with which we share a common environment the prospect looks hardly less bleak.

Such sobering prospects – whose realism will be doubted only by fundamentalist believers in progress – should occasion in both conservative and Green thinkers a mood of almost desperate humility. There will be no conversion to an ecological world-view that will deliver us from ourselves: we must make what little we can of the human animal as we find it. This means recognising that local environmental improvement can always be swept away by bandit states, by ecological terrorism or by Malthusian invasion: it is always precarious and ever endangered. In turn, for Greens, this should compel a revision of attitude to some recent technologies, including (hardest of all for Greens who see themselves as inheritors of earlier protest movements) the technologies involved in space-based defence systems. Fallible as the latter are, they are probably the best defence that we have in an intractably anarchic world against environmental catastrophes produced by weaponries of mass destruction. (Given the speed with which nuclear weapons systems can be reassembled, proposals for multilateral nuclear disarmament, like most arms control proposals, are of little avail. This is true even supposing – what is plainly false – that inspection and enforcement are always feasible. Such measures may have limited uses in specific contexts, as perhaps currently in negotiating between Russia and the Western allies; they do not solve problems of proliferation or obviate the need for space-based defence systems.) Green resistance to serious thought about the possibilities of such systems is only the clearest symptom of their refusal to contemplate the strategic–military dimensions of environmental conservation in our time. It is also an exemplar of the uncritically and unselectively hostile attitude of many Greens to new technologies with which, like them or not, we are saddled, and which we cannot hope to disinvent.

In part, such technologies as are involved in space-based defence systems are, like many others, prophylactic devices against other technologies which are otherwise uncontrollable. The task of using technology to tame itself is one that fate forces upon us. In this, as in so much else, Greens should heed the wise words of Lovelock, when he tells us that 'there can be no voluntary resignation from technology. We are so inextricably part of the technosphere that giving it up is as unrealistic as jumping off a ship in mid-Atlantic to swim the rest of the journey in glorious independence.'[91] Equally, Green hostility to the urban–industrial environment that modern humans have contrived for themselves misidentifies the real threats to their natural environment, which come from proliferating technologies of mass destruction, from farming, and, above all, from the growing deadweight of human numbers. As Lovelock has concluded: 'It seems therefore that the principal dangers to our planet arising from man's activities may not be the special and singular evils of his urbanized industrial existence.'[92] There can be no turning back from our current mode of life in cities, with its complex technologies; only a radical reform of them, with ecological stability as its aim. Protecting the environment from further human depredations will demand better technologies; it cannot be achieved by the Quixotist posture of trying to remove technology or abandon industrialism. Any people who attempted such a renunciation would soon be destroyed or conquered by others who had retained modern technology in its most invasive and destructive forms. This is a predicament that no ecological conversion can escape.

Green thought can learn from conservative philosophy the basic lesson of not looking after ultimate outcomes but, instead, of improvising humbly in order to avoid catastrophe and to stave off calamity. Green theory is an invaluable corrective of the Whiggish, anthropocentric, technological optimism by which all the modernist political religions are animated and which has, in the form of neo-liberalism, even infected most of what passes today as conservatism. From conservative philosophy, Greens must learn that the institutions of civil society are hard-won achievements, not to be casually thrown away for the sake of any ecological utopia. With all of their limitations and the needs that I have identified, which mandate their supplementation and restriction, the institutions of civil society – including market institutions, suitably amended – are the only set of institutions whereby any civilisation can in our age renew itself. The alternative to civil society – to an order of private property and contractual liberty, defined (and constrained) by a rule of a law that demarcates the spheres, and sets the boundaries, of autonomous social institutions – is only barbarism, in which both the human and the natural environments are laid waste. Our century is littered with the debris of political variations on Pascal's wager, in which people have gambled that the familiar conveniences of civil society can be transcended, and supplanted, by another order, whose outlines they could as yet only dimly perceive. All such wagers have proved to be bad bets. Greens would be more consistent, and more prudent, if they regarded the institutions of civil society, including the market economy, as elements in a social ecology or spontaneous order,[93] akin to those found in the ecologies of natural environments, which human reason can barely understand, let alone redesign. This is not to say that human environments – such as cities, or markets, for that matter – are invariably self-regulating, or that their workings cannot sometimes be improved upon by judicious intervention; but rather that intervention should typically take the form of alterations in the framework within which spontaneous activity occurs and which defines and limits property rights and contractual liberties, taxes and subsidies, and so on. In society, as in nature, we depend always on an order that we did not invent, and cannot re-create; our task can only be to remove the obstacles that we have ourselves put in the way of its natural healing, and, where this is not enough, to provide prophylaxis against hazards generated by our own virtuosity.

This may appear too humble a task for those who dream of ecological utopias, or who remain epigones of unlimited progress. In fact, the task of negotiating sensibly the transition to a stable social order is crucial. For latter-day Pelagians, it involves shedding the protective illusion of infinite improvement; for Greens, it means resisting the allures of arcadianism and utopianism. It is far from obvious that either the intelligence or the will exists among us in sufficient measure to make such a transition feasible. Behind the meliorist superstitions of the modern political religions and the Pelagianism that has conquered all of the traditional faiths, at least in the West, lies nihilism which, in becoming for the first time a mass philosophy, has also evoked its dialectical negation, fundamentalism, in many parts of the world. Further, contemporary science has itself assumed a fundamentalist form which – in the works of Monod[94] and Dawkins, for example – propagates a species of nihilism about nature and humanity's place in it. It is this species of scientism, in which fundamentalism and nihilism are conjoined, which allies itself with a sentimental humanism to give us the distinctive modernist world-view. Lovelock has justly characterised this view of things, and its narrow limitations, when he observes: 'Our humanist concerns about the poor of the inner cities or the Third World, and our near-obscene obsession with death, suffering, and pain as if these were evils in themselves – these thoughts divert the mind from our gross and excessive domination of the natural world.'[95] Certainly, ridding ourselves of a humanism that not only closes off any sense of transcendence but also lacks the reverence for nature and the tragic sense of life of genuine paganism is a precondition for any judicious assessment of our current environmental circumstances and prospects. It may indeed be that the Gaian vision, being free from the anthropocentrism which privileges humans in the universe and which even models the universe on humans, is the most appropriate antidote to this malady of the spirit that parades as enlightenment. It remains doubtful whether so subtle a vision can fill the spiritual emptiness of the masses of human beings who are lacking in transcendental faith and in respect for nature and for whom the promise of progress is proving a cruel joke.

Such a general condition of profound spiritual debility is ill-suited to the task of preserving the common environment that we inherit from our forebears and from nature itself. It may well be that a Gaian correction of the place of the human species in planetary ecology is the most likely outcome – even, perhaps, the least undesirable outcome – of current environmental trends. In the meantime, however, we are well occupied in doing good in minute particulars, in preserving what is left of beauty and wilderness in the natural world, and in doing what we can to tend and renew amenity and stability in the common environment of human settlements.

Notes

1 LIMITED GOVERNMENT: A POSITIVE AGENDA

1 Henry C. Simon, *Economic Policy for a Free Society*, Chicago: University of Chicago Press, 1948, pp. 41–2.
2 *Economist*, 20 August 1988, p. 52.
3 Ibid.
4 Michael Oakeshott, *Rationalism in Politics*, London and New York: Methuen, 1977, pp. 186–7.
5 I argue this point more systematically in 'After Liberalism' in my book, *Liberalisms: Essays in Political Philosophy*, London: Routledge, 1989.
6 Oakeshott, op. cit., p. 120.
7 I develop this argument more systematically in my book, *Liberalism*, Milton Keynes and Minneapolis: Open University Press and University of Minnesota Press, 1986, ch. 6.
8 I considered these questions in the context of a revised version of the liberal conception of the state in 'The politics of cultural diversity', my Latham Memorial Lecture at the University of Sydney, Australia, in September 1987. The text of this lecture was published in *Quadrant*, November 1987, reprinted as Chapter 18 of my book *Post-Liberalisms: Studies in political thought*, London: Routledge, 1993, and an abridged version appears in the *Salisbury Review*, Winter 1988.
9 Oakeshott, op. cit., pp. 40–1.
10 The so-called Rooker–Wise amendment (named after the two Labour Party MPs who tabled it) is a statutory requirement to uprate UK personal tax allowances in line with changes in the Retail Prices Index, i. e. allowing for inflation. It was first enacted in the Finance Act of 1977 and was later revised and expanded in the 1980 Finance Act.
11 See, especially, James Buchanan, *Liberty, Market and State*, Brighton: Harvester Press, 1986.
12 F.A. Hayek, *The Road to Serfdom*, London and Henley: Routledge & Kegan Paul, 1944.
13 F.A. Hayek, *The Constitution of Liberty*, London: Routledge & Kegan Paul, 1960, pp. 222–3.
14 Hayek, ibid., p. 126.
15 Samuel Brittan, *A Restatement of Economic Liberalism*, London: Macmillan, 1973 and 1988, p. 249.
16 F.A. Hayek, *Denationalisation of Money: An Analysis of the Theory and Practice of Concurrent Currencies*, Hobart Paper 70 (2nd edn, revised and enlarged), London: Institute of Economic Affairs, 1978.
17 For an argument to this conclusion, see M. Friedman and A.J. Schwartz, *A Monetary History of the United States, 1867–1960*, Princeton: Princeton University Press, 1963.
18 See Tim Congdon's excellent article, 'The Lawson Boom in the Light of the Crash', in *Economic Affairs* 8(3) Feb./March 1988, pp. 14–18. I should like to express my view that, although I reject on Hayekian grounds Congdon's positions on both methodology

and policy in monetary matters, his achievement in predicting the recent inflation, virtually alone among practising economists in Britain, is extraordinary and deserving of wider recognition. Rising inflation and interest rates in mid–1989 have further strengthened Congdon's historical analysis, which he has set out systematically in *Monetarism Lost: and Why it Must be Regained*, London: Centre for Policy Studies, May 1989.

19 James Buchanan and Gordon Tullock, *The Calculus of Consent*, Ann Arbor: University of Michigan Press, 1962.
20 James Buchanan and Geoffrey Brennan, *Monopoly in Money and Inflation: The Case for a Constitution to Discipline Government*, Hobart Paper 88, London: Institute of Economic Affairs, 1981.
21 Kevin Dowd, *Private Money: The Path to Monetary Stability*, Hobart Paper 112, London: Institute of Economic Affairs, 1988, pp. 58–9.
22 Hayek, *Denationalisation of Money*, op. cit., p. 77.
23 Hayek, ibid., p. 77.
24 Walter Bagehot, *Lombard Street: A Description of the Money Market (1904)*, New York: Arno Press, 1979, pp. 328–9.
25 Milton Friedman, 'Monetary Policy: Tactics versus Strategy', in J. Dorn and A.J. Schwartz (eds) *The Search for Stable Money*, Chicago: University of Chicago Press, 1987, p. 381.
26 Samuel Brittan, *How to End the 'Monetarist' Controversy*, Hobart Paper 90, London: Institute of Economic Affairs, 1981, p. 84.
27 Peter Brimelow, *Forbes*, 30 May 1988, p. 246.
28 Hayek, *Denationalisation of Money*, op. cit., pp. 102–3.
29 G. Stigler, 'Director's Law of Public Income Distribution', *Journal of Law and Economics*, April 1970.
30 See G.L.S. Shackle, *Epistemics and Economics: a critique of economic doctrines*, Cambridge: Cambridge University Press, 1972, ch. 1.
31 W.H. Hutt, *Politically Impossible?*, Hobart Paperback 1, London: Institute of Economic Affairs, 1971, p. 42.
32 John Stuart Mill, *On Liberty and Other Essays* (World's classic edn, ed. John Gray), Oxford: Oxford University Press, 1991, pp. 117–18.
33 J.S. Mill, ibid., pp. 118–19.
34 For a useful analysis, David G. Green, *Everyone a Private Patient: An Analysis of the Structural Flaws in the NHS and How They Could be Remedied*, Hobart Paperback 27, London: Institute of Economic Affairs, 1988.
35 David G. Green, *Challenge to the NHS*, Hobart Paper 23, London: Institute of Economic Affairs, 1986.
36 See Green's monograph, *Everyone a Private Patient*, op. cit. p. 58, fn. 1.
37 For a magisterial summation of his outlook, Isaiah Berlin, 'On the Pursuit of the Ideal', *New York Review of Books*, 17 March 1988, p. 18ff.
38 F.A. Hayek, *The Mirage of Social Justice*, vol. 2 of *Law, Legislation and Liberty: A new statement of the liberal principles of justice and political economy*, London: Routledge & Kegan Paul (one vol. edn), 1982.
39 I have discussed the relationship between Hayek and Kraus in my 'Hayek as a conservative' in R. Scruton (ed.) *Conservative Thinkers*, London: Claridge Press, 1987, pp. 249–59, reprinted as Chapter 3 of my book, *Post-Liberalism: Studies in Political Thought*, London: Routledge, 1993.
40 See my 'Classical liberalism, positional goods and the politicisation of poverty' in A. Ellis and K. Kumar (eds) *Dilemmas of Liberal Democracies*, London and New York: Tavistock, 1983, pp. 181–2.
41 James Buchanan, 'Rules for a Fair Game', in *Liberty, Market and State*, Brighton: Harvester Press, 1986, p. 139.
42 R. Nozick, *Anarchy, State and Utopia*, Oxford: Basil Blackwell, 1974.

43 James Meade, *The Intelligent Radical's Guide to Economic Policy*, London: Allen & Unwin, 1975, pp. 71–2. I do not intend to endorse Meade's proposal for taxing the annual value of houses.

44 J.S. Mill, *Principles of Political Economy*, 1848, London: Penguin, 1970.

45 James Meade, op. cit., p. 85.

46 Hayek, *The Constitution of Liberty*, op. cit., p. 321.

47 Barry Bracewell-Milnes, *A Liberal Tax Policy: Tax Neutrality and Freedom of Choice*, Economic Notes 14, London: Libertarian Alliance (reprinted from *British Tax Review*), 1988, p. 3.

48 Hayek, *The Constitution of Liberty*, op. cit., p. 307.

49 Home Office, *Report of the Committee on Financing the BBC* (the Peacock Report), Cmnd 9824, London: HMSO, 1986; and discussion of the proposal in both Alan Peacock's and Samuel Brittan's chapters in Cento Veljanovski (ed.) *Freedom in Broadcasting*, Hobart Paperback 29, London: Institute of Economic Affairs, 1989.

50 James Buchanan, *The Limits of Liberty: Between Anarchy and Leviathan*, Chicago: University of Chicago Press, 1975, p. 180.

51 J. Kornai, 'The Hungarian Reform Process', *Journal of Economic Literature* 24(4), December 1986, pp. 1687–1737. The quotation cited comes from pp. 1726–7.

2 A CONSERVATIVE DISPOSITION: INDIVIDUALISM, THE FREE MARKET AND THE COMMON LIFE

1 Michael Oakeshott, 'On being conservative', in *Rationalism in Politics*, London and New York: Methuen, 1977, p. 183.

2 Thomas Hobbes, *Leviathan* (Everyman edn), London: Dent, 1949, pt 2, ch. 17, pp. 88–9.

3 W.B. Yeats, *Selected Poems*, London: Pan Books, 1980, p. 179.

4 See Roger Scruton, 'In Defence of the Nation', in J.C.D. Clark (ed.) *Ideas and Politics in Modern Britain*, London: Macmillan, 1990, pp. 53–86. I have criticised Scruton's view in the same volume in my 'Conservatism, Individualism and the Political Thought of the New Right', pp. 81–102, reprinted as Chapter 19 of my book, *Post-Liberalism: Studies in Political Thought*, London: Routledge, 1993. An excellent statement of conservative communitarianism, to which I am much indebted, may be found in Robin Harris's *The Conservative Community: The roots of Thatcherism – and its future*, London: Centre for Policy Studies, 1989.

5 John Stuart Mill, *On Liberty and Other Essays* (World's Classic edn, ed. John Gray), Oxford: Oxford University Press, 1991.

6 See F.A. Hayek, *Law, Legislation and Liberty, 2: The Mirage of Social Justice* (one vol. edn), London: Routledge & Kegan Paul, 1982, p. 112: 'the only ties which hold together the whole of a Great Society are purely "economic"'.

7 The term Areopagitic refers, of course, to Milton, and is used in a political context to characterise ideal liberalism by J.R. Lucas in his *Principles of Politics*, Oxford: Clarendon Press, 1966.

8 Philip Larkin, 'Days' in *Collected Poems*, London: Marvell Press & Faber and Faber, 1988) p. 67.

9 I have elsewhere suggested how the NHS in Britain might by an evolutionary development turn into a system of private care for all who seek it. See my *Limited Government: a Positive Agenda*, London: Institute for Economic Affairs, 1989; pp. 00–00 of the present volume. That argument should not be interpreted as a rationale for under-funding the NHS in its present, or likely future, form.

10 For evidence that individualism is in England immemorial, see Alan Macfarlane, *Origins of English Individualism: The Family, Property and Social Transition*, Oxford: Basil Blackwell, 1978.

11 The term 'radically situated selves' originates, so far as I know, in Michael Sandel's *Liberalism and the Limits of Justice*, Cambridge: Cambridge University Press, 1982.
12 Oakeshott, op. cit., p. 65.
13 On this, see *Correct Core: simple curricula for English, maths and science*, prepared by Sheila Lawlor, Policy Study 93, London: Centre for Policy Studies, 1988.
14 *Community Care: Agenda for Action*, Report to the Secretary of State for Social Services by Sir Roy Griffiths, London: HMSO, 1988.
15 Isaiah Berlin, *The Crooked Timber of Humanity: Chapters in the History of Ideas*, London: John Murray, 1990, especially 'The Pursuit of the Ideal'.
16 G.L.S. Shackle, *Epistemics and Economics: a critique of economic doctrines*, Cambridge: Cambridge University Press, 1972, p. 239.
17 See Joseph A. Schumpeter, *Capitalism, Socialism and Democracy* (4th edn), London: Allen & Unwin, 1952.
18 See P. Smith (ed.) *Lord Salisbury on Politics*, Cambridge Cambridge University Press 1972).
19 This is a point illuminatingly explored in George Santayana's neglected conservative classic, *Dominations and Powers: Reflections on Liberty, Society and Government*, New York: Charles Scribner and Sons, 1951.
20 I owe the expression 'the politics of imperfection' to Anthony Quinton's book, *The Politics of Imperfection: The Religious and Secular Traditions of Conservative Thought in England from Hooker to Oakeshott*, London: Macmillan, 1976.
21 See Donald Livingstone's excellent book, *Hume's Philosophy of Common Life*, Chicago: University of Chicago Press, 1984).
22 David Hume, *A Treatise of Human Nature*, London: Penguin, 1969, p. 319.

3 THE MORAL FOUNDATIONS OF MARKET INSTITUTIONS

1 Joseph Raz, *The Morality of Freedom*, Oxford: Clarendon Press, 1986.
2 John Stuart Mill, *On Liberty and Other Essays* (World's Classic edn, ed. John Gray), Oxford: Oxford University Press.
3 On this, see J. Kornai, 'The Hungarian Reform Process', *Journal of Economic Literature* 24 (4), December 1986.
4 For an introduction to public choice theory, see James Buchanan and Gordon Tullock, The Calculus of Consent, Ann Arbor: University of Michigan Press, 1962.
5 See F.A. Hayek, *Individualism and Economic Order*, London: Routledge & Kegan Paul, 1976, chs 2, 4, 6–9. For an excellent history of the Austrian calculation debate, see D. Lavoie, *Rivalry and Central Planning: the Socialist Calculation Debate Reconsidered*, Cambridge: Cambridge University Press, 1985.
6 Michael Polanyi, *The Logic of Liberty*, Chicago: University of Chicago Press, 1951.
7 Paul Craig Roberts, *Alienation and the Soviet Economy: the Collapse of the Socialist Era*, 2nd edn, New York and London: Holmes & Meier, 1990.
8 G.L.S. Shackle, *Epistemics and Economics: a critique of economic doctrines*, Cambridge: Cambridge University Press, 1972.
9 I owe this formulation to Michael Oakeshott, *Rationalism in Politics*, London and New York: Methuen, 1977.
10 G.L.S. Shackle, op. cit., pp. 239, 240.
11 James Buchanan, 'Jack Wiseman: A Personal Appreciation', in *Constitutional Political Economy* 2(1), Winter 1991, p. 4.
12 In so far as Austrian economic theory neglects, or seeks always to explain away as by-products of government intervention, the endogenous breakdowns of coordination in markets theorised by Keynes and Shackle, it becomes seriously misleading.
13 See, also, Peter Rutland, *The Myth of the Plan*, London: Hutchinson, 1985; and James Sherr, *Soviet Power: the Continuing Challenge*, London: Macmillan, 1987, pp. 27–30.

14 As I shall note later, it is far from being the case that Soviet (or post-Soviet) military technology was uniformly less advanced than that in the West: on the contrary, with the important exception of some of the computer technologies that go into space-based defence systems, it was (and still is) often in advance of its Western counterparts.

15 For a decisive demolition of this species of rationalism, see Oakeshott, op. cit., p. 96, fn. *et seq.*

16 On this see A. Navrozov, *The Coming Order: Reflections on Sovietology and the Media*, Claridge Blast 4, London: Claridge Press, 1991, p. 12.

17 For further evidence on this point, see my paper, *The Strange Death of Perestroika: Causes and Consequences of the Soviet Coup*, European Security Studies 13, London: Institute of European Defence and Strategic Studies, 1991, pp. 20–21.

18 A. Alchian, 'Uncertainty, Evolution and Economic Theory', *Journal of Political Economy* 58, 1950, pp. 211–22; H. G. Manne, 'Mergers and the Market for Corporate Control', *Journal of Political Economy* 73, 1965, pp. 110–20; S. G. Winter, 'Satisficing, Selection and the Innovative Element', *Quarterly Journal of Economics* 83, 1971, pp. 237–61; P. Pelikan, 'Evolution, Economic Competence, and the Market for Corporate Control', *Journal of Economic Behaviour and Organization* 12, 1989, pp. 279–303.

19 Pelikan, ibid., pp. 281–2.

20 An unfettered market for corporate control may have negative as well as positive effects on the economy. The German and the Japanese examples suggest that market competition may not be inhibited, and long-term planning may be facilitated, by an environment where stock market fluctuations are less important in their impact on firms than in Anglo-American style economies. This is an important point I cannot pursue here.

21 I take this to be Raymond Plant's view, as expressed in his contribution to *Citizenship and Rights in Thatcher's Britain: Two Views*, Raymond Plant and Norman Barry, Choice in Welfare 3, London: Institute of Economic Affairs Health and Welfare Unit, 1990, and in Plant's pamphlets, *Equality, Markets and the State*, Fabian Society Tract 494, January 1984 and *Citizenship, Rights and Idealism*, Fabian Society Tract 531, October 1988.

22 For an argument that it often does not, see E.J. Mishan, *The Costs of Economic Growth*, London: Pelican, 1967.

23 G.L.S. Shackle, op. cit.

24 I have myself stated this objection, more systematically, in *Liberalisms: Essays in Political Philosophy*, London: Routledge, 1989, ch. 12; and in my *Post-Liberalism: Studies in Political Thought*, London: Routledge, 1993, ch. 20.

25 For the best untechnical discussion of value-incommensurability, see Isaiah Berlin, 'On the Pursuit of the Ideal', in *The Crooked Timber of Humanity: Chapters in the History of Ideas*, London: John Murray, 1990. I try to clarify further this difficult idea in my *Post-Liberalism: Studies in Political Thought*, ibid., ch. 20.

26 For a good statement of this view, see David G. Green, *Equalizing People*, Choice in Welfare 4, London: Institute of Economic Affairs Health and Welfare Unit, ch. 4.

27 On Berlin, see my 'On Negative and Positive Liberty', in my *Liberalisms*, op. cit., ch. 4.

28 For a comprehensive argument that negative liberty has little or no intrinsic value, see Joseph Raz, op. cit., chs 14, 15.

29 Raz, ibid., p. 207. I have myself argued for a conception of freedom as autonomy in my *Liberalism*, Milton Keynes and Minneapolis: Open University Press and University of Minnesota Press, 1986, pp. 58–61.

30 See A. Hirschman's *Exit, Voice and Loyalty*, Cambridge, Mass: Harvard University Press, 1970.

31 F.A. Hayek, *The Constitution of Liberty*, London: Routledge & Kegan Paul, 1960.

32 See Joel Feinberg, *Moral Limits of the Criminal Law, 2: Harm to Self*, Oxford: Oxford University Press, 1986, ch. 18.

33 See Loren Lomasky, *Rights, Persons and the Moral Community*, Oxford: Oxford University Press, 1987, pp. 247–50.

34 See Raz, op. cit., chs 14, 15.

35 For a critique of Rawlsian legalism, see my *Liberalisms*, op. cit., ch. 10.

36 On this, see my *Liberalisms*, op. cit., postscript.

37 See Plant's contribution to *Citizenship and Rights in Thatcher's Britain: Two Views*, op. cit., especially pp. 20–2.

38 Raz, op. cit., ch 9.

39 Raz, ibid., p. 235.

40 Raz, ibid., p. 240.

41 L.P. Hartley, *Facial Justice*, Oxford: Oxford University Press, 1987.

42 Hayek, *The Constitution of Liberty*, op. cit., pp. 90–91; R. Nozick, *Anarchy, State and Utopia*, Oxford: Basil Blackwell, 1974, pp. 167–8.

43 On this, see Bruno Bettelheim, *The Children of the Dream*, London: Macmillan.

44 Hayek, *The Constitution of Liberty*, op. cit., p. 87.

45 On this, see my *Mill on Liberty: A Defence*, London: Routledge & Kegan Paul, 1983, ch. 3.

46 From the standpoint of the present argument, according to which 'justice' is a short-hand term for a miscellany of practices and procedures having in common only a regulative ideal of fairness, there cannot be a theory of justice – though there can be a theory of law.

47 J.S. Mill, 'On Liberty', in *On Liberty and Other Essays* (World's Classic edn, ed. John Gray), Oxford: Oxford University Press, 1991, p. 87.

48 Hayek, *The Constitution of Liberty*, op. cit., ch. 6.

49 F.A. Hayek, *Law, Legislation and Liberty*, 2: *The Mirage of Social Justice* (one vol. edn), London: Routledge & Kegan Paul, 1982, pp. 115–20.

50 J.S. Mill, *Principles of Political Economy*, London: Penguin, 1970, p. 350: 'the distribution of wealth. That is a matter of human institution only. The things once there, mankind, individually or collectively, can do with them as they like.'

51 See B. de Jouvenel, *Ethics of Redistribution*, Indianapolis, Ind: Liberty Press, 1990, Introduction by John Gray.

52 On this, see D.K. Willis, *Klass: How Russians Really Live*, New York: St Martin's Press, 1985.

53 See Hayek's *Individualism and Economic Order*, op. cit. I have discussed Hayek's argument in my *Hayek on Liberty*, Oxford: Basil Blackwell, pp. 13–16, 21–6.

54 David Miller, *Market, State and Community: Theoretical Foundations of Market Socialism*, Oxford: Clarendon Press, 1989.

55 For Mill's 'competitive syndicalism', see his *Principles of Political Economy*, op. cit., pp. 118–41.

56 On this, see A. Schuller, *Does Market Socialism Work*,? London: Centre for Research into Communist Economies, 1989; and V. A. Naishul, *The Supreme and Last Stage of Socialism*, London: Centre for Research into Communist Economies, 1991.

57 For the best statement of this analytical Marxist critique of classical Marxist conception of exploitation and alienation, see G. A. Cohen, *History, Labour and Freedom: Themes from Marx*, Oxford: Clarendon Press, 1988, chs 6–9.

58 See Miller, op. cit., ch. 3.

59 Nozick, op. cit., p. 163.

60 For a brilliant discussion of this and other aspects of neutrality, see Raz, op. cit., ch. 5.

61 Gerald F. Gaus, 'A Contractual Justification of Redistributive Capitalism', in J.W. Chapman and J. Roland Pennock (eds) *Nomos XXXI: Markets and Justice*, New York and London: New York University Press, 1989, pp. 89–121. Gaus also notes (p. 121, fn. 89) that the oft-cited Mondragon cooperative in Spain generates adequate levels of income 'only because of its very special circumstances, in particular its nonmobile labour force'. See Keith Bradley and Alan Gelb, 'The Replication and Sustainability of the Mondragon Experiment', *British Journal of Industrial Relations* 20, 1982, pp. 20–33. If immobility is a precondition of worker-cooperative viability, what becomes of the freedom of workers?

62 David Miller, 'Market Neutrality and the Failure of Co-operatives', *British Journal of Political Science* 11, 1981, p. 328.
63 Some of these difficulties have been acknowledged by Miller in 'A Vision of Market Socialism', *Dissent* Summer 1991, pp. 406–15.
64 Anthony de Jasay, *Market Socialism: A Scrutiny: 'This Square Circle'*, Occasional Paper 84, London: Institute of Economic Affairs, 1990, p. 21.
65 See, in particular, Walter Lippmann, *The Good Society*, London: Allen & Unwin, 1938; and H. Simon, *Economic Policy for a Free Society*, Chicago: University of Chicago Press, 1948.
66 A.M. Honore, 'Ownership', in A.G. Guest (ed.) *Oxford Essays in Jurisprudence 1*, Oxford: Oxford University Press, 1961.
67 James Buchanan, 'Tacit presuppositions of political economy: implications for societies in transition' (unpublished).
68 Norman Barry, *Welfare*, Milton Keynes: Open University Press, 1990, pp. 78–82.
69 The term 'compossibility' is owed to Hillel Steiner, but originates in Leibniz's monadology. See H. Steiner, 'The Structure of a Set of Compossible Rights', *Journal of Philosophy*, 1977; and, on non-conflictability, Joel Feinberg, *Social Philosophy*, Englewood Cliffs, NJ: Prentice-Hall, 1973, pp. 95–6.
70 This is a point acknowledged by Barry, op. cit., p. 79.
71 See H.L.A. Hart, *The Concept of Law*, Oxford: Clarendon Press, 1961, pp. 184–95.
72 Raz, op. cit., chs 7, 8. It may be worth noting that the welfare state could be given a derivation in contractarian terms. For an example of this, see Christopher Morris, 'A Hobbesian Welfare State?', *Dialogue* 27 (1988), pp. 653–73.
73 See Raz, op. cit., pp. 235–44.
74 See Chapter 1 of the present volume, pp. 28–9.
75 See Chapter 2 of the present volume, pp. 60–1.
76 Raz, op. cit., p. 242.
77 I developed this argument myself in 'Classical Liberalism, Positional Goods, and the Politicisation of Poverty', in A. Ellis and E. Kumar (eds) *Dilemmas of Liberal Democracy*, London: Tavistock, 1983, pp. 174–84.
78 Raz, op. cit., p. 242.
79 See Chapter 1 of the present volume.
80 See my *Advertising Bans: Administrative Decisions or Matters of Principle?* London: Social Affairs Unit, 1991.
81 See, on this, K.R. Popper, *The Open Society and Its Enemies*, vol. 1, London: Routledge & Kegan Paul, 1945, ch. 9.
82 Raz, op. cit., chs 14, 15.
83 For a perfectionist defence of liberalism, see V. Haksar, *Liberty, Equality and Perfectionism*, Oxford: Oxford University Press, 1979.
84 On this, see Chapter 1 of the present volume, p. 42–3.
85 The term 'wanton' originates with H. G. Frankfurt and is explained in my *Mill on Liberty: A Defence*, op. cit., p. 75.
86 On this, see Chapter 2 of the present volume. See, also, David Willett's excellent *Happy Families: four points to a Conservative family policy*, Policy Study 120, London: Centre for Policy Studies, 1991.
87 Raz, op. cit., p. 309.
88 See Hayek's *Monetary Nationalism and International Stability*, London: Longman, Green, 1937. I have earlier argued for Hayekian currency competition on the ground that money may in the conditions of the contemporary British economy be unmeasurable: see Chapter 1 of the present volume. I have since been persuaded by the arguments of Tim Congdon that this Hayekian objection to monetarist policy may be unfounded. On this see T. Congdon, *Monetarism Lost: and Why it Must be Regained*, London: Centre for Policy Studies, May 1989.
89 See T.W. Hutchinson, *The Politics and Philosophy of Economics: Marxists, Keynesians*

and Austrians, Oxford: Basil Blackwell, 1981, ch. 5, 'Walter Eucken and the German Social-Market Economies', pp. 154–75. See also Lord Keith Joseph, *The Social Market Economy*, London: Centre for Policy Studies, 1981.
90 Hutchinson, op. cit., p. 160.
91 Hutchinson, op. cit., p. 168.
92 Hutchinson, op. cit., p. 17.
93 The spirit of the German Social Market Economy School has been well captured by E.Y. Neaman, who observes:

> It was hardly a coincidence that behind Ludwig Erhard's concept of a *Sozialmark-twirtschaft* (social market economy) lay the conservative cultural criticism of capitalism of Erhard's mentor, the philosopher Alfred Müller-Armack. In an influential book of the era, *Diagnosis of Our Times* (1949), Müller-Armack pleaded for a synthesis of two opposing forces: the ruthlessness of the market and the Christian concept of brotherly love. Müller-Armack's stress on the *social* side of the market equation typifies the general ambiguity of the German liberals in the post-war period. The founders of the social market economy, known as the 'Ordo' group, after the economic journal of that name, were sceptical of unhindered market capitalism. Thinkers like Wilhelm Röpke and Alexander Rüstow advocated a social market as a collective healing process, by which social harmony should be instituted and traditional values, such as the sanctity of the family and Christian morality, preserved. Even the so-called Fribourg Group, economists who were more pragmatic and politically minded, saw the social market as a kind of objective mechanism which would regulate the collective in the most efficacious manner. They were not opposed to government intervention as long as its aim was to make competition even more effective. Thus, for example, government subsidies for the poor to pay rent were seen as enforcing the social market, but rent control was not.
>
> The 'social state' (*Sozialstaat*, the same appellation used by Gottfried Feder) was built on four fundamental pillars after 1945: (1) old-age pensions; (2) health and accident insurance; (3) employment-creation and unemployment insurance; and (4) family support.... In contrast to the past, the Basic Law (*Grundgesetz*) of 1949, which is the closest the Federal Republic has to a constitution, made the state responsible for protecting its citizens from social insecurity (E.A. Neaman, 'German Collectivism and the Welfare State', *Critical Review* 4[4], Fall 1990, pp. 607–8).

The crucial point is that the social market economy model conferred on citizens an entitlement to protection from insecurity.
94 For evidence on this point, see Julian Le Grand, *The Strategy of Equality*, London: Allen & Unwin, 1982.
95 Hayek, *The Constitution of Liberty*, op. cit., p. 323.

4 AN AGENDA FOR GREEN CONSERVATISM

1 C.S. Lewis, *The Abolition of Man*, London: Macmillan, 1947. The citation occurs in Herman E. Daly (ed.) *Toward a Steady-State Economy*, San Francisco: W.H. Freeman, 1973, p. 323.
2 See Chapters 2 and 3 of the present volume.
3 The expression, 'rationalism in politics', is, of course, Michael Oakeshott's.
4 Garret Hardin, 'The Tragedy of the Commons', *Science* 162, 13 December 1968, pp. 1243–48. The citation occurs in Herman E. Daly, op. cit., pp. 137–8.
5 This is acknowledged in Hardin's book, *Nature and Man's Fate*, New York: Mentor Books, 1959, ch. 11.
6 For a discussion of the Prisoner's Dilemma, see Russell Hardin, *Collective Choice*, Chicago: University of Chicago Press, 1987.

7 The best version of this argument for market institutions is to be found in Michael Polanyi, *The Logic of Liberty*, Chicago: University of Chicago Press, 1951, ch. 8.

8 Yablokov's estimates were reported in the London *Independent* of 24 January 1992.

9 As quoted in the London *Sunday Times*, 7 July 1991.

10 Ibid.

11 Stefan Hedlund is an Associate Professor of Soviet and East European Studies at Uppsala, Sweden, who presented a paper on Soviet environmental degradation to the Washington-based National Security Information Center in June 1991.

12 *Independent*, 24 January 1992. The *Independent on Sunday* of 15 December 1991 contains a much more detailed account by Mark Hertsgaard of the secret 'Mayak' nuclear complex at Chelyabinsk; it mentions the cover-up by both Soviet and Western authorities of the nuclear disaster at the Mayak waste dump in 1957, during which around twenty million curies of radioactivity – four times the amount released at Hiroshima – were released into the local environment.

13 See Hertsgaard's report, ibid., for details.

14 Hertsgaard, ibid.

15 Hertsgaard, ibid.

16 See Vanya Kewley, *Tibet: Behind the Ice Curtain*, London: Grafton Books, 1990.

17 See Murray Feisbach, *Ecocide in the USSR*, New York: Basic Books, 1992.

18 Stefan Hedlund, 'Red Dust', London *Sunday Times*, 7 July 1991.

19 As reported in the *New York Times*, 2 August 1992.

20 The term 'inherently public goods' I owe to Joseph Raz, who explains it in his *The Morality of Freedom*, Oxford: Clarendon Press, 1986 pp. 198–9.

21 Michael Oakeshott, *Rationalism in Politics*, London and New York: Methuen, 1977, p. 171.

22 There are some penetrating observations of the consequences of this point for moral and political thought in Stuart Hampshire, *Innocence and Experience*, London: Penguin, 1989.

23 That human individuals are tokens of which forms of life are the types is argued in the last chapter of my book, *Post-Liberalism: Studies in Political Thought*, London: Routledge, 1993.

24 See my *Post-Liberalism*, ibid.

25 I have criticised the use of the Kantian conception of the person in recent Anglo-American political philosophy in my 'Against the New Liberalism', *Times Literary Supplement*, 3 July 1992.

26 See Chapter 3 of the present volume.

27 Ibid.

28 See Arne Naess, 'Green Conservatism', in Andrew Dobson (ed.) *The Green Reader*, London: André Deutsch, 1991, pp. 253–4.

29 For a good statement of this truth, see Edward Goldsmith, *The Way: An Ecological World-View*, London: Rider, 1992, chs 22, 64 especially.

30 James Lovelock, *The Ages of Gaia*, Oxford: Oxford University Press, 1988.

31 Goldsmith, ibid., pp. 367–8.

32 I discuss the incoherence of the idea of progress, in the context of incommensurabilities among human goods and evils, in Chapter 20 of my *Post-Liberalism*, op. cit.

33 See Ivan Illich, *Limits to Medicine: Medical Nemesis: The Expropriation of Health*, London: Penguin, 1976, chs 1–3.

34 I have discussed Herder's rejection of the melioristic interpretation of human history in my *Post-Liberalism*, op. cit., especially in chs 6, 20.

35 F.A. Hayek, *The Constitution of Liberty*, London: Routledge & Kegan Paul, 1960.

36 George Santayana, *Dominations and Powers: Reflections on Liberty, Society and Government*, New York: Charles Scribner and Sons, 1951, p. 340.

37 J.S. Mill, *Principles of Political Economy*, vol. 2, London: John W. Parker and Son, pp. 320–26. The citation is reproduced in Herman E. Daly, op. cit., pp. 12–13.

38 Lovelock, op. cit., p. 178.
39 Hardin, *Nature and Man's Fate*, op. cit., pp. 289–90.
40 On this possibility, see Lovelock, op. cit., p. 178ff.
41 On the conflict between high population density and individual liberty, see Jack Parsons, *Population versus Liberty*, London: Pemberton Books, 1971.
42 I refer to José Ortega y Gasset, and his book, *The Revolt of the Masses*, New York: W.W. Norton, 1957.
43 Nicholas Georgescu-Roegen, 'The Entropy Law and the Economic Problem', in Herman E. Daly, op. cit., pp. 37–49.
44 Goldsmith, op. cit., p. 300.
45 See my paper, 'From post-communism to civil society: the re-emergence of history and the decline of the Western model', *Social Philosophy and Policy* (forthcoming).
46 For an excellent account of the introduction of poverty into Ladakh via development programmes which were animated by conceptions of modernisation, see Helena Norberg-Hodge, *Ancient Futures: Learning from Ladakh*, London: Rider, 1991.
47 This is a point well discussed by E.J. Mishan in his *Costs of Economic Growth*, London: Pelican, 1967.
48 On this, see F.A. Hayek, *Denationalisation of Money: An Analysis of the Theory and Practice of Concurrent Currencies*, Hobart Paper 70 (2nd edn, revised and enlarged), London: Institute for Economic Affairs, 1978; and Kevin Dowd, *The State and the Monetary System*, New York: St Martin's Press, 1989.
49 G.K. Chesterton. The citation appears in Herman E. Daly, op. cit., p. 148. No source is given, but I believe that it comes from Chesterton's book, *The Outline of Sanity*, London: Methuen, 1926.
50 Hilaire Belloc, *The Servile State*, Indianapolis, Ind: Liberty Press, 1977, p. 107.
51 The reference is to Feisbach's study. See note 17, above.
52 I have argued, in Chapter 3 of this volume, that market socialism, as a 'third way' between capitalist and socialist institutions, is systemically unstable.
53 See Chapters 1, 3 of the present volume.
54 I have discussed reform of inheritance taxation in Chapter 1 of the present volume.
55 F.A. Hayek, *The Road to Serfdom*, London and Henley: Routledge & Kegan Paul, 1944.
56 I believe that the idea of a negative capital tax was advanced by A.B. Atkinson but I have been unable to trace the source.
57 I have argued, in Chapter 3 of the present volume, that the current apparatus of the welfare state could in most countries be substantially dismantled, while the needs of the most disadvantaged and vulnerable were satisfied better than at present.
58 See Chapters 1, 3 of the present volume.
59 Daly, op. cit., pp. 160–63.
60 Daly, op. cit., p. 158. The proposal for 'child licenses' which Daly discusses originates with Kenneth Boulding, in the latter's *Economics as a Science*, New York: McGraw-Hill, 1970, p. 149.
61 Lovelock, op. cit., pp. 171, 110.
62 Lovelock, ibid., p. 173.
63 Lovelock, ibid., p. 174.
64 Lovelock, ibid., p. 178.
65 Goldsmith, op. cit., p. 373.
66 Robert Waller, 'Prospects for British Agriculture' in Edward Goldsmith (ed.) *Can Britain Survive?*, London: Sphere, 1971, p. 133.
67 Walker, ibid., p. 135.
68 Goldsmith, op. cit., p. 291.
69 Ivan Illich, *Energy and Equity*, London: Calder & Boyars, 1974, pp. 30–31.
70 I owe these figures to Wolfgang Zuckerman's *The End of the Road*, London: Lutterworth Press, 1991.

71 See Richard Rogers and Mark Fisher, *A New London*, London: Penguin, 1992. The quote comes from the London *Sunday Times*, 14 February 1992.
72 Rogers and Fisher, op. cit.
73 See, on this, Jane Jacobs's book, *The Death and Life of Great American Cities*, New York: Vantage Books, 1963.
74 I have not traced the expression but I believe that it originates with Russell Kirk.
75 Illich, *Limits to Medicine*, op. cit., p. 50.
76 See Chapter 3 of the present volume.
77 On this see the writings of E.G. West.
78 Ivan Illich, *Deschooling Society*, London and New York: Harper Row, 1970, pp. 20–21.
79 Illich, ibid., p. 19.
80 For Mill's suggestion, see J.S. Mill, *On Liberty and Other Essays*, (World's Classic edn, ed. John Gray), Oxford: Oxford University Press, 1991, pp. 117–19.
81 See Illich, *Limits to Medicine*, op. cit.
82 Illich, ibid., p. 92.
83 Illich, ibid., p. 272.
84 Illich, ibid., p. 235.
85 Illich, ibid., pp. 271–2.
86 Paul Feyerabend, *Three Dialogues on Knowledge*, Oxford: Basil Blackwell, 1991, p. 75.
87 Michael Oakeshott, *Hobbes on civil association*, Oxford: Basil Blackwell, 1975, p. 151.
88 Hardin, *Nature and Man's Fate*, op. cit., pp. 296–7.
89 Lovelock, op. cit., p. 212.
90 John Aspinall, *The Best of Friends*, London and New York: Harper & Row, 1976, pp. 132–4.
91 Lovelock, op. cit., p. 138.
92 Lovelock, op. cit., p. 121.
93 I do not mean here to endorse the Hayekian conception of spontaneous order, with its attendant erroneous theory of cultural evolution. I refer instead to Polanyi's account of it in his book, *The Logic of Liberty*, op. cit.
94 For J. Monod's views, see his book, *Chance and Necessity*, London: Collins, 1972.
95 Lovelock, op. cit., p. 211.

Index